Still Upright & Headed Downstream

Collected River Writing

If adventure is activity on one's personal frontiers, then John Lane has spent his life on those frontiers. He enters them through rivers rapid and meandering: through prose, poetry, teaching, and social justice. He takes us off waterfalls in Mexico, down his beloved Chattooga River, on urban creeks renewed by communities, in swamps capturing alligators, and in wounded landscapes through which piedmont rivers flow, cleansing themselves and all who travel them. His message is clear: you can go home again into nature to rediscover what has been lost and found repeatedly.

—Gordon Grant, Director of Education,
North Carolina Outward Bound School

Lane is a teacher, and his essays and poems teach us just how much rivers matter. Rivers have stories to tell too, and John Lane puts those stories into words. Lane understands the natural and human history of the rivers of the South and understands the culture of rivers at a deeply personal level.

—Joe Pulliam, riverman and
cofounder of Dagger Canoes

John Lane combines the prose and poetry of a gifted writer with the insights of a dedicated teacher and environmentalist, and the love of being on the water of a lifetime paddling enthusiast. His writing exhibits his love of being on the water whether in a kayak on a class IV/V river, poling or route finding in a tandem wooden canoe on a low-water river, exploring the suburban rivers around his Spartanburg, SC, home, or catching alligators by hand from the bow of a canoe at night. Serious paddlers will recognize John as one of their tribe.

—Payson Kennedy, pioneer paddler and founder
of the Nantahala Outdoor Center

If any author comes close to cracking the code to the enigma of why folks are drawn to the black-rock dangers and white magic of fast, free-flowing water, it is John Lane.

—Richard Bangs, founder of Sobek Expeditions

"A writer who would obviously paddle first and theorize later, Lane prefers the river speak for itself."

—*The Atlanta Journal-Constitution*

A kayaker's soggy-seated perspective...Lane writes with muscle and insight.

—*The Charlotte Observer*

John Lane's poems are built from the muscle-memory of being on the river. Because of that, his writing is not just about rivers; it is made of rivers, their rocks and ripples, currents and eddies.

—T. S. McMillin, author of *The Meaning of Rivers*

Lane artfully applies his poetic sensibility to the river itself.

—*Publisher's Weekly*

From the viewpoint of both whitewater paddler and poet...mastering the tricky intersection of water and rock.

—*Wall Street Journal*

A man who can write with the force and the power of the currents he describes.

—*Smoky Mountain News*

Lane lends eloquent weight to the metaphoric assertion that life is a river.... In an age that values faster and faster travel, Lane...affirms the great value of floating and observing, providing meaningful testimony to the merits of focusing on a deeper level to one's life journey.

—*Booklist*

Lane has a fluid eye in a 'world where time moves in more than one direction and no landscape holds steady for long,' and it's energizing to see through that eye, open as it is to both light and darkness.

—*Kirkus Reviews*

UNIVERSITY

MERCER UNIVERSITY PRESS

Endowed by

TOM WATSON BROWN
and
THE WATSON-BROWN FOUNDATION, INC.

STILL UPRIGHT &

HEADED DOWNSTREAM

Collected River Writing

JOHN LANE

MERCER UNIVERSITY PRESS
Macon, Georgia

MUP/ P636

© 2022 by Mercer University Press
Published by Mercer University Press
1501 Mercer University Drive
Macon, Georgia 31207
All rights reserved

25 24 23 22 21   5 4 3 2 1

Books published by Mercer University Press are printed on acid-free paper that meets the requirements of the American National Standard for Information Sciences—Permanence of Paper for Printed Library Materials.

Printed and bound in the United States.

This book is set in Adobe Caslon Pro.

Cover/jacket design by Burt&Burt.

ISBN   978-0-88146-827-4
Cataloging-in-Publication Data is available from the Library of Congress

CONTENTS

One: *From the Center*   1
    Why I Love Falling Water   3
    Pilley's First Law of Rapids   6
    Down the Sometimes River   10
    Silver Creek Paddles   13
    Waterfall Logic   20
    Death by Water   23

Two: *First River Poems*   29
    At Cherokee Ford, South Carolina   31
    The River Falling   32
    Along the Little Betsie   33
    At Relia's Garden   35
    The Fear Program   36
    Above Bone Ring Lake   38

Three: *Excursions*   41
    Sardis   43
    Gradient   57
    Lake Conestee   74
    Confluence: Pacolet River   81
    Youghiogheny   95
    Sols Creek Falls   109
    Paddle to the Sea   116
    River Time   119
    $35 Million River   122

Four: *River Poems Downstream*   137
    No Water in the River   139
    If You See the River   140
    First Spring Flood   141
    Teaching the River   142

Ridge Music   143
The Half-Finished House   144

Five: *Ripples Outward and Inward*   147
   ReGenesis: Seeking Wildness in a
      Damaged Southern Landscape   149
   A Week of Mexican Waterfalls   165
   Meet the Creek   177
   Watershed Thinking   188
   On the Chattooga   190

Six: *The Mad Kayaker Poems*   199
   Hears the River Flood   201
   Teachers His Wife to Roll   202
   Surveys His Gear   203
   Dreams of Waterfalls   205
   First Psalm of the Mad Kayaker   206
   Votes His Values   208
   Plants a Garden   209
   Watches His Sons on the River   209
   The Drought   210
   The Old Wet Suit   212

Seven: *Mostly Flat Water*   213
   Keowee   215
   The Upper Broad River: A Pastoral   229
   Urban Reedy River   237
   May the Wind Take Our Troubles Away   241
   Canoe and Alligator   252
Eight: *Recent River Poems*   259
   Thinking Like a River   261
   The Habits of Crayfish   262
   Suspension Bridge   263
   No Water in the River   264
   Trout in a Tank   265

Intellectual Watershed   266

Coda   267
      Meanders, Toeholds, Scour Holes, and
            Oxbows: Some Notes on a River Life   269
      Origins of Writing and Publication
            Histories   278

Biography   289

ACKNOWLEDGMENTS

Many thanks to those who have accompanied me on these watery excursions into the "nearby nature" of my own backyard and the wilder place further away.

Thanks to all my periodical editors through the years. These poems and essays appear mostly, but not entirely, in chronological order beginning in the early 1980s and continuing to 2020. For a complete composition and publishing history see "Origins of Writing and Publication Histories" at the book's conclusion.

For support of time and money while writing several of these narratives I'd like to thank Wofford College and the Spartanburg Water and Sewer District. Many thanks also to the folks at the National Geographic Society for trusting me to paddle rivers on their dime. And rivers of thanks to these friends—the late John Pilley, Lee Hagglund, Randy Riddle, Franklin Burroughs, Terry Ferguson, Venable Vermont, Lynn Brandon, Angus Morrison, Craig Andrews, Chris Lechner, Ellen Goldey, Dave Hargett, Gerald Thurmond, G. R. Davis, Thomas Pierce, Dixon Bynum, Wes Cooler, Aliston Reid, Ab Abercrombie, and Brent and Angela Martin. And to another raftload of old friends—Tom Harvey, Ben Fleming, James Johnson, James Jackson, Tom Visnius, Wayne Dickert, Tom Decuir, Arlene Burns, Bob Beazley, Mark Zwick, Scott and Mary Danials, Slim Ray, the late John Dolbeare, Nick Williams, Teresa Gryder, Kent Ford, Steve Liebig, Nance Petit, John Barbour, Ed and Marlys Daugherty, Mervin Readman, Brett Poirier, Bob Hathcock, Bunny Johns, Bill Hester, and Janet Smith.

And finally, as always, to Betsy, who keeps me upright and has been paddling with me for many watery miles.

ONE

FROM THE CENTER

WHY I LOVE FALLING WATER

Most weekends you can find me in the mountains west of Asheville or in the foothills west of Walhalla, South Carolina. I search out the places where rivers, mostly with Native American names, fall through the hard rocks of the Blue Ridge. That's where the glint and sparkle of white water break soft greens and mud reds of flowing streams.

These are not the coal-dark rivers, slow and thick as pitch, of the Low Country; they are not even the clay floes of Piedmont counties gathering the eroded country fields from smaller streams. My rivers hang like lace in the early fog among laurels and junipers.

When I get to the river, I take down the blue kayak from the car racks, shuck my flatland clothes, and outfit myself like a Greek warrior. If it's cool, I pull on my wet suit, feeling slick as an eel, then layer myself with a red paddling jacket and blue life vest. I pull on my black shoes called Reef Walkers, find my nose-clip, snap on my helmet. Then I pull on my spray skirt, a rubber gasket to keep the river out, and carry the boat and paddle down to the edge of the water.

I slip into the bobbing boat, legs first, like sitting in a green bean, so thin and tippy. The boat pauses in the current, and I sit deep for steadiness. I nose into the moving water.

But like most manners of love, kayaking is not easy. To paddle with skill takes an attention as deliberate and practiced as any true human affection.

I call my shoulder, the one that hurts when it rains, Painted Rock. It was there, years ago on the Chattooga, where I made the wrong stroke and ended up kissing smooth stones on the bottom of the falling river.

My wrist is Delebar's Rock on the Nantahala. As a novice, I eddied in a shallow pool above the rapid, drifted back, and flipped. The rapid, which now seems so tame, that time rolled me into the cold water. I paddled for shore; my wrist bent back by the current. It throbbed for days.

My knee, the right one, has a name too. It's called Little Corky on the Green. That's where I jammed it up into the deck of my boat trying to roll my bean upright after flipping in a curling wave. Next day, I stuffed kneepads with foam rubber, hobbled, waited for the next weekend to take the pain away.

I came up with a name for this sport I invented: full-contact kayaking. Early on in my kayaking, every river was a roller derby when I headed downstream. It took a summer to get out of bumping into river things. Rocks. Trees. Other boats. I was a worshipper of collisions.

But one weekend on the Nantahala it all changed. The current was a jade swirl as always, but I finally had done enough groundwork. I leaned out instead of fearing for my balance, caught the river headed for the sea, and floated with it. The strokes, so foreign at one time, seemed part of my arms, back, and waist. The paddle was my extended hands; the boat, my body.

I was learning to love rivers. I gave up my life for two or three days each weekend to feel the water bend around my boat, the rocks break and scatter a smooth stream in front of me. I'd learned to make the right movement of my being. The right movement took me where I wanted to go.

That's why I fell in love. Rivers make me realize I'm in the world, moving through at the length of my own seated body times two. Each moment is an edge with two clear sides. I make the wrong choices, and I'm on the rocks or caught in a place I should not be.

In the life I live, Monday through Friday, I'm encouraged to do three things at once, not one. One thing at a time is all I can afford to do on the river. One motion done well, followed by another perfect motion. That's how I get downstream. That's how I stay upright in all that churning.

Paddling is like learning to live with friends or lovers. With the wrong choices, there is sometimes pain. But to live within the responsibility of this choosing is to make it a part of a balanced world. Like the water snake on the river's bank. Like the rapid in equilibrium with the river's flow around the next bend. Like death in our own lives moving toward us a day at a time.

But this paddling of wild rivers looks like a loss of common sense to those who don't know rivers. Much as divorce looks to those on the outside, caught in the backwash. Why would I want to throw my body into a plastic boat and invite the river to twist me around a steady rock?

Hiking is much safer, you'd think. Biking. Shark wrestling? Why not take up one of these?

There are other ways, most good, to get close to the earth, to be alone with it, but rivers are mine.

My little friend Hailey, three-year-old poet with an ear for people's situations, once listened to me tell my Painted Rock story. She twisted her hands, looked up.

"John, this time find a soft river," she pleaded.

The rivers are getting softer every weekend. I'm learning to love them, and they seem to be falling for me. I sit by their grinding waters and listen for what they have to say. When I paddle down them, I look deep within the still pools behind rocks. In the rapids, those places where the river kisses resistant rock and then backs away, I hear the roar of wildness and make out pure vowels of something other than me, and I'm moved to do the right thing.

Someone told me once that there are only two types of kayakers, those that swim and those that are about to. Talking to experts, this seems a little extreme. Many great boaters with midnight runs down Section IV of the Chattooga and hands rolls at Pillow Rock on the Gauley to their credit have been many, many years without being "out of their boats."

But the other night at supper I listened to two expert paddlers talk about how helpless they've felt at times when the moment did come when they had to swim out of a hydraulic. "It had been so long—seven years—since I'd been swimming that my body did not know what to do. I was gasping for air and my eyes were as big as plates," one of them said, remembering the fear, stirring his ice cream around in disbelief.

To paddle a kayak is to live constantly between curiosity and fear. When I first started paddling, I sat at the top of most rapids with a death grip on my paddle, no matter how small the drop. I had no Eskimo roll at that time, no way of flipping the boat back upright if I leaned upstream or missed a brace. Each drop was Niagara Falls, and I had about as much control over my boat as I would a barrel. Fear had the upper hand.

Sitting in an eddy once at the top of a rapid called Little Corky, on the Green River in North Carolina, I once watched three friends turn to make the drop. "How do I run this one?" I asked the woman who was the last to follow.

"Upright and downstream," she informed me, leaning on her brace like a racer. I would not gain access to Holy knowledge by questions, only by action, by following. I gripped the paddle tighter and waited for curiosity to take over.

I have been upright and downstream in many rapids, riding the swirls and holes of several rivers like the Ocoee and the

Nantahala a hundred times. My fear was slowly replaced by skill acquired through many hours of watching water move over a rocky riverbed. I thought I replaced the fear, feeling a curious question at the top of each drop, "Can I make it through?" That is, until I learned Pilley's First Law of Rapids.

"If you run a rapid enough, no matter what your skill level, it'll get you sooner or later," John Pilley, a man with probably close to a thousand river trips, told me once, sitting in an eddy at the top of Seven Foot Falls on the Chattooga. I did not want to believe him, looking over the edge at the churning hydraulic below me, as the water pushed against a rock wall to the left of the river.

But Pilley took the drop and I followed soon after, willing to play the odds on our years of paddling. What Pilley was saying is that in paddling, no matter how good you are, there still remains the possibility of error in each difficult rapid; there is no sure thing. A little fear—respect, some call it—should remain as much a part of a river trip as curiosity.

An experienced white water paddler pushes the odds well in his or her favor through years of skill, but the force and intent of the river is constant, something the human body cannot claim. To paddle Class IV and V, and especially Class VI, white water is to live within the possibility of human error, which might result in a swim through a rocky riverbed, or something even more serious. Like auto racing, the deaths in white water sometimes count among them those who are most skilled.

The last weekend of the season in 1984 I had Pilley's Law brought home to me in a most embarrassing way. During the Customer Appreciation Festival weekend at the Nantahala Outdoor Center in Wesser, North Carolina, there is a hot dog contest on the Nantahala River. Each contestant gets two runs through a forty-foot-long series of ledges know as Nantahala Falls. In the early seventies, this rapid was rated a Class V at high water, but in the last fifteen years the number of people running it and advancements in skill levels and equipment have dropped its rating to a Class III.

I had run the rapid close to fifty times that year alone, since the river is only twenty minutes from my house. I had even made an effort to lose my fear and develop a curiosity about the "top hole," the one place in the falls where there is any real danger. Many times, I had dropped from the small eddy to the hole's left and played at that near end, doing spinning turns and then heading downstream, losing my fear little by little.

I had seen the top hole grab rafts and swimmers and recirculate them three or four times before spitting them into the downstream current and the waiting safety ropes. Once I'd even seen a man come out face down to be revived downstream. But watching, I had formulated my own opinions. If a kayak got into the hole the bulk of boat and body would push you downstream. It was only rafts and frightened tourists who would be kept by the river god in the top hole.

It all happened so fast, like an auto accident, but there was no doubt about it, I was upside down in the top hole; I rolled once and found myself sideways, bracing downstream. I could hear the guy on the bullhorn who was announcing the contest telling the crowd that I would probably surf there and then pull my way out.

"He's getting some high scores with the judges," he joked as I worked to stay upright. Then I flipped again, banged my helmeted head on a rock so hard I let go of my paddle, and decided to take my chances out of my boat.

The boat stayed in the hole with me, circulating around as I was plunged on the upstream side of the boil, only to be swept along the bottom, popped up and head back upstream for another recirculation. Just like the tourists. My boat and me.

I remember thinking, Where are the safety ropes? as I circulated several more times, getting tired and running out of ideas as to how to get out of the hole.

I'd tried to swim to the edge where there was plenty of downstream water; I'd tried swimming hard each time I'd reached the furthest point downstream in my circulations. But no ropes came. Suddenly I relaxed and my body was popped "waist high" someone on the shore told me later, and I was on the way downstream.

Needless to say, I didn't do very well with the judges, although my swim was the most exciting thing the audience saw that day. Little did they know they were also seeing a river law being proven. Pilley's First Law of Rapids stands unchallenged with me until someone comes up with a unified theory of rivers and river running that can explain what made me get right back in my boat twenty minutes later for my second run. Very quickly, the curiosity kicked in.

DOWN THE SOMETIMES RIVER

In southwestern North Carolina, the Fontana Dam was scheduled for maintenance by the Tennessee Valley Authority in the late fall of 1985. By December, for the first time in many years, stretches of the Little Tennessee, the Nantahala, and the Tuckaseegee appeared from under the draining waters of the lake. The reappearance of a river brings out a different sort of spirit in river runners, especially if it is the end of the summer season. The day I paddled the lower Nantahala, my first Sometimes River, I went down with a group of river guides. I watched a playfulness emerge that is burned out of many guides by mid-July.

The last rapid on the Nantahala before the river catches up with the TVA's impoundment is called "Worser Wesser." River trips end upstream of this twenty-foot drop through blasted granite left by the railroad when they diverted the river years ago. Worser Wesser is legend among paddlers of the Nantahala. The first time I came to the Nantahala, in 1974, the leader of our trip, John Pilley, stopped at the overlook above the rapid and told us how we would run it. We shook in our tennis shoes. Funny joke, we thought to ourselves, three hours later when we pulled out well above Wesser, changed clothes, and headed to the restaurant for hot tea.

Sometimes in high-water springs, I've been told Lake Fontana backs halfway up the falls and makes it into an easily runnable five-foot drop. But high water or not, most river runners don't think beyond the horizon line of Worser Wesser. This is usually the end of the white water world on the Nantahala, but it is the beginning of the Lower Nannie, the Sometimes River.

The day we paddled down the lower Nannie—five kayaks strong—we played for a little while at the bottom of Worser

Wesser; then we headed downstream toward Almond boat dock before the river disappeared again into TVA's idea of recreation.

As I dropped deeper into a part of the Nantahala gorge I'd never seen before, I had a strange sensation. I had the sense of transportation, the excitement of discovery. This was not a normal river trip. This effect, I soon realized, was caused by the lake's water line getting farther above my head. The old lake created a desert below its surface, and in receding had revealed high, red canyon country right in the Smoky Mountains.

There is another way in which this stretch of river is like some western streams. Out West, a stream might only run two months a year. The rest of the time the canyons are dry draws. Here, our Sometimes River sleeps for half a century under the thick pad of a lake, to emerge with a dropping instead of rising water level. There were only three or four rapids along the two-mile stretch of the Sometimes River, all Class II at best. This did not matter. In one rapid with a good drop and a slightly turbulent hole at the bottom, I sat in an eddy with friends and made up names for the places the river picked up speed—Popgun; Make My Minute; Here Today, Gone Tomorrow.

I stopped and surfed each new standing wave, no matter how small. December surfing is a floating, steady joy. By late in the fall, Lake Nantahala, the source of the daily releases, is so low that the water is no longer Alaska cold, and the air temperature is still warm. Loren Eisley, the poet and scientist, said once, "If there is magic on this planet, it is contained in water." December is a good time for magic, to have a mind for water.

This Sometimes River was a perfect place to practice river Zen, river Being. I worked back and forth in the elbow of the river. Time collapsed around my boat, broken into the thousand glittering folds of aerated water. Each second was no more than a brace against no-time, becoming lost in the crook of the river. I was a calm center connected to the flow of the river by more than the bottom of my boat. Out from there, I was only one small part of a larger whole. The air, gorge walls, winter trees were all just extensions, parts of a larger being. When I pulled off the wave, back into the eddy, I was unsure how long I had surfed. Moments? Days? Centuries? I wondered, When the lake rises does a wave cease to exist?

SILVER CREEK PADDLES

The steep slopes on either side of the Silver Creek paddle shop in southwestern North Carolina are studded with yellow poplars straight as paddle shafts. Outside the shop, the narrow, noisy bed of Silvermine Creek is thick with grey cobbles. After a good rain, if the creek was a few yards wider, Homer and Margaret King, the shop's owners, could boat the one mile down to the Nantahala River.

Unlike the local people who are constantly leaving the mountains to find work, many young "post-professionals" like Homer and Margaret have migrated here into southwestern North Carolina. Dissatisfied with employed life in cities and suburbs, some simply prefer a life of paddling, rock climbing, and mountain biking and hiking to that of a year-round paycheck. Some came to work for the Nantahala Outdoor Center, one of the largest white water outfitters on the East Coast and one of the largest seasonal employers in the area, located at the confluence of Silvermine Creek and the Nantahala River. Homer and Margaret King each drifted from an earlier life— Homer as a visual artist, Margaret as a lawyer, then MFA student and costume designer in the dance program at Florida State—to come to the Smokies. They met in 1979, guiding rafts for Nantahala Outdoor Center, and now, years later, they were up to their armpits in the wooden-paddle business.

Homer and Margaret do not run a craft shop. There is no Eric Sloan working slowly with chisels and planes. In the Silver Creek shop are band saws, belt and disk sanders, a large press for making laminates, a table covered with rasps and mill files, and a lattice of shelving filled with hundreds of four-by-one-inch wood strips cut in twenty-inch lengths for paddle blades. Deep in the shop, a compressor switches on every twenty seconds. After the men finish sweeping, the odor of sawdust rises from piles in the corners.

There are only a few custom or "top-end" wooden paddle makers in the United States. Mitchell, River Styx, Sea-One, Dagger, Backlund, to name a few—and Silver Creek. Several of these paddle makers produce so few paddles that it may take years to receive an order. Many river outfitters, world-class, and weekend paddlers consider Silver Creek the finest among the "available" paddles, those you can order sometimes out of an existing stock. For years, when the shop was very small, Homer and Margaret built about four hundred paddles a year. They made what they could to sell in a few retail stores or took special orders. "There were always more orders than paddles," Homer says. Only in the past year and a half have they expanded the shop. They bought ripsaws, planers, and shapers. This basic woodworking machinery gave the shop the capacity to make many more paddles yet allowed time for the hand work necessary to make a beautiful paddle. This year they'll finish fifteen hundred.

Margaret has been away all day working up a specification sheet and cover letter to send to twenty-seven retail outlets they hope might carry their paddles. "Before, all we did was make paddles. Now we've got to market them," Homer adds.

Homer had no formal training in woodworking or production technique when he started making paddles in 1980. He sat around for a year, as he puts it, "with my thumb in my ear." He finally solved the problems particular to making paddles by visiting furniture plants and using their solutions for his application—within Silver Creek's means. "We had a one-room shop and I couldn't make paddles as a production item." Now, with the new addition, their crew, and many long days, they have a production item.

Homer never had a real love for wood before he started the shop. But what he did have was a love for rivers and paddling. "I made several wooden paddles in college—out of necessity. I couldn't afford to buy another when one broke. Painting and ceramics—my major—taught me to be a good technician, a problem solver. So I copied a paddle I owned. When I arrived here, I saw a market for a high-end wooden paddle and started the business."

Homer considers what he had said and corrects. "I also started building paddles because there was nothing else to do in the winter. Back then, in October, you either invented some work or left." His voice was lyrical—measured—as he counted paddles to be finished the next day. "I never thought I'd stay this long."

Swain County is a hard place to make a steady living. Unlike the last ten centuries, when the native people farmed the four river bottoms and hunted and gathered in the highest mountains east of Colorado, 82 percent of the land is government owned and known variously as the Great Smoky Mountains National Park, the Cherokee Indian Reservation, Nantahala National Forest, the Blue Ridge Parkway, and the Tennessee Valley Authority.

In the paddle shop, three men sweep and move paddles from one room to another, finishing the day's chores. Four carts of wooden kayak paddles in various degrees of completion sit beside the door. There are fifty blades in each cart.

Earl McMahan, a local man who has worked at Silver Creek for about a year, has seen the employment problems of the southwestern mountains throughout his life. When Earl was young, his father took the whole family to Catawba County, North Carolina, to look for work. They stayed four years. A few years later, Earl had to leave the county to get work himself, but returned home when the shoe factory, in nearby Graham County, closed down because of import competition. Now Earl stands in the late afternoon sun and builds paddles for a sport he's never tried.

The economy of Silvermine Hollow, with its double handful of year-round residents, has always been connected to wood in some way. Wood and water. In the first quarter of the century, a wooden flume ran along Silvermine Road. The old-timers used the creek's natural gradient to float chestnut logs down from the higher end of the hollow. Chestnut bark, used in leather tanning, was big business. At the bottom of the run the men loaded the logs and bark on flat cars headed up the gorge to Murphy, North Carolina. There are eleven one-lane bridges, a sawmill, and several churches on Silvermine Road between the Silver Creek shop and the Kings' house. Two sawyers wave as Homer's truck passes. In the back of the truck is a thin layer of sawdust, a pile of hardwood scraps, and a kayak.

From the outside, in the falling light of evening, the Kings' house looks like a Walker Evans photograph. "Welcome to our tar paper shack," Homer says. There are paddling gear, two rocking chairs, and a pile of wood for the stove on the wide porch. "Home Sweet Home," states a little sampler in the front door window.

Inside, work has been done. Much work. Mostly work with wood. The space has the easy, functional feel of most hand-built or recovered houses. There is a loft above, a small office in one corner, a TV and VCR in another. On the wall is a framed print of Einstein riding a bicycle.

The house had been abandoned for years when Homer found it. When he brought Margaret up the creek to see where they were going to live, she sat in the front yard and cried. They rented it for ten dollars a month from a man in Florida who had plans to burn it down. There were layers of old newspaper on the walls. They stripped away thirty years' worth of news to get down to the stud walls. Homer wired, added plumbing, and trimmed the inside with truckloads of pallet wood from a local lumberyard. "We used a variety of species," he jokes. "Mostly cheap hemlock."

Back to talking wood, Homer explains the woods they use at the shop. "First of all, we use too many species of wood to be a sensible production operation. Various species give character to the blades. They give a unique look to the lay-up," Homer says, cracking a tray of ice cubes for drinks. Homer buys as many woods locally as possible, including basswood, cherry, and yellow pine; but some woods—such as ash, which is used in the shafts, and walnut, for edging and color—are best bought up North. "Northern climates grow healthier trees. I think the soil must be better."

Even though Homer and Margaret still hang on to "insensible" production techniques—mostly on aesthetic grounds—they have worked out many of their early production problems through trial and error. "The paddle is an ever- changing product. There's an evolution in its growth. I enjoy working out the problems of making them," Homer adds. As an example, he describes the evolution of the tips of the blades. They once used to be held on with small, spring clamps while the epoxy was drying. Now the tips are laminated onto the blade core using large air bladders. The compressor kicking on keeps constant pressure on the tips, one more step toward creating a perfect wedding of form and function.

One paddler friend of mine disagrees; he says that when he buys his Silver Creek, he'll never let it touch water or rock, forgetting function. "I'll hang it over my mantle like a tapestry," he claims.

Two cars come up the gravel road. Each time, Forest, Homer and Margaret's two-year-old boy, says, "Mommy?" He alternates between crying and chasing the cats. Homer says the toddler has picked up a cold at day care. Forest cries to confirm. Finally, another car slips up the hollow, and Forest drops the cat and runs to the front door.

It is Mommy this time. Margaret enters, excited. She has finished the spec sheets to send out to white water dealers in the next day's mail. She somehow gathers her tired child, finds the letter she has written, begins to think about supper, and launches into Homer's continuing discussion of paddle making. But mostly, she's excited about the letter. She's afraid to let me read the cover letter, which she worked on too long. Her conversation is breezy and articulate, but she keeps saying she doesn't quite know how to catch words on the permanence of a page. "I finished law school and practiced a few months. Imagine me spending all day on a cover letter," she says, and finally shows a copy to Homer, then to me, starts supper, then begins to answer a question I'd asked earlier in the day.

"For most, the economy here is subsistence," Margaret says. "The tourists come, then leave, and the bottom falls out for seven months. One reason we build boat paddles is because we live in Swain County. You know as well as I do that you have to figure out something to do with your life," she says while cutting up some broccoli for supper. She thinks for a moment, and then continues. "It makes it hard to decide if we really want to stay here forever. You worry about your kid going to school, coming home with double negatives in every sentence. And your friends end up saying 'I'm tired of guiding rafts' and there's not much else for them to do in these hills."

Both Homer and Margaret have mentioned close friends leaving because of the lack of steady work in the county. The stability of any community is based on employment of its people. In Swain County there is a "surplus workforce," as the State Office of Economic Development calls it. The lack of winter work makes migrants out of even the most community minded. One man at the Nantahala Outdoor Center calls himself an "outdoor sports migrant worker." It's much easier to go to Colorado and work the ski slopes than create a winter life in the hills.

"You have to feed yourself," Homer agrees.

"We could do other work to feed ourselves," Margaret says, "but it wouldn't be work close to our hearts."

For most of the young migrants in southwestern North Carolina, feeding themselves is not the real problem. Most are well educated; many are trained in a skill they could sell elsewhere. Most are here because of the land and water. Margaret could practice law in Bryson City, ten miles away. And Homer, she jokes, could "get a job at Clampett's Hardware."

Water falling over stones brought both Homer and Margaret to Swain County. Out of that love of falling water they built a life, then a business. They seem to have found—almost by circumstance—what the Buddhists call "Right Livelihood"—a direct, living exchange between work and self. But there's nothing mystical about it, both my friends insist. "No matter how much I like what's evolving with each generation of paddles, it's still only a paddle," Homer says.

"But Homer," Margaret disagrees, putting food on the table. "It all circles back to the fact that you enjoy using a good paddle."

WATERFALL LOGIC

It would take five seconds, but I'd be thinking about it all summer. Late June. Cool mountain evening with the light filtering through Whiteoak Falls, the last cascade before Whiteoak Creek drops forty feet into the upper Nantahala River in western North Carolina. The creek was only two kayaks wide yet created the kind of waterfall where tourists take pictures. The falls dropped almost vertically in two broken, rocky shafts. Most of the water went left, piled up against the dark cliff wall in a startling slide, then continued the final twenty feet to the shallow bottom pool. The right side was rocky, scrappy and more difficult, with little flow for paddling. "A cliff lubed with water," a friend had called it. Until recently the numerous paddlers in the area had looked, but never considered running it. There were demons. Death. Paralysis. Enough to keep most paddlers' boats on their cars.

Waterfalls have always been powerful images in the human psyche. Early American landscape painters never tired of painting Niagara Falls, and the Japanese always had those thin ribbons of water hanging from cliffs in Sumi painting. Lao-Tse talks of waterfalls and the poet William Carlos Williams compares the falls on the Passaic River to a man's passion.

For years Whiteoak Falls seemed a powerful embodiment of the mental, physical, and spiritual limits of paddling. Forty feet of snarly vertical drop. Then a local expert paddler ran it successfully in the winter of '89 and suddenly, like the breaking of the four-minute mile, people started asking if they could do it. Finally, one evening in late June, two friends, John and Jeff, headed up to Whiteoak Falls to run it too.

There were four of us who would watch. We clambered over the wet rocks as John and Jeff paddled slowly down the creek above and pulled their boats to shore in the calm water overhung by rhododendron. They stood looking down for a moment. It was like an image from a film. Quiet. Almost slow motion. "We could see somebody die today," I remember another friend whispering.

My two friends were both experts, two of the best paddlers in the East. They had rolled the dice many times in their paddling careers and at worst come up with only scrapes and a few cuts. They were the equivalent of Ted Williams poised just out of the path of a hundred-mile-an-hour fastball, or in the metaphor I prefer, St. George facing off against the dragon.

I knew that John did not consider the run overly risky. He had explained to me earlier how he had come to the decision to run Whiteoak. He was twenty-eight and had been raft guiding the Chattooga River since he was twelve. Sixteen years on difficult rivers. There were some things that his years of paddling told him he could control. First, he was aware Whiteoak had been run before by another expert boater, and he knew that he could make all the particular moves. For John these were the rational elements in his decision.

He admitted that there were irrational elements, food for the demons: whom you were with, how you felt, and whether or not you were afraid to die. These three elements, along with the two rational ones, would determine the outcome of any difficult paddling challenge for John.

Jeff was just out of college. His experience did not go as deeply as John's, but he seemed to lead the charmed life of the young. I had seen him paddle a hard stretch of water once and he seemed to bounce smoothly past all the holes like a puppy. He was known for paddling old used boats he'd pick up for practically nothing, and at Whiteoak he had chosen to borrow an old Hydra Dragonfly, a boat most consider too long for waterfalls.

John and Jeff worked their way down the cliff face and stood with us and charted their routes. John decided to take the rockier right side and pointed exactly where he wanted to hit after the first twenty-foot drop onto a shallow water-covered ledge. His hand fluttered past that spot and continued to describe his route to the final pool below. It looked impossible to me. One wrong move on the approach and he was taking what he had described to me as the greatest risk of this kind of paddling: "moderately high impact injury," a compressed disk or broken ankles when the boat hits bottom.

Jeff said he would choose the left route, where the water piled up on the cliff. One friend of mine had taken his boat to the top of the Whiteoak Falls days before in high water and pushed it off to see the route it would follow. It had gone left and disappeared at the bottom.

John and Jeff started back up toward their boats. Steve, another friend who was along, headed down to the bottom of the waterfall to set safety. He was silent and serious as he worked over the wet rocks in his Tevas carrying the yellow rope.

I stayed still. Looking up at Whiteoak Falls I thought of Jesus, Buddha, and all the great religious traditions that teach through supreme paradox, the journey, hardship, the dragons, and devils we must meet along the way. In order to gain your life, you must lose it. Above me, twenty feet closer to heaven, were two friends in kayaks getting ready to drop over a big cliff padded with about a hundred fire hydrants worth of water.

John went precisely where he said he would go. It took five seconds. We watched as the Noah Jeti he paddled came down the left side, hit hard in the first shallow pool, corrected slightly, and took the second drop. From where I stood, I could tell it was successfully over by the look on Steve's face below me. He smiled and held his throw rope high in a ritual sign. For John this dragon was dead.

Jeff watched and waited. He shook his head. "Not this home boy," he said, and we all assumed he'd shouldered his boat and walked up the path to the county road. We all began to walk away. Minutes later, as we loaded in the cars, Jeff paddled out of Whiteoak Creek, the nose of his Hydra crushed by impact at the bottom of the falls. He wasn't hurt. He had done the run after we all left, the young buck calling on all his magic and charm.

DEATH BY WATER

In the first dream I remember I'm running down a drainage ditch (I was maybe five at the time) followed by a rising wall of rushing water ready to overwhelm me. We were living in Southern Pines, North Carolina. It was the year my father committed suicide, so the dream might be easily explained in terms of personal apocalypse, but it's the water I focus on when I remember it. Water can be so many things—source, purifying agent, flux, infusion, salvation ("water of life"), and grave. Jesus walked on the water, and the Buddha in his assumption sermon saw a mountain lake (with clear waters, sand, shells, snails, and fishes) like a path to redemption.

"If anything will level with you, water will," the poet A. R. Ammons says somewhere. Wordsworth, in the sixth section of "The Prelude," calls a white water river he's walking along in the Alps "tumult and peace, the darkness and the light." Water is an aspect of my own interior landscape I often return to, a landscape feature of my own psyche that remains central to the understanding of my world as roaring river.

"There is an opening downward within each moment," James Hillman says early in *The Dream and the Underworld*, "an unconscious reverberation." I am a kayaker, and I know nothing loves down more than a river. Hillman says later, in "Praxis," in a section about dream images, that there are at least five rivers associated with Hades: "the frigid Styx; the burning Pyriphlegethon; the mournful, wailing Cocytus; the depressive, black Acheron; and Lethe," the stream of "Remembering and Forgetting." If there is *topo* in Hades, as Hillman argues, then there must be whole watersheds below. Hillman fails to mention whether any of these Hades rivers have significant stretches of white water, but I would bet the Lethe, in its upper reaches, falls through some heavy gradient.

Entering water, Hillman says, "relaxes one's hold on things and lets go of where one has been stuck." To enter too deeply in water for a kayaker is Hades. That's why we learn the Eskimo roll, to keep from staying down for too long. We know too well what Hillman knows, that moving water, like soul itself, has within it a special relationship to death. Ocean. Lake. River. They all rage and they all can kill. Call it physics or try to explain it away through luck and hydrology, but if people associate with moving water long enough, there will be tragedy.

I was paddling the Big Laurel Creek on a summer day in 1989 when I learned my lesson about what tragedy moving water can conjure. After ten years of paddling I had achieved a degree of mastery of the kayak. I lived in a paddling community and boated with other people of similar skills. We felt capable and assured of every move. I had not yet been touched by Hades.

It was a difficult isolated run through a beautiful Appalachian creek gorge. I remember the water was high, but we had a perfect run. We were all advanced paddlers (I think there were four of us) and so each rapid was a challenge, but not a real nightmare factory like white water can be if someone in the group is unprepared for the difficulty. One of the people I was paddling with was Bunny Johns, then vice president of the Nantahala Outdoor Center (NOC).

The Big Laurel empties into the French Broad just above Frank Bell Rapid, the last significant drop on that river. Our take out that afternoon was the NOC French Broad Outpost. When we paddled through the last rapid, a river-wide ledge called Surprise, we eddied out in front of the outpost. A guide was waiting for Bunny. Soon she was on the phone, already privy to a tragedy unfolding on the Tuckaseegee, a river close to the

NOC's main outpost in Wesser, and a river often used for beginning kayak clinics.

We quickly lashed on our kayaks, packed our gear, and drove back toward Wesser; Bunny filled us in on what had transpired on the Tuckaseegee. The day had started normal enough with the routine beginners' kayak clinic, but in the first hour out on the first river day things turned terrible quickly. The clinic leader, a very experienced instructor, had led the excited novice paddlers through a simple Class II rapid near the top of the river; though slightly bold from high rains, there should have been nothing really dangerous on this easy river. As best as Bunny could figure from limited information, one student, a man in his early thirties, had somehow tangled his boat in something obstructing the river and quickly drowned. His body had not been recovered, so there was no chance to revive him.

It turned out later that the junk was an industrial conveyer belt probably washed out of a landfill upstream by the high water. The long stiff abrasive belt had been lodged between two rocks, invisible, pulsing to the surface in a standing wave in the middle of the rapid.

The belt (we saw later, watching from the shore) would appear every three or four minutes. The man was the unlucky one to intersect his kayak with it. His plastic boat folded around his legs and he was drowned. The boat, his body, life jacket, and spray jacket all washed off, but his body disappeared, swirling down into the muddy rain-thickened river. I had paddled the same river that week and run the exact route, so it could just as easily have been me or the instructor, or any one of several dozen boaters who probably ran the river that week.

The rescue squad was there when we arrived, about two hours after the drowning. Bunny gathered what information she could at riverside and then departed for the main outpost to begin contacting the man's family and organizing the company for the search and investigation into what exactly had happened on the Tuckaseegee that morning.

I understood the odds of the situation. The drowning was an event rare as a one-hundred-year flood. NOC is considered one of the most professional outfitters in the world, renowned for their safety precautions and technical training of clinic partic- ipants. There was never, from the beginning, any suggestion that the guide or the center had been negligent. "The Harvard of white water instruction," the clinic program had once been called by *Outside* magazine. The blame could be placed nowhere. The water had worked its dark logic with an unsuspecting kayaker.

I was still dressed to paddle, so right away I drove to the put in with a group of NOC guides who had brought a raft. A half mile upstream we launched the raft and paddled quickly down- stream and did all we could do; we began to look for the body. Payson Kennedy, the president of the company, was in the raft, and he pulled us along with strong strokes in the boat's bow. I remember the silence as we floated down that short stretch of the Tuckaseegee. Usually rafting is very carefree, but this short trip had the smell of death and tragedy hanging all about it.

We swung the raft back and forth across the rapid (several guides had already set up safety ropes to ferry us back and forth through the swift current) and probe with long sticks for the body. We did this for hours the first day with no success.

I came back every day after work (I worked in the store at that time) and continued to ride in the raft, to probe the river bottom with a long pole. One day the rescue squad brought in a diver and he paddled back and forth in deep eddies like a trout, looking for some sign of the kayaker's body. On shore the scene took on the feel of a Southern wake, as restaurants brought food for us and the rescue squad. The hoods of trucks were spread with biscuits, hamburgers, ham, and deviled eggs. There were urns of sweet tea set up in the shade, and we drank deeply of them on our breaks.

Day after day we did not find him. The rescue workers as- sured me the corpse would "float up," probably a week into the process, when the natural chemistry of necrology countered the natural cooling of the river. One day family members showed up at the site of the drowning. It was an awkward and terrible time, and I prayed that we would not find the body that day, but that he would be recovered among strangers instead.

Each morning that week we sent out two kayakers to paddle slowly the six miles downstream to Bryson City, scouting the bank for the missing body. When the word came six days into the search that the kayakers had spotted the body, we jumped into a raft and stroked the three miles downstream. We ran all the rapids in silence, a floating ambulance or hearse bound for the scene of an accident. After a half hour we saw the two kayakers standing on a small beach on river left, looking awkward in their river gear. The rescue squad had worked down to the river on river right. The kayaker's brother-in-law was waiting as well. They all stood helpless to recover the body. What separated them was twenty yards of swift current. They needed our raft to ferry them across so they could retrieve the body.

We grounded the raft on the small beach. I glanced at the snag. I could see the man's body caught on a dead limb of the tree, resting in the branches of a tall tree blocking a left bend of the river. I had been told that the dead look very dead, but I was not prepared for what I saw. I could see the top of his head and his black hair flowing peacefully in the current. I could see the top of his right shoulder where the river had stripped it of clothing. It was ghostly white. There was no smell.

Two guides from NOC ferried the coroner across in a canoe. He had to declare the kayaker dead before the work could begin to recover the body. We waited in the raft as a canoe came across with the coroner.

As soon as the coroner had done his work he jumped in the raft, and we pointed it into the current and ferried across to where the rescue squad stood waiting. Two of the squad members were dressed in a yellow suits with rubber gloves and wore masks over their mouths. They tossed a black body bag into the raft. I could see silver grommets so the river water could drain freely out. The dead kayaker's brother-in-law climbed in the raft as well, along with the men in the yellow suits. They all settled in and we ferried in reverse, back to the small beach. The two rescue-squad members climbed out and waded into the current to recover the body.

In a vivid dream I remember from around the time of the drowning I'm driving past a flooding river. I get out and look down into the colliding current. It's obvious I can't paddle such difficult surging water, but just as I'm ready to leave, a single kayaker starts down with great skill and caution. When I look closely, I realize it's me. In the dream I know now that I am riding one of the rivers of Hades.

That moment on the Tuckaseegee was James Hillman's "opening downward;" it was when I was swallowed up by Hades the first time. It is when I stopped being a kayaker in some significant way. Simply put, one kayaker in me died and another was born when I saw what happened to the dead man. But in some deeper way, that was the first time I came to terms with what Hillman calls "the subtle kinds of death." The physical death of the kayaker affected me deeply, but it was the tiny deaths within—I was a college professor and a writer for good after that—that set me to different purposes.

The two rescue-squad members made the recovery quickly and capably. They untangled the dead kayaker from the tree, slipped his body into the bag, and zipped up the heavy black zipper and floated their burden to the beach. The glance at his shoulder was really the most I ever saw of him. The nightmare week finally came to an end when we grabbed a corner of the bag and hefted it into the middle of the raft. The Tuckaseegee was my own river Styx. The men in yellow climbed in. We nosed the black rubber raft into the current a second time, experienced boatmen keeping our steady line across the river, swinging us all—living and dead—efficiently to the other shore.

TWO

FIRST RIVER POEMS

At Cherokee Ford, South Carolina

Above the Broad River, a hawk
sleeps in the wind, then banks
and wakes, looking for snakes
or rabbits out in the heat.
Power lines wading the shallows

on treated pine poles could
be Whitman's cavalry crossing
the ford, or only the complex
of light and color attracting
the hawk's yellow tilted eye.
Unlike the hawk, I am caught

by a purely human equation:
to balance what the creature sees
with my apparition of the past
and the line's transgression
of gullied landscape, to find
a point of rest within the three—

but now, out of time, small eddies
of light catch the hawk's eye.

The River Falling

Once, we slept in oak woods,
zipped our two bags together, pulled free
of flannel shirts, shucked jeans,
counted the sad light of planes
flying to Asheville until the darkness
of dying oak leaves offered up some light.
All night Bradley Falls argued the moon down.

That morning, we climbed down,
took off our clothes, listened
to a song of water leveling with stone.
You sat in a hole where the river once
licked its own bed. I squatted, pressed silt
in my palms, caught round stones dragging
the creek bottom. The fall sun was up,
cliff-high, a star in a stub oak.

I squinted, spoke,
"You know I could be this river, easily
live my life between two places, two women."

You watched the falls, the perfect sadness
of the river falling. I swear the wet air
hummed, water dug for something to hold.
Then you turned, said,
"Then go, the seed's in us all, this leaving."

Along the Little Betsie

for Nikki and Dan

If in your indifference you have mistaken
these lines for a river in northern Michigan return
to the beginning of the poem. Or if you find brown trout here,
eddies, or caddisfly larvae drifting along
the margins, cast them out like abstraction.

There will be no river in this poem. No remnant wilderness
encountered, or left behind. Return to the beginning
if you admit disappointment at the poverty of
narrative or image, rhyme or meter, the poet's common speech
in which we fool or startle the world's approach.

If you have followed this far and see two ducks
hiding in shallows, admit they are only ducks
in the imagination, not named, given genus or species.

Snow falling. Early afternoon. I am walking in the woods
along the Little Betsie. Hear the snow like a broom
sweeping a hardwood floor? Are you so easily fooled?
Return to the beginning. How can it be
a broom sweeping the woods that slope to a river
not in this poem? I hope you are not there
on the banks of the Little Betsie, for you are here,
if my speech has trailed you this far.

For those among you who have yet to see a river
you do not need my permission to proceed.
But if a river flows here for you, return once more
to the beginning and do not repeat your mistake.

You can make no mistake; if you see a river
between here and there, you will return again.

If you are somehow here, so full of joy to have lost
the Little Betsie, you have learned a new skill, to clear
things up, the difference between what is
and what is not, like the river, far from you
which in your indifference you have allowed to be.

At Relia's Garden

In memory of Aurelia Kennedy (1935–2019)

I love to weed with Relia
When she wears her Chinese hat.
Her face peeping from shadow
Underneath. We weed and talk
Of a simple plan, how all years
Grow together like this garden
Hanging on the hill.

Relia says the Cherokee
Have no word for weed,
But we new settlers have many—
Mornings clearing the nutgrass,
Crawling vines,
But compositing what we can.

We weed to clear a place
For long green zucchini, fingers
Of beans, and direct the good
Spirit of nitrogen upward
From the old cow manure.

I love to work the full beds—
Where new vines wander the weather
Of mountain days. All morning
Our hands pass, slow and loving,
Directed again and again
To the good ground.

The Fear Program

When I taught kayaking we called any beginner
afraid to submit to learning the Eskimo roll
"signing up for the fear program." The part that got
them was when they realized their head had to dip
below the lake water. The awareness began to leave,
chilling their eyes to frozen cherries in a bowl.

I watched them as they snapped the buckles
of life vests, slipped the spray skirts over their hips
like a tight skin. There were always two or three.
Sometimes a man I would never guess who'd sit,
his knees shaking, as others slipped in the long
kayaks to test their fit. We would still be high
and dry, miles from the rolling lake, but he would
wait until all the others tried their pastel boats
back and forth in the dust before finally committing.

That man knew kayaking could kill him,
no matter how professional we were and sure.
It was not like signing up for tennis, or racquetball.
The physics of water and blind chance can wrap
a boat around a rock in the smallest of currents.
Even the best paddlers make mistakes. But it's worth it,
life's a river, and I'd rather have a roll in any situation
I'd float into downstream, with death the takeout.

"What's my name?" I'd yell at rank beginners
we tipped over in kayaks. We'd be right beside
them, rolling them upright with our shoulders,
no risk, only dark lake water, the spinning boat,
and their own desire. "John," the ones comfortable
with the darkness said. "What?" said those who'd learn

in a day or two. "Ugh." The sound of the fear program.
I still hear it when I come up against something
that sets the watery darkness moving deep in me.

Above Bone Ring Lake

for John Dolbeare (1957–1989)

Dolby, I thought of you as I worked up over
weather-split stone here in the Bighorns.
Thunderstorm brought you back above Bone
Ring Lake, cross-country bushwhacking.

You'd be headed higher for the ridge top too,
goat-jumping, stone-to-stone. I'd like to climb,
fast as you, but I breathe hard, a summer of talk
instead of paddling water, walking ragged land.

I've learned to love the way the mind eats
at the body, sets stiff muscles on brittle edge,
makes me want to give out just as wild flowers
spring up among standing snags of an old burn.

The living sure as hell are with us, but you
dead are too, lying around like fallen silver trunks,
brittle bones stacked against lodge pole pines.
Your presence never left me, mountain-spirit,
scree-in-the-hills, home on this distant range.

Stone, wind, and water-born, this place
called you out of my back country silence,
out of the oracle gurgle of hidden streams.

I slow down, search the boulder field for you,
and the light above—strange conjunction of ridge,
trail, and memory: your ashes, moving still,
somewhere near the sea by now, dropped in
the Nantahala, mixed with wild flowers

and the true mourning song of forty friends.

Are you hiding in this godless scrabble of down logs,
left by weather, fire, or age for me to kick or straddle?
You laugh—a jay, crow?—as I break through my lungs'
Summer-off-the-mountain pain and push on up,
through the pine's brittle branches, the stones'
cracked orbits, the slick moss slime.

Your dead voice is the wind pounding my mortal ears—
"Don't hang back. Climb, John, Goddamn it, climb."

THREE

EXCURSIONS

SARDIS

Easter Sunday and it's windy and cold for April in the Deep South. To make matters worse, squall lines have been blowing up from the Gulf all morning, hanging tattered clouds so low and thick they look like the soaked inside of a cotton bale. I'm on a three-day book tour—Memphis, Jackson, Oxford, Mississippi—for *Chattooga*, a book about the river made famous in part by a Southern writer named James Dickey. It hasn't really been a triumphant tour. On Saturday afternoon in Memphis the Davis-Kidd chain store where I was scheduled to sign forgot to order the books from the publisher. I stood around for twenty minutes while an embarrassed clerk searched for two copies the computer said they had somewhere in the store. My one other stop in Memphis that evening was at an independent bookstore where, upon arrival, I discovered they'd closed early for Easter. There was a small handwritten sign in the window next to a nice pile of my unsigned books that said, "Gone Fishin'." I am still hopeful concerning stops in Jackson and Oxford on Monday. The bookstores there—Lemuria in Jackson and Square Books in Oxford—are legendary in their hospitality to writers. Other writer friends who'd done this very tour told me I would not be disappointed with either.

Since I'm so close, I've told a Mississippi buddy I wanted to paddle something of what's left of Faulkner's river bottom that made up his *Big Woods*. Getting in touch with moving water will salve all my tour wounds and relax my tired mind. Dixon has set up a six-mile, half-day paddle downstream from the Sardis Dam, on what little free-flow is left of the Little Tallahatchie River, which becomes the Tallahatchie thirty miles downstream after its confluence with the Coldwater River. It's no wilderness, but it will give me a window cracked open on what Faulkner calls the "tall and endless" woods.

William Faulkner made up a mythical Mississippi county with the unpronounceable American Indian name of Yoknapatawpha, and James Dickey did the same with a North Georgia river called the Cahulawassee. Both mythical places have lived in my imagination parallel to real places. Both landscapes—the real and the imagined—have their appeal. Today I'll add the real Little Tallahatchie River to my life list of rivers I've paddled and figure out the connections to the myth of Faulkner's "Big Woods" as I float down.

Is it Faulkner's Big Woods drowned under Sardis Lake? Not really. The big bottom of "The Bear" isn't any more a real place than Jefferson or Frenchman's Bend or old Sutpen's Hundred. Dixon assures me, though, that southwest of here is where the real Faulkner is known to have hunted and camped along a real Mississippi river, and surely he used his experience in the Little Tallahatchie river bottom to create "The Bear" and several other stories. "Write what you know"—that's what we tell our students in creative-writing classes.

I've driven out of Memphis south on I-55 parallel to the Big Muddy. After an hour I get off on Highway 315, approach, and cross Sardis Dam—a vast mowed greensward of earthen construction so long (more than a half mile) that the Army Corps of Engineers has made a park out of the base of it with football and soccer fields. I cruise over the causeway and see that the dull brown lake is on one side humming with motorboats. The recreation space is down-slope on the other. The whole complex is like a snapshot of twentieth-century engineering logic—drown something dynamic and wild like the Little Tallahatchie River, offer car camping, fishing, boating, chalk off a playing field or two, and call it "green space."

In the Deep South there's little natural about a big lake. The terrain of Mississippi remained glacier-free in the Pleistocene and, if not manipulated, the local water does what it's done for hundreds of thousands of years, eventually finding its way to the Gulf of Mexico. Even the oxbow lakes on the Mississippi are ephemeral in geologic time, cut-off meanders filling in every few thousand years to form bogs, dells, swamps, and finally covered with thick riparian forest of cypress and tupelo. Check out any North Mississippi lake holding enough water to drop a ski boat in, and at the outlet you'll find a water control system of some sort, a low earthen levee cutting across the stream flow, a shallow concrete dam, or a bigger dam made of earth, rock, masonry, concrete, or some combination of the above.

I don't like dams, but I have to admit I'm probably in the minority. Impoundments have been around awhile. Some say as little as 1/100th of all the water on the planet is available to us, not salty or frozen in glaciers, and that tiny bit of H20 is often not in the right place for us humans to do with it what we need for survival—drink it or use it to ensure ample crops. Human engineering of water flow dates back to the Egyptians, who built irrigation systems. When, in *Monty Python's Life of Brian*, a member of one of the numerous liberation fronts during the time of Christ answers the rhetorical question, "What have the Romans ever done for us?" he only needs one word—"Aqueducts." It even gets a laugh out of me.

Who could dislike aqueducts? Architecturally, an aqueduct looks more like a Roman temple than does Sardis Dam. Their elegant arches show some classic sensitivity to place. They survive as ruins and in some rare instances still do what they were designed to do 2,000 years ago—move water from a place of abundance to one of scarcity.

Once human beings start engineering it's hard to stop. There's a direct line from a marble dam built in India in 1660 for water impoundment and crop cultivation to the huge contemporary hydro projects like China's Three Gorges Dam, trapping whole river drainages under their vastness. If you're a hydraulic engineer with a hammer in your hand—in this case with enough knowledge to build a dam—it doesn't take much to see dams plugging the vast river systems webbing the planet as your nails.

I know my feelings of disdain for reservoirs flow from a place of Western economic privilege. China argues they need the Three Gorges Dam for hydropower to fuel their future and pull billions out of poverty. I trust when I turn on my tap at home in South Carolina that water will flow forth. When I eat a salad, I know some engineer has long ago guaranteed the lettuce will be irrigated in a semi-arid California field. But it isn't these human uses that I seriously question. It's our need for impoundments like Sardis; it's the desire so many Army Corps of Engineers impoundments in the South articulate—rivers drowned for flood control, recreation, and aesthetics.

Construction on Lake Sardis began in 1936 as flood control for the southern Mississippi River Valley after the great flood of 1927 swamped the whole vast floodplain of the Mississippi delta from the bluffs in Arkansas to the bluffs in Mississippi, a distance of more than fifty miles. In the wake of that famous flood, the Army Corps of Engineers built these now familiar dams, floodways, spillways, and levees; they did channel stabilization and channel mapping. They cut meanders on the Mississippi, shortening the river's route to the Gulf by 152 miles. They tamed the river and any tributary that might offer trouble again.

In the 1930s there was little doubt that "flood control" was desirable. Most years, people die from floods and property is lost. Who could argue that if engineering floods is possible, we should not do it? Recently though, "control" has been substituted for "management," and the prevailing wisdom (even in the Army Corps of Engineers) is that bigger dams make for greater damage once a big flood does come. Is it possible that the era of large dams for flood control and development has drawn to a close?

A few hours alone in a rental car have given me way too much time to think about all this and made me way too cynical about taming rivers and landscapes with reservoirs like Sardis. "God would have done it, if he had the money"—that's what they say about the federal agency's makeover of the world in its own image since 1865. As I drove out of Memphis, I pondered the South fallen off from what, as an old romantic, preservationist anarchist, I long for. I mourn all the species lost to development, the logging, the crude runoff from paving the continent, the engineered rivers in the Mississippi River Valley, and the man-manufactured lakes holding back the waters bound for the Gulf.

Though the name of Lake Sardis slightly echoes one of Faulkner's most famous families, Sartoris, I don't think the 1950 recipient of the Nobel Prize would recognize much of his native county now. Dixon says Faulkner knew Lake Sardis and even opposed it at first. He wrote a letter to the local Oxford paper articulating his views on what the Army Corps of Engineers called "progress." It's not hard to hear echoes of Faulkner's uneasy relationship with progress in the first few pages of "The Bear" from *Go Down, Moses*, first published in 1940, the year Sardis Lake's floodgates closed and water began to back up over the big bottom. In "The Bear," Faulkner describes the modern countryside around the bottom as "a corridor of wreckage and destruction" and compares progress moving through it with "the ruthless and irresistible deliberation of a locomotive, the shaggy tremendous shape." Dixon guesses that by the 1950s Faulkner seemed to have made his peace with the lake. He often escaped from his increasing fan base by retreating to a houseboat named "Mingagery" he kept at the Sardis marina. As one biographer said, "He spent a good deal of time on his boat, sulking, avoiding contact with the world." There's even a famous picture of the Nobel Prize winner plying the waters of Sardis Lake on a sailboat he owned called the "Ring Dove." As far as I know there are no photos of Faulkner in a canoe floating downstream toward Batesville on the Little Tallahatchie.

What would William Faulkner make of the interstate highway system that brought me here or the campers parked at the foot of the 15,000-foot dam? Driving in I saw a little slice of what's left of Faulkner's countryside—dogwoods in bloom, abandoned farmsteads, closed cinderblock country stores only a few generations removed from one like Flem Snopes might have run, a stray black dog working the roadside for whatever scraps he can find, a vista out over newly plowed fields of the hill country around Oxford, and the dark silence of a far way hardwood tree line in the distance. But there is also the new rural South— on the way down, signs advertised Mallard Pointe Golf Course halfway to Memphis, and a convenience store called "The Dam Store" anchored the turnoff for the resort on the lake's western shore. As I pull into the Sardis Dam parking lot, I think how for Faulkner the past pools in the present, wetting down the future, and never evaporates. From reading his novels and stories I know nothing's purely downstream in Faulkner's world.

I've arrived a little early, so I park the rental car and wait for Dixon's pickup. He's told me to look for a crew cab Toyota Tacoma, but it would be easy to spot the truck anyway because of his canoe. "By their racks, ye shall know them," said a bumper sticker I once saw on a paddler's car. I'm a little cold—dressed like a touring writer for the raw, wet, windy spring day. Though I know I'm going paddling I haven't packed well. I thought in April a pair of shorts and a tee would do. Leaving the motel at 6:00 A.M. I slipped on all three dress shirts I'd brought and a wind shell, but it's still not cutting the wind and chill. While I wait, I walk down and look at the Sardis spillway to keep warm. It's wide open, booming—a massive plug of heaving delta water from the impounded Tallahatchie River coming through every second. This chilly Easter morning locals fish the riprap banks. Just downstream a smaller, quiet lower lake spreads out, and three aluminum skiffs trawl down toward where the river flows out over a low-head dam. There's no shortage of reading material as I wait. A "posted limit" sign reminds the fishermen and fisherwomen they are allowed seven black bass or crappie per day.

Soon I'm walking back up the ramp to the parking lot, and Dixon's truck pulls in, followed by another car, a Chevy truck with a camper top and canoe on top. When Dixon's window comes down, I hear birdcalls coming from the cab. We shake hands though the open window and Dixon knows I'm a little confused by the birdcalls, and he explains that the bootleg bird-call tapes are a habit he picked up while he was writing his thesis at Mississippi on Audubon. "My wife nearly left me over these damn tapes," Dixon says. "I still don't know 'em all. Get in, we're gonna run the shuttle first."

When I'm in the warm cab and buckled in, Dixon nods back to the following Suburban and says he's brought a graduate school friend, Greg, along to paddle, says Greg is working on the prosody of English poetry. "A strange passion in Faulkner country," I comment, and Dixon just laughs. "It's a big department."

Dixon takes off, and we head back down Highway 315 to a cut-through gravel road that parallels the river five miles downstream to the next bridge, where we'll drop Greg's truck. Dixon says we'll stop along the way and walk a boardwalk through a tupelo swamp, something he thinks I should see if I'm going to visit Mississippi searching for Faulkner's big bottom. Unlike me, Dixon's dressed for the weather. He's two or three layers topped by a golden hunting jacket. He's got a ball cap to top off his head, blue jeans, and worn-out L.L. Bean "duck boots" to protect his feet from the wet morning as we paddle. Pulling into the parking lot for the boardwalk Dixon explains how it's not predicted to climb above 50 today and will stay windy. "Raw spring day," is how he puts it, looking at my underdressed torso. "I've got a second paddling jacket. You're gonna need it."

Dixon, Greg, and I walk from the parking lot toward the boardwalk. The sun's out, and it's warmer. Greg's a friendly guy, dressed like Dixon for the weather. Dixon tells him I've commented on the oddness of a scholar of English poetry prosody in

Faulkner country, and Greg makes it clear that when not study-
ing English poetry he gets in as many canoe expeditions as possible, day trips and overnights, the rhythm of canoe paddling
blending nicely with all the conventional rhythms of poetry. On
the way in Dixon says both he and Greg get to walk here more
than they get to canoe. This boardwalk is only twenty minutes
from Oxford and affords a nice escape from graduate school. He
directs my attention to two large clusters of buckeye growing
near the parking lot already boasting a showy display of red dangling blooms. I wish for a moment I had a concordance of all
Mississippi writers so I could see ways they've used plants in
their fiction. Is there anywhere in Faulkner where a character
comments on buckeye blooming in the spring? Does Eudora
Welty weave the buckeye into any story, or does a range map of
her fiction leave the buckeye high on the bluffs above the river?

When we enter the swamp proper Dixon points out tupelo
leafing out in the marginal forest, and I know I'm in the Deep
South. The rough buttressed trunks of the tupelo are dark gray-
ish, still wet from the rain blowing through in waves this morning. Is this the remaining Mississippi equivalent of the mythic
forest Faulkner found "somber, impenetrable" in "The Bear"?

We circle out on the wooden boardwalk to the middle of
the swamp, and it terminates at two large observation platforms.
Taking up the center of the swamp is a large beaver pond. I look
around. Two great blue herons fish in the shallows just far
enough away to stay undisturbed by our presence. A kingfisher
cackles as we pause. Dixon has brought his field glasses and
swivels them to his eyes and scans the distant tree line where he
knows from his other visits here there is a beaver lodge.

"Look at that," Dixon says, in a moment or two, pointing
toward the middle of the pond. With my bare eyes I can see
what looks like two muskrats on steroids that have risen out of
the pond to frolic on a hummock of brush. "Nutria," Dixon says.
"Two big ones. It looks like they are grooming each other." Dixon hands me the glasses, and I watch intently. They are not Old

Ben, the bear of the big bottom, but the wild nutria will have to do for megafauna today. As I watch, Greg gives me a little natural history. The rodents—close kin to beavers and muskrats—were introduced to the Gulf states as a furbearer from South America in the early 1900s. They've worked inland from freshwater marsh to marsh for a hundred years, helped along the way by a storm surge or two. Herbivores, they eat pickerelweed, cattail, and arrowhead, and in the winter gnaw the bark from wetland hardwoods. Nutria have long yellow incisors like beaver and graze up to 25 percent of their body weight in a single day.

Dixon adds that they are not beloved wildlife in the Delta. They destroy wetlands with their voracious grazing of aquatic plants, and the young are sexually mature in only four months. If nutria is an indicator species for anything it's how quickly things can get out of control when we try to engineer natural systems for our own good. The nutria is sort of a dark twin to Faulkner's bear roaming the big bottom for generations in spite of, as Faulkner beautifully puts it, "man's puny gnawing at the immemorial flank" of the bottom. Now we've gnawed practically everything away and sent in the mercenaries—the nutria, the Asian clams, the kudzu, and the Japanese honeysuckle—to gobble up and colonize what's left.

On the drive down to the takeout bridge we pass still active farm fields, newly plowed. Dixon points out an old abandoned silo with "white power" scrawled in black paint across the curving concrete. As we pass closer, I see it's also riddled with large-caliber bullet holes. "Well, it's still Mississippi," Dixon says, laughing. The scene chills me a little though, a hangover from *Mississippi Burning*. Violence is always right here, in imagination, just below the surface in the countryside—bullet holes and racist slogans—and any protection afforded the outsider drains away.

———

We drop Greg's truck at the takeout, transfer his boat, and drive back to the Sardis Dam. With gulls circling overhead and a two-foot dead gar, empty-eyed, bobbing at the water's edge, we put in at the boat ramp on the lower lake. Dixon and I push his four-teen-foot Old Town tandem canoe out from shore as Greg steps in his Mad River Intrepid canoe setup to paddle solo. A bass boat launches right as we do, and the local boys can't resist get-ting in a little shot at our mode of travel. "You boys might be needing a tow back," yells the Mississippi Bubba in camo bib overalls as we begin to stroke across the lake.

First two miles downstream the Tallahatchie, set free from the Sardis impoundment, meanders through forested banks of what Dixon calls "the corps land," and if I squint it's possible to imagine I'm paddling some primordial bend in an ancient Southern river. I ask Dixon where the Delta officially begins, and he repeats historian David Cohen's famous comment from 1935—"In the lobby of the Peabody Hotel in Memphis," then gives me the answer I'm looking for—"twenty miles southwest, but ecologically, it's right here. It's a fringe delta stream and shares many of the delta's characteristics—tupelo and other bot-tomland hardwoods, but it's also got the Northern Mississippi species like the dogwood."

I make a survey of the ecological zone we're passing through. It's a species of hardwood I'd expect along the shore. The dogwoods Dixon has mentioned are blooming in the under-story. Swallows work the surface of the river for insects. Then the trees disappear, and the vista opens up into newly plowed farmland, and the banks, upstream held in place by trees and understory vegetation, are now deeply eroded where the farmers have planted row crops right up to river's edge. "They all know about best-management practices," Dixon says. "But they choose to ignore them."

For an hour or so we talk about whatever is passing—a deer breaking through a thicket, great blue herons fishing in the shal-lows. Halfway down we take Greg's lead and follow him up a tributary creek coming in from the left bank. When we enter, it narrows down to ten feet, but we begin to see more birds in the denser cover—kingfishers, green herons, more great blues. Before we turn around, we even begin to see the distinctive flared trunks of some mature cypress.

As we float, Dixon talks about how much he loves a day on the river, any day. I ask if he's ever taken his canoe out on the Mississippi, and he recalls a race he'd been in, the only time he'd ever really paddled the big river in a canoe. He also talks about a long wild trip on the Pearl River in southern Mississippi he and Greg have been planning—six days, all the way to the Gulf, from Jackson on down. He seemed to anticipate these canoe trips the way the narrator of "The Bear" anticipated the yearly journey into the Big Bottom to hunt. The Big Bottom might be gone, but the yearning to get out in the dense woods is still around.

We've soon left the little tributary, and we're back to the river proper and headed downstream. We stop for water and some crackers on the only gravel bar we've seen—all river sand everywhere else. Here, the water rushes over a beach of dull cobbles, not so much many-colored as variations on a shade of brown, and Dixon mentions that Tallahatchie is an American Indian word that means either "river town" or "rock river." I pick one up the size of a baseball and feel the curve worn smooth by tumbling. The smoothness is a fossil of passing time, this chunk weathered or eroded out of an outcrop somewhere north of here and rolled along the river to end up at our feet.

Dixon says twenty miles southwest the Little Tallahatchie enters the Delta proper and begins its run over deep sediments laid down by thousands of years of Mississippi floods, the rich black alluvial soil where the blues grew alongside cypress, cotton, and soybeans. The Delta loam downstream birthed a culture, birthed a way of life, but the hill country we're floating through south of Lake Sardis did all right as well. It birthed Faulkner, an intellectual industry, birthed a place inhabited by stories, what historian Don H. Doyle calls "the most Southern of all places."

I'm out of place here, a native of the upper South plunged deep for a day in a landscape and topography I'm unfamiliar with. Though I can name a few, the riverside trees are still a little foreign, as is the weight of the air, the pitch of the horizon. If Doyle is right and Faulkner's Yoknapatawpha County, laid mythically on top of Dixon's real life Lafayette County, is the essential South, then I have a right to feel like I'm a visitor. I settle back to appreciate it. I look south with the flowing river. The sun falls in glittering slats across the surface. The water surges over the cobbles at the edge of the bed.

But soon time it's time to come back to the river and its flow, step in the boats and let the current take us downstream. Knowing too much can tear you from the moment, can get you lost in ideas and speculation, and when you finally do look around you have to blink hard to get some focus again. As we head downstream, I see the ridges are a quarter mile distant from the channel here. In the old days, before flood control, the river took every inch of the space between the ridges in high flow. Now the corps controls the river through the spillways at Sardis Dam. I ask Dixon if he's ever seen the river high, and he says higher than this, but not much, not out in the fields laying down silt like it used to every spring. This makes me think about the river moving us downstream and the action of the ancient current. I remember how the river channel is almost completely absent from Faulkner's account of hunting in the Big Bottom. You know the river's there because it has to be, but McCaslin never describes it. McCaslin's attention is on the woods, still thick and mysterious in the floodplain before the loggers take it down, not the river running through it.

But today we are canoeists, not hunters, and so we make our recreation in the river channel. For Faulkner, "The Bear" is a eulogy to a lost way of life, a time when once a year men retreated to the pure Mississippi wilderness to hunt for a month at a time living in a camp. We retreat with river running, paddling stretches of territory where it's possible to forget the university and the soccer fields and the spillways and the dams upstream. Outdoor recreation has become our passage, our deliverance from town life.

As we float along, Dixon gets quiet, listening for birds he can recall from his Audubon tapes, and it gives me time to conjure some half-baked theory about when Faulkner wrote and how it was like a last big wild river being dammed. All those Mississippi stories from Chickasaw and Choctaw times, forward flowing around and through him, finally ending up in more than a dozen novels and a hundred short stories. Now, fifty years later, he's a cultural lake, an impoundment of ideas and images and stories, and all the graduate students at Mississippi and all over the world are out sport fishing on Lake Faulkner.

Soon we see the bridge in the distance, and we know the five-mile float is over. There's a local fishing next to where we take out, and Greg drops a paddle as he steps from his canoe. We watch it circulate in a strong eddy just out of reach. If it were warmer we'd just jump in and grab it, but we made it this far high and dry. Finally, we borrow the guy's fishing net to pull the errant paddle back to shore.

We haul the boats to the truck through an old cotton field. From where we take out the Little Tallahatchie flows another forty miles to join the Mississippi River. What's the river like the rest of the way? Dixon ties down the canoes, says it flattens out, slips down the Yazoo Bluffs, joins the Yazoo River, and then the Yazoo slides out on the vast Delta floodplain, bends into deep meanders, and slows down to a sluggish crawl south before disappearing ceaselessly into the Mississippi's deep dark flow.

"One big field curving into the body of the continent," that's how Dixon has described his home country, the lower Mississippi Delta. We get in Greg's truck to drive back to Sardis Dam, where I'll rejoin my book tour. I'm renewed by paddling, even this small taste of it on the Little Tallahatchie, and remember it will soon be time to join up with my literary life. I've got a book tour to finish. I remember even the rivers work hard for a living in Mississippi, absorbing fertilizer runoff, pesticides, anything from industrial agriculture that drains off crops and soil. Critics have said that Faulkner viewed nature as something mysterious, frightening, and exhilarating. What would Faulkner think of our day on the remnant river?

As we rode back up to Sardis, I registered with Dixon and Greg a little exhilaration brought on by our canoe trip, but other Faulknerian themes would have to go unfulfilled. I was never really frightened, and the only mystery for me was why the corps dammed so many Southern rivers like the Tallahatchie in the first place. Was it simply another chapter in what Faulkner called "man's ramshackle confederation against environment," or is flood control and recreation on the big lake worth the loss of wild rivers? Laurence Buell argues that Faulkner probably had not developed anything we would recognize as an "environmental imagination" until after the writing of *Go Down, Moses*, and not long after the book's publication.

North of where my car waited most of the Little Tallahatchie now sleeps under the waters of progress, and the floodgates of Sardis Dam spill a little of what's left of the ancient river at the feet of bass fishermen. Faulkner obviously believed in the country of the imagination, and I try to bring myself to trust it the way he did. Maybe this essay about a day's paddling redeems what's lost in this country, with recreational canoeing acting as a fit substitution for hunting. What's left of a real river once you dam it? What remains of a scrap of storied wilderness once the logging trains, the skidders move in on it? These questions rattle around among us in the cab of the truck as we skirt the river, headed back toward where I've parked the memory of Faulkner's Big Woods.

GRADIENT

Even the upper end of the river
believes in the ocean.

—*William Stafford,*
from "Climbing Along the River"

My friend Frank has rigged his garage for the storage of canoes. He has three, one a light, modern Kevlar model and the other two, beautiful wood-and-canvas Maine Guide canoes. His boats are lovingly maintained. As we survey his collection, I see that there is space for one more canoe in the rafters just in case the need or opportunity arises to acquire another. I have no doubt that in Frank's mind the space will be filled with wood and canvas. These lovely craft are an anachronistic habit of mind Frank doesn't seem predisposed to abandon.

When I stare into the rafters of Frank's garage at his wood-and-canvas canoes, I admit they puzzle me. They are the sort of craft phased out at summer camps before I was born, when aluminum took over the canoe business after World War II, and yet here they sit in Frank's garage, stored carefully, maintained exquisitely, and as he reminds me, paddled frequently. I know that part of my bemusement is practical. An aluminum canoe, like the battered one I own down South, can lean, oxidizing, against an outside garage wall, home to possums, but a wood-and-canvas canoe, like a good guitar, calls to be put to use and has to be kept out of the weather.

Frank's two wood-and-canvas canoes call my own loyalty to watercraft into question. I'm a generation younger, and I grew up paddling white water in metal and synthetic boats, beginning with aluminum, which was soon replaced with plastic, fiberglass, and more recently, Kevlar. I've bumped over rocks and dragged boats through cobbles and gravel patches with no concern for damage to my craft. Paddling with Frank this week, I will not have the luxury of contemporary sloppiness. Every bump of Frank's canoe, during carry or paddle, will be noted, if not by a smudge on the white canvas bottom, then by Frank himself, who will fix the boat before it's returned to the rafters.

I'm up in Maine to paddle white water, and this is how Frank has it planned: we'll take two canoes with us for my first excursion into the North Woods, several hours up the Kennebec from his house near the coast. Frank's crafts of choice for the trip are the functional, fast Kevlar model and the heavily rockered fifteen-foot wood-and-canvas Maine Guide canoe, called a Templeton or a Comstock, built for Frank by Fred Reckerds near Rockwood, Maine, at the south end of Moosehead Lake. The wood-and-canvas canoe was developed in Bangor, Maine, during the 1870s based on Penobscot birch-bark canoes, and the construction principles are similar—thin, flexible ribs and planks covered with canvas instead of bark. In Maine people still paddle them, though in the Southeast, where I'm from, you're more likely to see a wood-and-canvas canoe in the rafters of a summer camp dining hall or pressed into service as a salad bar in the occasional backwoods roadhouse.

Frank and I are both writers, though very different in our paddling and prose styles. Frank's sentences are elegant and dense. His output is measured. He's published only two books in twenty years. I'm prolific. My writing is more like a spring river in full flush. It's in the area of subject matter that we tend to converge. We both have written books about floating Southern rivers and collections of reflective essays with human culture and natural history at their often-watery cores. When we get together, every year or so, we end up paddling and talking more about canoes than we do writing. Looking up into Frank's rafters I realize it might be the same thing—writing and paddling. Frank does everything with the same balance of practicality and joy that I see displayed in the rafters of his garage.

I have an afternoon and then a full day before my flight back to South Carolina. Today, Frank wants to introduce me to the ancient art of canoe poling, and so we'll take the two boats up, drive a logging road to where it ends at a put in called Spencer Stream, and pole the Kevlar canoe in the Class I ripples on a river ominously called the Dead. Next day, we'll get a local guide to shuttle us back to Spencer Stream and paddle tandem in his wood-and-canvas canoe sixteen miles from the put in to the Dead River's confluence with the Kennebec at the Forks.

Preparing to leave Bowdoinham, I help hoist the Kevlar canoe out of its rack in the rafters, and then Frank lowers the bow of the canoe on pulleys and line from the ceiling. He slides the stern from its high crosspiece and settles the boat on his shoulders and the center paddling thwart. Walking with the canoe he looks like some sort of Greek monster Hercules might have encountered, two legs and a humongous beak and crest. The Reckerds (he often calls the boat by its builder's name) rocks on his hidden shoulders as he crosses between the early sun and me. After a short walk Frank slides the canoe on the Chevy truck racks and ties it down. I've learned to stop asking if I can help. It's something Frank loves to do alone, a necessary selfishness of an aging canoeist.

The canoe, like corn and the Clovis point, is a product of the New World. The force at work on the aboriginal mind to shape the canoe was most likely travel of differing distances, some of them quite epic. In the southern Piedmont and mountains, travel, even for the aboriginal populations, was essentially trail walking, so we as adaptive souls had little trouble taking to the interstate highways.

Gradient was to be avoided in laying out trails. The earliest ones followed the contours of hills and hopped from valley to valley through gaps. Traveling game originally sought the ease of low gradient, and so 18,000 years ago early hunters tracked their prey and adapted these passages. The car, as anthropologist Edward T. Hall suggests, evolved as an extension of the feet, a certain sort of dream in men's minds. The interstates followed, extending the trail to rubber tires and petroleum. Canoes and rivers interest me more than cars and highways, though much of my time is spent driving interstates to reach rivers and the places (put ins we call them now) where access is easy.

From the St. Lawrence southward on the Atlantic slope, dugout canoes (the aboriginal word "kenu" means dugout) were also used for travel and war. Some were more than a hundred feet long, hollowed from the single trunk of a pine, poplar, or cypress. Mostly dugouts were heavy, but some were also so small it's said a woman could heft one on her back and walk from stream to stream. These canoes were hollowed out by fire and ax and on the coasts often painted bright colors. Huge painted dugout canoes carrying twenty-five paddlers on each side and up to eighty-five warriors attacked De Soto in the 1560s, mixing beauty and death in the industry of canoes on the Southeast coast. The wood-and-canvas canoes of Frank's are a long way from the dugouts of the early Southeast, but to me they seemed just about as distant.

Travel was something that was not to be taken lightly in the cold and rocky northern waters where the birch-bark canoe developed thousands of years ago. As a combination of elements goes, cold and water can be deadly. Two paddlers in a canoe upset far from shore might have five minutes of clear panic before the bliss of hypothermia sets in. On a river, in rapids crazy with spring rains, the canoeist might face similar conditions complicated by rocks and current. In all high country, gradient is a given consideration as a river flows toward the coast. The trail, one could argue, led forward to the interstate, the foot to the wheel, but the river trails still offer in most places their primary courses, and the canoe is an original human response to those conditions.

From Labrador to Alaska, as far north as Kodiak and south, continent wide, until the diminished size of the white birch limited its production, the birch-bark canoe appeared as a response to the landscape. There is a sophistication, a maturity, to canoe design. The bark canoe is seaworthy enough to endure waves of large lakes and tides, light of draft enough to glide through the shrunken rivers and streams of midsummer, capacious enough to carry a large load on a long expedition, easy to repair, and light enough to portage. No doubt there is beauty in its long lines. High in quality of material and workmanship, the birch-bark canoe took on different forms. Near the mouth of the Yukon River, where there is turbulence, the craft was pointed at both ends like a kayak and even partially decked over. In eastern Canada, the bow and stern of the canoe were raised and rounded.

When constructing a bark canoe, large strips are formed into a "skin," and then a skeleton of spruce ribs and decking is fitted to the shape, the craftsman working from the outside in. No nails are used, the craft predating the introduction of metal to these cultures. The canoe is held together by gravity, spruce gum, and for lashing, the roots of the white pine.

It's not far from bark to the natural ingredients Frank prefers and preserves in his paddling preferences—wood and canvas. It's definitely less of a leap from birch bark to a wood-and-canvas canoe than from wood and canvas to aluminum, sort of like the distance between a turned maple bowl and a beer can.

As we'd stared up into the rafters, Frank had qualified his attraction to wood and canvas. It's more, he'd said, than their Luddite appeal. Wood and canvas canoes, he explained, have the best balance "between rigidity and flexibility of any material." Wood and canvas, he'd said, is surprising in this way. "The bottom can flex up three inches or more before ribs begin to splinter, if you are able to go over the rock at reduced speed." He pointed out this may be worth remembering as we work our way down the Dead.

———

After loading the canoes we drive inland, following the Kennebec, one of Maine's biggest rivers. Although I only have a day and a half to burn in Maine's backcountry, Frank wants me to experience the river from the seat of one of his Maine guide canoes. The two canoes—the Kevlar Mad River and the custommade wood-and-canvas guide canoe—ride securely on top of his truck. As we drive a road along the Kennebec River, Frank explains what he sees as the differences in Northern and Southern canoeing. In the North, where the lightweight birch-bark canoe was developed, the canoe became an extension of the aboriginal and later the European culture. It was a working craft perfect for a water land of lakes and rivers. "The norm up here," he explains, "was the long canoe trip involving a lot of rough water."

In the South, the wood-and-canvas canoe, the industrial descendant from birch bark, was adapted as recreational equipment, camp gear, in the 1920s. These recreational wood-and-canvas canoes were kept at mountain lake cottages and summer camps all along the East Coast. It was in the southern Appalachians that adventurous camp directors and canoe instructors began to develop white water programs and paddle the boats on local rivers. From his base of operations at Camp Mondamin for Boys and Greencove for Girls, Frank Bell Sr. explored many of the white water rivers in the Southeast from the seat of a wood-and-canvas canoe as early as the 1920s. By the late 1950s canoe instruction and programming at a half dozen camps, with legendary instructors like Fritz Orr Sr., Ramone Eaton, John Delabar, and Hugh Caldwell, included ambitious white water trips on the Nantahala and Chattooga Rivers. My friend Frank says he took philosophy classes in the early 1960s at Sewanee University from Hugh Caldwell and finds it strange that as a student he had been unaware of his professor's summer employment in the mountains east of Sewanee as a white water canoe instructor and explorer of many of the region's now premier white water runs.

It's ironic, I point out, how Southern suburban children in the 1950s and 1960s were exposed to running white water at summer camps, and from there it was only a short distance to an Atlanta poet and advertising executive, James Dickey, imagining four suburban men with canoes tied to the roof of their International Scout heading into the Southern mountains for a weekend of retreat and adventure that ends so famously tragically in the novel *Deliverance*. The men living in rural Maine would never be so unfamiliar with their rivers as Dickey's locals seemed to be, Frank says, and in 1960 wood-and-canvas canoes in the back-yards we are passing would have been as common as bass boats.

Frank's right. To the locals up here we might not look as much like Burt and the boys to the rural folk we pass with these canoes on the truck. I can tell he doesn't like the comparison. There's something he's cultivated in his love for boats and boat-ing that's in a different watershed than what's driven millions upriver to float down various "Deliverance rivers" all over the country since 1973. Paddling is craft—even art—to him. When Frank describes paddlers he makes distinctions such as, "He's an experienced paddler but not a good paddler." As I listen, I won-der what sort of canoeist I'll look like to him by the end of the trip.

Midday we arrive at the Forks, the confluence of the Kennebec and the Dead, a timber and fishing town now sharing space with raft buses and the business of industrial white water. One mile upstream from the Forks is Moxie Stream, a small turbulent tributary that free falls toward the Kennebec gorge. When we arrive at the junction of the rivers, Frank first drives me on up there to see some "kayaking water," a stairstepping series of Class IV to V rapids the locals like to run. In the pull-off there is a truck with racks on top and two kayaks. "Manually propelled ATVs," Frank says, joking about the tiny yellow and red boats as we pass.

As we stand and look down at Moxie Stream, Frank wants to make it clear, though, that it's not entirely on aesthetic grounds he prefers canoes over kayaks. It's practical. "A canoe is less able to handle extreme white water like this," he says. "But it is a lot more versatile. You can take long trips with it, fish from it, run moderate white water in it, and carry it around immoderate white water, stand up in it, pole it upstream." And the sport of kayaking has little connection now to its origins. As Frank puts it, "Kayaking is an art form enormously refined from some single aspect of its original purpose." Recreation, he says, taken one way, means going back to beginnings.

Even though I've kayaked for twenty years I share some of Frank's disgust at where the passion for new boat design and a higher degree of "playability" has led the industry of white water. When I see the tiny "play-boats" tied to the racks of young boaters, I see that now the sport has closer ties to surfing and skateboarding than it does to traditional canoeing. "Materials, design, and technique" are the elements one historian of white water delineates as the through-line for white water boating from deep past to dawning present. As these elements changed, so changed the activity. When I began to paddle, kayaks were thirteen-feet long, molded from cross-linked polyethylene plastic, and designed primarily for "river running." The crafts had rounded bottoms, no sharp edges or rails, and tips so sharp we used tennis balls on them to keep from impaling our paddling partners in eddies. And technique? To paddle a kayak safely downstream you needed similar strokes to that of canoeing. Four basic strokes could get you in a kayak from put in to takeout—forward, back, pry, and draw. The only technique specialized for the kayak was the Eskimo roll, a way of righting the boat, but "rolling" was not an essential for river running.

These days kayaks are designed for a host of "rodeo moves" with names that sound right out of gymnastics, rollerblading, snowboarding, skateboarding, and surfing—McTwist, pirouette, whippet, loop, airwheel, clean 360, cartwheel, flat spin, and olie.

Many paddlers have abandoned rivers, instead spending all afternoon on one wave near a "park and play" spot.

Boats are so small they can now fit out of sight in the hatchback of an SUV. I've always felt I sound like a geezer when I begin to talk this way. Turning my back on the present of boat design and use sounds to me a little like an old man longing nostalgically for the past. As what John McPhee in *The Survival of the Bark Canoe* once called "a canoe-man," Frank doesn't care for the little kayaks either, but I know from what he's said in the past that he believes nostalgia is a sort of selective amnesia. I like to think Frank's disgust is based more on aesthetic and moral grounds.

Late that afternoon we drive the sixteen-mile gravel road to the confluence of Spencer Stream and the Dead. We'll leave from this put in for our paddle back to the Forks tomorrow, but today, Frank wants to show me a little about poling in the Kevlar canoe. The road ends at the river-wide thirty-foot horseshoe Grand Falls, and it's there we take the canoe and pole off the truck and play for an hour or two in the fast water. "Canoe poling is like paddling in that it is self-evident and anybody can do it, but doing it well is another matter, and it's remarkable what a skilled person can do, upstream or down," Frank says. I watch as he stands in the canoe with the long aluminum pole in both hands like a thin jousting stick. Then, the pole extended hand over hand along the stream's rocky bottom, Frank effortlessly moves the canoe upstream across a tongue of fast water and into an eddy on the other side.

Then Frank does it again, climbing thirty feet up the small rapid toward the falls. I watch him several times as he sets his angle, acquires speed for the ferry, and leans slightly into the downstream pole and crosses the current. I'm not sure I can do it, though I know I will soon have a chance. As I watch I try to figure out the advantages of poling over paddling and finally set-

65

tle on the contact with the stream's bottom and the ability to climb small rapids effortlessly. Frank says the experts can pole up Class III white water and I'm sure it's true.

I'm not so sure I believe Frank's assertion that the technique is "self-evident" and worry I will make a fool of myself when he hands me the pole. The whole thing reminds me a little too much of my one attempt at punting on England's Cam River while in Cambridge one summer. That long-ago afternoon I remember I had little skill at moving the boat with any grace or accuracy in spite of hundreds of tourists all around for role models.

When I'm finally holding the pole and standing in the canoe, I find some of the basics of poling second nature—the angle I need to set for crossing the current, reading water, knowing where to enter the stream. It's the balance and where to place the pole that throws me off. I find myself hunkered in the boat in an attempt to lower my center of gravity. In five minutes of poling my thighs and lower back are so tight I don't think I can survive very long. From shore Frank tells me to relax and stand up more.

After five or six attempts to climb the small rapid I swing the canoe to shore and step out. I've poled successfully only in content not form. I've achieved my goal of poling upstream, but I can feel in my body how uncomfortable I've been the whole time. The Zen Buddhists never talk about "beginner's body," only "beginner's mind." Learning a new physical skill at forty-five is not a comfortable thing. I can see from my poling sampler that expert's status or even intermediate in this skill would be a lofty goal. Frank says it's been a great skill to learn in his late fifties and early sixties, and he says he's finally on his way to feeling comfortable with a pole in his hands. As we load the boat on the truck to drive back to the Forks, I'm thinking I'll be glad to get a paddle back in my hands tomorrow on the Dead in spite of the radical change in equipment I'll experience with the wood-and-canvas canoe.

———

Next morning, we hire a local to shuttle Frank's truck back to the Forks. Once we're on the Dead, there will be no road crossings for sixteen miles. As we drive up, Frank points out that if something happens and we smash the boat up on the rocks we'll have to walk out a mile or so through the woods to get to the put in access road we're now driving. This paddle will take me as deep into "roadless" as I've ever been in a watercraft. We'll have the river to ourselves, though. We're paddling on one of the Dead's "low-water" days with only natural flow. None of the thrill seekers will crowd the river. On peak release days from April to October the dam releases 1,500 to 5,500 cubic feet per second. On these days the Dead is one of the most popular white water runs, with some of the 90,000 who run Maine's rivers each year floating it.

Our shuttle guide, a local store clerk from the Forks, drops us and our boats and gear at the put in and wishes us luck. He drives away leaving us standing in the parking area. I'm a little self-conscious, dressed like a kayaker in spite of my change of craft for the day. I've strapped on my helmet, including dangling nose plug for rolling, pulled on my blue nylon dry top and my blue splash pants. Topping it all off are my bright blue rubber booties with white soles. Everything I'm wearing would have to be bought at a white water outfitters shop. When I go on a river I'm always specialized, geared up for the sport I love. Frank, in contrast, could comfortably walk into a bait and tackle shop and buy a lure or two or paddle downstream in his canoe. He's dressed more like a Maine guide—heavy tweed wool pants, a plaid cotton twill shirt on which the collar has been worn down to white batting, and L.L. Bean duck boots. His only concession to the industry of white water is a beautiful new gray Patagonia paddling jacket he says he's acquired at a Friends of Merry Meeting Bay auction. Warming his head is a Duke Forestry School cap, a gift from his daughter who went there. In the wood-and-canvas Templeton are two Tide bottle bailers with the tops cut out, a fly rod in a case, four paddles, Frank's big green dry bag with our lunch, and my smaller one with paddling gloves and a black kayaking beanie, in case my head gets cold.

The raft companies headquartered at the Forks advertise this river as having the longest stretch of continuous white water in the East, and looking downstream from the put in I can see why. The gradient is steady, and the stream's bed is thick with boulders. As we stand on shore, Frank points out how we'll work our way to the far shore for our descent through the first rapid, Spencer Rips. When I'd asked a kayaking friend who knows the Kennebec watershed about paddling the Dead on natural flow, he'd said, "Oh no. Way too bony." Frank seems to think it's just right, though, for what we want, a sixteen-mile run down to the Forks with conditions much like a trapper might have experienced a century before—enough water to float the wood-and-canvas boat but in the descent the challenge of a math problem at every moment. Where to run though the cobbles? Where to find enough flow to make the gradient work for us? Sitting in the bow of the canoe on the Spencer Stream side of the river, I'm already a little tired thinking how many choices we will have to make to get safely downstream. The river is fast, and it will be no pleasure float. I step into the canoe and sit in the bow seat, resting my feet on the varnished ribs of the bow with the planking underneath. The Templeton is a lovely craft, and I make my vow to the river gods to do my part to keep it whole on this descent. We peel out into the current and work our way across to the other shore, and I look back upstream at Grand Falls and tuck the sound of its falling current into my memory.

Spencer Rips is a fast series of three-foot waves at the termination of a tilted cobble run. In the eddy at the bottom Frank says the raft companies like the big Class III to IV compression waves that form on the surface as the release passes over the rocky bottom here. It's a good indication they'll get their money's worth on the Dead. He reminds me again what we'll experience today is much more technical with less than 1,000 cubic feet per second of natural flow spilling through boulder gardens that are pretty much continuous for sixteen miles. I realize as we work downstream it's the ultimate canoe run, especially in Frank's fragile wood-and-canvas canoe.

After we paddle through Spencer Rips, the first half of the Dead blurs into one continuous morning of white water. I know there are named rapids somewhere in the riverbed below us, but they are hard to pick out. I'm working so hard all I can do is recite what should be here—the Minefield, Humpty-Dumpty, the Basin, Elephant Rock. I've read the guidebook, and I know that Enchanted Stream enters the river from the left, and I want to see a tributary with such a mythical name, but the banks in the distance dissolve as I focus on the ten or twenty feet in front of the canoe.

From the stern Frank sets the general course, calls out the direction we need to go, and I respond with my minor corrections using bow or cross-bow strokes. The Reckerds, the most heavily rockered of any of Frank's canoes, responds quickly to the corrections. I've heard canoe instructors joking how any tandem craft should be called "the divorce boat" since paddling one in white water is often fraught with conflict, but so far Frank and I make a happy old odd couple, and I honor his commands. I cherish the clear channel he always guides us toward. Only once do we hear the rifle-shot sound of a wood rib cracking as it comes into direct contact with a cobble in its path. Mostly we manage to keep the boat in the swift water and off the rocks.

Halfway down we need a break from the nonstop "reading" of the white water, so we pull over in a big eddy and walk a mile along an old logging road. My land legs return quickly and so does my land-mind. The contrast of the trail to the river is perfect for reflection. Watery road and logging road—each of them trails to somewhere interesting. I adjust my vision to terrestrial surprises and start to think horizontal again after a morning of looking for whatever challenge is out ahead. Frank points out there might be ruins along the way from the logging business that has been Maine's main industry since before Thoreau took his trip into the woods in the middle of the nineteenth century, but we see none of the cribwork fallen into the underbrush. I comment that it's a young woods with maples six-to-ten-inch girths thickly crowding the trail. Frank says they may be older than I think, that trees in the north woods don't grow as fast as those woods down south I hold up for comparison. After we head back for the river, Frank points out the fiddlehead ferns everywhere and how the markets back home in Bowdoinham will soon be full of them. Back at the boat we eat our lunch on the bank next to a shaded eddy. We have turkey sandwiches, gorp, oranges, and oatmeal cookies.

When we start down the river again there is little space for reflection, but it creeps in anyway. I think about canoes and kayaks the rest of the way. "Every force evolves a form," the Shakers say. There were many aboriginal responses to travel by water, each appropriate to the situation: the kayak and umiak, rafts of rushes lashed together and abandoned on the far side of a deep ford, hide boats stretched over frames of birch saplings, crude bark canoes constructed for single crossings and left for the return passage, loose windfall logs pointed for the other shore. To craft is to manufacture with care and attention to detail. To build a craft to survive is to know just how much attention a particular situation demands, so that craft and survival evolve as a dance of conditions.

None of these watercraft, as far as the literature shows, were constructed for recreation, as many kayaks and canoes today are. They were crafted for work of various forms—hunting, fishing, gathering, travel. Estimates are that an aboriginal kayak or birch-bark canoe may have survived five seasons or so under the pressures of utility, a dugout, many decades, particularly the cypress models of the Southern coast.

Paddling techniques can't be carbon dated, and there are no fossil remains, no artifacts. We can only extrapolate backward into the past from boat and paddle designs. Most paddles were built for power and speed—a tapered blade at one end, a grip at the other. In my living room I have a five-foot aboriginal paddle carved from a single piece of tropical wood in Suriname. I spotted it stashed with one of two others in the bow of a twenty-foot dugout canoe. It was used, I observed, for drawing the boat to shore or emergency propulsion when the outboard failed to fire and the boatman was forced to recover the virtue of the paddle stroke.

Before outboard motors were affixed to the sterns of dugouts in the last surviving backwaters of boating, they would not have required a sophisticated array of strokes. A forward stroke purposely applied, a crude draw, and ruddering steerage would have sufficed in Suriname or South Carolina for moving the boat from point to point on a black-water river or a calm bay. Dugouts, as a cultural form, are stable craft, sitting steady in the water, but do not lend themselves to the rocky rivers. It is in these rocky rivers where the bark canoe proved valuable.

The first day in a canoe course you learn a canoeist's technique for making a boat go straight—the classic J stroke. The stroke could easily have been perfected in the far north by aboriginal paddlers crossing lakes in high winds, digging hard for each inch of forward momentum against the backdrop of birches and pines along the shore. The cross-bow draw I'm using to move us through rapids may have been discovered descending through gradient like the Dead's, steep enough to wrap a boat around a long run of current and glacial till. Much of this is speculation, but it is of the sort that derives from floating rivers like the Dead.

Almost five hours after we put in at Spencer Stream we approach Poplar Hill Falls, the last set of rapids before we reach

our takeout near the Dead's confluence with the Kennebec. I
look back from my bow seat and see the first concern on Frank's
face. He says he wants to get out and scout this one, a formidable drop even at these low water levels. As we stand on the bank
and look downstream, I can see the gradient is much steeper
than the twenty-nine-feet per mile of what's upstream. At higher
water levels Poplar Hill Falls would be a solid Class IV rapid.
Even with natural flow I can still see large waves and holes, particularly on the left side. Frank looks it over, and we both agree
we should probably run left. The holes and waves are bigger
there, but it's much less bony, and the chance of flushing
through upright is much higher. We don't think much more
about it. We simply get back in the boat and push off into the
current.

The roar of water falling over stone is distinct and drowns
out what anxiety I may have. Frank sets the line and we commit
to the run. We are moving faster than we have all day. It's as if
we're on a tabletop tilted downstream. Frank calls out "left" and
"draw right," and we're in the middle of it, the water breaking
over the bow of the canoe, but we stay upright. By the time we're
through the worst our boat is practically swamped but afloat.

"This is the most like Southern white water of anything
we've paddled today," I say to Frank, who is bailing water with
the Clorox bottle. "I'm exhilarated!" Frank smiles. I can tell he's
happy we're safely at the bottom, but I get the feeling Poplar Hill
Falls was not his favorite part of the run. To revel in the adrenaline settling back to normal levels is a little too much like recreational rafting for him, too akin to those boys running waterfalls
in their kayaks, to those tourists who come on fat-release days to
conquer the Dead. Frank revels in the work of bailing to keep us
afloat just as he worked at the steady job of edging a wood-and-
canvas canoe down the Dead like the old Northwoods trappers
and traders used to. I take off my helmet and can't wait until we
get to the truck and I can change into some regular clothes. Paddling this canoe on the Dead is the most difficult thing I've ever

done on white water. I think how much fun the recreational paddlers I know in the Southeast would have doing this but realize it would be almost impossible to get them here to this anachronistic moment—two grown men in a wood-and-canvas canoe half-filled with river water successfully running a rapid near the craft's limits. But there are a few, just like there are bow and crossbow hunters and golfers who enjoy playing with wooden shafts. When we get to shore Frank takes off his blue Patagonia paddling jacket, revealing his old work shirt, dry as a bone. We are connected backward through our passions.

LAKE CONESTEE

Dave Hargett's dream for Lake Conestee isn't really visible from the parking lot of the Racecar Speedy Mart. The impressive nineteenth-century stone dam on the Reedy River in Greenville, South Carolina, is in clear view, though, and the boarded-up textile mill, closed twenty years ago, crowds in everyone's line of sight just off Conestee Mill Road. To anyone driving past, the eighteen of us—two Wofford College professors, fifteen college students, and Dave—look a little suspicious standing among the fire ant hills and stunted pines on the ridge above the river.

It's early fall, and in only the minute or two we've stood with our freshmen looking out over the Reedy River, we all consider something beautiful: a great blue heron and redtail hawk crossing paths low above what's left of the lake behind the dam. Appreciation of beauty in the natural world is something easy to teach. Convincing these students that they are somehow responsible for understanding and even correcting the sort of environmental disaster that is contained in the story of Conestee is more difficult and will take far longer than an afternoon visit.

Dave is up for it, though. He's sent us links to the Conestee website, and with my colleague Ellen Goldey's expertise as a toxicologist, we've sorted through pages of environmental history. Slender and dressed comfortably for the field in chinos and hiking boots, Dave could just as easily be leading a bird walk as briefing a class on Conestee. He waves his arms and begins to tell us of the vision that has possessed a handful of people who have seen the potential here: a long corridor of greenway stretching for twenty-five miles from Furman University all the way to this depressed site.

We've prepped our students for the Conestee field trip, told them that environmental visions in South Carolina have been few and far between. It's a state known more for a Bible Belt faith in "economic development," no matter what the cost. A few families got rich off ventures like Conestee Mill, but the working people in the Upstate have suffered mightily through two hundred years of Industrial Revolution—first the clear-cutting iron industry, then the positioned textiles, and now real estate speculation. Unlike the ruling class, the poor have little to show for their role in what former Supreme Court Justice William Brennan once called "the war against the world." Wages have remained low, and the old industrial communities—once thriving, though poor communities—turned blighted when industries left, chasing even cheaper wages overseas.

The waterways of Upstate South Carolina have shown the strain of "progress" maybe most of all. Nearly all the rivers and creeks in the region are classified impaired by the South Carolina Department of Health and Environmental Control (DHEC). All are unsafe to drink, and most aren't fit for swimming. Some still can't support aquatic life, thirty years after the Clean Water Act was meant to put a stop to wholesale exploitation of these waterways for greed and profit.

The discussion and this field trip are part of two required general education courses, biology and humanities, linked around a theme, in this case, "The Nature and Culture of Water." Ellen, in a former life, worked as a researcher for the Environmental Protection Agency, so she has a keen interest in toxins and has taught the students enough chemistry and freshwater ecology concerning the site to grasp its complexity as an industrial "brownfield." Holding down the role of humanities professor, I've spent my class time talking about Upstate environmental history, about issues of environmental justice and the complex set of values that allow a community to dam a river and then, in a little more than one hundred years, destroy the lake behind the dam.

Two of the students, Thomas and Amelia, took the linked classes as freshmen, and now they're back as rising sophomores to assist. They help the students grasp the material, give the linked courses some continuity through their two-year participation, and shoulder the weighty titles of "preceptors" for the courses. Today, their main role will be as kayak wranglers as we take the students out on the lake.

Dave, a local environmental engineer and activist, drives us behind the Speedy Mart and through a chain-link fence to a launch site on the impoundment's east lobe. We unload our boats—enough kayaks for us and the students and Dave's canoe—and Dave gathers us at the water and fills us in on the research to make the place real. He knows the history of this watery landscape, how in the 1940s, Lake Conestee (Cherokee for "beautiful water") was hundreds of acres of open water, a power source for the mill since the 1830s. It was also a recreational centerpiece for the community and a source of supplementary protein for the workers—fish and turtles.

Now, aerial photos show a fifty-year-old river-bottom forest maturing over thick sediment laid down by the Reedy during Greenville's busiest industrial decades. There's clay here from the clearing of the land for early agriculture, eroded off the Donaldson air base in the 1940s, the I-85 construction project of the late 1950s, and the industrial boom of the 1960s, all before there was any sediment control. And not only sediment came down the Reedy River channel to this first major dam below Greenville proper: there are also all the compounds used to create our current "standard of living"—heavy metals, lead, zinc, copper, PCBs, and pesticides in vast quantities, all "stored" here behind the thick Conestee Mill dam.

The students take notes as Dave tells us about the vision for "Conestee Park" as we look back upstream toward the horizon line marking the spot where water courses down the old dam's face. What Dave sees when he looks toward the dam is the silted-in lake above, a place with boatable water and wildlife habitat. What Dave and the Conestee Foundation, the nonprofit that has purchased the lake, dream will be here are hiking and biking trails and an ecological education center on the three hundred acres of slough, island, shoreline, and mudflat near what he says will be the urban center of the city of Greenville in a decade.

We fit everyone in their kayaks. Thomas and Amelia go through a safety talk and check to make sure all the personal flotation devices are snug and secure. These are stable lake kayaks, so we don't see any trouble with navigating the calm lake and river. Howard, a large basketball player, can't get his feet in his boat, so we switch him into a longer one. Amelia makes a joke about how if Howard's boat somehow sinks he can paddle one of his sneakers back to shore.

As we launch our boats, I sort the complex smells of this place: peat or sewage? Somewhere below in the sediment is what Dave calls "black mayonnaise," a layer of sludge laid down years ago before Greenville treated the discharge from its sewage plant positioned a few miles upstream since 1892. This shit savannah, this delta of deadly compounds, holds all the sins of the industrial Upstate, washed downstream and deposited like sand where the current slowed behind the Conestee Dam. As we paddle upstream, I learn, once again, that we're all downstream from something, somebody.

On the water it's like paddling in Africa, not Upstate South Carolina. The Conestee sloughs open up into bays fringed by yellow periwinkle and a backdrop of mature oaks and poplars. Dave points out that the periwinkle, though beautiful, is not native. It's an intrusive weed species. Ellen agrees but notes that it's hiding all the Conestee trash—cans, Styrofoam, bottles, balls of every sort: football, golf, soccer, basketball, anything that will float.

We cruise around the bay, and I'm baffled by how much something can change in my mind from ugly to beautiful by just cruising into the middle of it. From shore this old silted-in industrial reservoir looks like a wasteland, not a wonderland, or "oasis," as Dave keeps calling it. Then there is a whistle of a redtail hawk upset as we cruise close to where a nest is hidden. The bird's call brings me back to Dave's dreams. I hear something and turn—a turtle big as an old black skillet lumbers down off the bank into the water.

After the hawk has fallen silent, we all portage over a narrow strand of hardwoods like early explorers, dragging our boats from the bay where we put into an old river channel and paddle upstream. Birds everywhere! They seem not to mind the sewage sludge below, though tissue samples from fish this summer will show more of what we can't see, hope isn't happening. Ellen circles everyone together and reminds them that what we're hiking over is what toxicologists call "biomagnification," concentrations of contaminates all the way up the food chain, a little Rachael Carson nightmare, right here in our own backyard. The bird life is abundant: little green herons, great blue herons, cormorants, all eating fish. Dozens of "woodies," the wood ducks whose boxes rise upward every few hundred yards of shoreline, cruising these waters and grazing the duckweed. Along the shore are the ones we can't see: tracks of deer, raccoon. Dave tells me stories of seeing otters swimming in these very waters.

We land the boats, gather the group, bushwhack a few yards, and hit a well-traveled four-wheeler trail circling an island in the old lake's north corner. There are red flags through the woods, signs of an archeological survey showing that Archaic and Woodlands people lived here, working quartz and imported chert, making pottery, hauling in soapstone from quarries in the Upstate. This high spot on the island is where Dave hopes to put some sort of structure for environmental education, above the wetlands and the river. I look around and note the loveliness of these neglected woods. Full summer's green expanse closes in around us.

Back on the river Thomas, leading the way in his kayak, follows a pair of wood ducks. Some of us get close enough to see the way they drag one wing in the water, faking injury to draw us away from their young ones hiding in the mats of flowers. So much life here! These cycles go on—birth, the raising of the young. And what of our young? Why have so few seen wood ducks perform to protect the summer's brood? "One hundred thousand school children are within a thirty-minute bus ride of this place," Dave says.

I look back at our line of kayaks strung out along the Reedy River. We are like a flock of brightly colored waterbirds following Dave in his green canoe. Headed back to the launch site, we slosh through the flowers and mud to cut through to the bay we started in. We slide our boats behind us, and several of us sink down in the sludge, knee-deep. The week before, we'd introduced the class to the Earth Charter, several hundred cascading pledges packed into a teal-and-white trifold brochure. We told them this charter was the result of years of negotiation among nations to articulate the complexity of a world environmental vision. 'We stand at a critical moment in Earth's history," the Earth Charter states in the preamble, "a time when humanity must choose its future."

We had discussed how difficult it is to find common ground among all the world's citizens, and now in this place I think of Thomas Berry and his book *The Dream of the Earth*: "We are returning to our native place after a long absence, meeting once again with our kin in the earth community." I remind myself that the promise of the Earth Charter and Thomas Berry's earth community includes these wood ducks and the hawks as great citizens of this watery commonwealth. These dreams even include the bacteria working at the sludge below the lake's neglected surface.

As we land our boats, I hear the water over the Conestee Dam just downstream, see the top of the old abandoned cotton mill. There is so much beauty here but also so much uncertainty about what is under the surface. That's the ugliness—what we don't know, what we can't afford to clean up. I take one last look at Lake Conestee before loading the boats. It's as if the whole long history of our exploitation of the Piedmont is contained here in these images, these sounds. It will take decades of deep earth dreams to restore Conestee to a vision of wholeness, but those who have learned to love the lake seem up to it. We'll return here each year and float these sloughs and listen for the hawk's call.

CONFLUENCE:
PACOLET RIVER

The Blue Ridge Mountains, visible from Spartanburg, South Carolina, on a clear day, have always had the nostalgic force of a song for my family. Stories told by my aunts and uncles in the early 1960s confirmed that we had come from there. They told me how my great-grandparents migrated from mountainous Rutherford County in North Carolina to work in Spartanburg's numerous Piedmont cotton mills at the end of the nineteenth century. With time off from shift work and a little gas in the ramshackle car, my mother would often take me back there to cool down on a summer day.

On those childhood outings we traveled up US Highway 176, the original road from Spartanburg into the mountains. As it approaches the mountain front, the highway follows the course of the North Pacolet River. As a child I loved how the narrow two-lane climbed the slopes of Big and Little Warrior and Cedar Mountains in steep switchbacks. Local historians say it follows an ancient game trail along the dizzy gradient of the river and marks the descent of an American Indian trading path walked for thousands of years to reach the Piedmont Plateau. On the other side of the river is one of the steepest railroad grades in the eastern United States, and now, just east of the old highway, Interstate 26 carries commerce quickly across the flank of Tryon Mountain and over Howard Gap onto the Hendersonville Plateau.

My mother would load me in our beat-up, cantaloupe-colored DeSoto convertible with the white ragtop and head out for those cooler mountains. It was water she was headed toward, cool water falling over stones. We would pick up her younger brothers, the twins Bobby and Billy, in Saxon, a mill village on the city's outskirts. As my mother remembers, back then they were "into loafing," young boys often laying off from relentless work in the cotton mills.

One of the twins, with his white T-shirt, ducktailed hair (it was the 1960s), and Pall Mall in his mouth, would drive the DeSoto. The other twin would sit in the passenger seat twisting the AM from station to station. Mama and I would sit in the back, her black hair pulled back secure from the hot Piedmont wind by a patterned rayon scarf. After crossing into North Carolina and negotiating most of the Saluda Grade, a switchback highway, my uncle would park by the side of the road in a narrow pullout crowded on one side by a sweating gneiss cliff and on the other by the highway. For each trip, Mama packed fried chicken, deviled eggs, potato salad, and sweet tea for me. There would be some hidden Budweiser in the trunk. We would sit roadside at a small concrete table and picnic.

Back then I never thought of that river as going somewhere, falling toward sea level.

Then we'd work our way down to the roaring North Pacolet, and I would slide over the rocks left by ice wedging and flood in the channel. It was always as if it had been laid out like a carnival ride (or today's water parks) simply for my enjoyment—big slick rocks, falling water, overhanging rhododendron. When the sun dropped below the gorge walls, we would retrace our steps up to the highway, pack up the DeSoto, and head back down into the mill village.

These are my earliest memories of water—of escape and relief. It's said the Cherokee, who claimed what would become Spartanburg County as their territory, went regularly to water to purify. For them each river was "the Long Man," with its head in the mountains and feet dangling in the ocean far away. I look back now at the irony of that cantaloupe-colored DeSoto named after the first Spanish explorer who, in 1540, looped decisively through this territory. Traveling a Piedmont river like the Pacolet (probably the Catawba), DeSoto set the tone for the future, looking for gold and trailing a herd of pigs.

It's now November, and I am back on the Pacolet, though thirty miles downstream from my childhood picnic spot. I'm floating the river this time, not playing among boulders and waterfalls. At this point along its course the Pacolet has become wide and shallow with very little exposed rock as it makes its way over the wide Carolina Piedmont, an area of steep hills but few extremes in elevation or scenery. I've realized recently that I've somehow missed this river my entire life. I am an expert kayaker, and challenging rivers were always somewhere else, never close by. Twenty years ago, when I began white water kayaking, I always had to head west from Spartanburg and climb into the mountains where there were steeper gradients. (Once it leaves the mountain front, the Pacolet drops only an average of five feet a mile. In contrast, the Chattooga, seventy miles west, can drop as much as two hundred feet a mile.) In this way my kayaking adventures reflected my youthful picnics. I'm older, less driven by adrenaline, and paying attention to nearby places as never before. Now, Piedmont rivers like the Pacolet are appealing for the first time, and I've made a vow to paddle them all over the next few seasons.

There's not much time left this year to keep my vow. We've already had the first hard frost. The tulip poplar leaves have already turned yellow and fallen. I am paddling with my partner, Betsy, and the youngest of her sons, ten-year-old Russell. We've packed a lunch of sandwiches, apples, and soft drinks. It's my equivalent of the childhood picnics, minus the beer. We are on the northern edge of Spartanburg, in a rural area near Interstate 85. We plan to put in with our sea kayaks and float the river from Bud Arthur Bridge Road to the old abandoned Converse cotton mill where my uncle Tommy once worked, a distance of about five river miles. Though I've never paddled it before, I've been told the stretch just downstream from where the river crosses the interstate (maybe thirty miles from the river's origin) is marked by only one road crossing, a house or two, and a mining operation for sand. I know the current will be steady, and there is abundant wildlife: wood ducks, mallards, great blue herons, hawks, and kingfishers frequent the stretch.

The stretch will make for a pleasant fall paddle. The air temperature is in the 70s. The river is maybe a hundred feet wide, clear, and two feet deep. Looking at my topo map before we left I could see that the river sweeps through two large meanders. The bunched-up lines tell me there are steep, north-facing bluffs along the way, probably covered with mountain laurel (a species common to the Blue Ridge, but no stranger to cool Piedmont river bluffs) and dark hardwood. Though we will only be three miles from the city limits of Spartanburg, I know it will feel like we are surrounded by wooded country thick with mature oaks and poplars.

A friend will pick us up downstream later in the day, and so we leave my truck parked near the bridge, slide the brightly colored plastic kayaks like otters (sometimes still seen on the Pacolet) down the steep, long approach our paddling friends have told us about. I wrestle each kayak down as far as possible and let go. The boats bounce to an angled stop short of the river. I laugh at how difficult it is to get into the flow. "It seems a resource, so the public should have some sort of access short of skydiving," I say.

When I stop and listen, it's possible to pick up the sound of a small wild shoal one hundred yards upstream. The water is noisy as it works its angled descent over the exposed country rock; and beyond that, hanging in the air like static, is the sound of hundreds of cars and trucks humming over the expansion joints on the interstate. Just above us is one of the busiest stretches of highway on the East Coast, and yet in a few moments we will push off from shore and Huck Finn our way downstream in a rhythm as old as any human impulse. Floating, my kayaking friends call it.

"Let's go float a river," they say.

On the topo map the Pacolet's two main branches are laid like a tuning fork against the South Carolina Piedmont and the mountains to the west. Along its sixty-mile journey, before the confluence with the Broad River in Union County, the river falls over many (though widely spaced) sets of shoals. They are often designated on the map by double bars piercing the blue line of the river. Before railroads rendered the river redundant for transportation, these shoals made long-distance navigation on the Pacolet difficult but created many "mill seats," topography with enough fall to generate power for early industry. This natural power, and the jobs it created in cotton mills, is what drew my family down from the mountains to Spartanburg County. It was a confluence of need and geography that formed our connection to this river and its many tributaries.

Along the Saluda Grade, where we had parked to picnic, the north fork of the river falls precipitously for fifteen miles through rhododendron, laurel hells, and mixed hardwoods and conifers (hemlock, sweet birch, white oak) on slopes too steep to log. The North Pacolet's noisy descent now comforts porch sitters in vacation cabins and finally flattens out near Tryon (where F. Scott Fitzgerald spent summers in the mid-1930s) and flows swiftly through old farm country in what's known as "the isothermal belt," an area traditionally associated with milder winter temperatures and fewer days of frost, though no one has confirmed this scientifically.

The South Pacolet, the other prong of the tuning fork, is much shorter and less extroverted, falling off the lower slopes of Hogback Mountain as a series of narrow creeks. Then it quickly ceases its mountain song as it meanders quietly among Piedmont hills, abandoned peach orchards, old field succession, and the first hints of suburban sprawl.

Confluence of uses, confluence of memory, I think as we begin our float on the main branch of the river. In high school I water-skied on Lake Bowen, the reservoir formed on the dammed South Pacolet River. Lake Bowen is the source of Spartanburg's drinking water and is tightly ringed with waterfront vacation homes. Powerboats and Jet Skis rage over the surface three seasons a year, the latter expelling a flume of ruddy lake water as they push into the tiniest coves and inlets.

No one in my family had made it beyond mill work at that time, so we could not afford this affluent form of fun on a regular basis. (Those fried-chicken picnics and self-propelled slides down a slick rock were mostly what I knew of water recreation.) It was through the generosity of high school friends from across town that I once strapped on a ski belt, snapped on water skis, and waited as the Evinrude torqued the prop into high enough rotation to pull me from the grip of the Pacolet's impounded flow.

I remember gliding over the lake's waters, my arms and legs stiff with exertion. It was an unnatural motion for me. There was too much trust of machinery. It didn't take long for me to tire, swerve, and plow into the lukewarm surface of the water. My buddies cheered as I fell, and they circled the boat back to pick me up. Another boy entered the water for his turn on the skis. Sitting in the stern, recovering my senses, I remember distinctly the sharp bite of petroleum fumes and a rainbow sheen spreading in the bilge pooling in the boat.

Soon after we enter the current in our kayaks, I point upstream toward the sound of the traffic and say that we can paddle up toward the gravel roar of the small rapid and play there. Russell's not appeased. When I say "river" he always thinks of rapids. Russell wants his floating to be punctuated by drops and waves. He's young and still on the adrenaline program. He wants to know if there is white water downstream and acts disappointed when I admit it's doubtful. I try to explain that this is not the Blue Ridge, but instead a Piedmont stream with less of the gradient that produces white water than its mountain counterparts. I guarantee him it will be swift water, though, and he will not have to paddle much. "Just float," I smile. He likes that, and we float into the current and head downstream.

Betsy is glad to hear there won't be any significant white water. The summer before, we were floating a calm mountain river punctuated with occasional rapids, and the curling edge of a wave caught the stern of her boat and dumped her in the cold current. We rescued her, but she still remembers the sting of the cold water. She likes to float but would rather not swim on this warm fall day.

Just downstream from our put in, as we pass under the Bud Arthur Bridge, we see the first signs of one of the river's historic functions: trash heap for the locals. Someone has thrown two of the newspaper dispensers for the Spartanburg daily paper off the bridge in the river. "Somebody must have frisked them for their quarters," Betsy speculates. I nose my boat up to one. It has been in the river for a long time, unmoved by recent floods. A sheen of algae makes it look more like rock than machine. I peek through the machine's gate into the paper compartment. It's too dark to see anything, but I tell the story of a radial tire a friend picked up on one of the Pacolet's tributaries during a river sweep once. Inside lived a three-pound catfish.

Remembering the catfish in the tire reminds me that this is a living stream, with bass, bream, riffle beetles, gilled snails, sow-bugs, dobsonflies, crayfish, a whole world beneath the surface. It wasn't always so for a river once as impaired as the Pacolet. I know that as recent as the 1960s the textile mills along its length dumped their raw sewage directly into the river.

My uncle Tommy, who worked for decades inspecting cloth and marking it in the cloth room downstream in the Converse cotton mill, likes to tell the story of camping on the wide sandbar at Poole's Bend, a large, sweeping meander on the Pacolet a few miles below the mill. He and some buddies ran a trotline and pulled in a washtub full of catfish. "We skinned some to cook over the fire that night. When I opened them up, they smelled like sewage. I couldn't eat catfish for fifty years."

Russell, floating ahead of us, is more interested in the white-and-turquoise wreck of a Jet Ski that has somehow landed in the river than the catfish probably living below its surface. He gets excited. "Maybe we can fix it up?" he asks. I only think how the infernal machine probably washed downstream from Lake Bowen in a flood and how its owner pushed the noisy thing all over the lake in the summer. I am strangely hopeful we'll see more and can pretend they are wreckage of some lost world. "It's like *Planet of the Apes*," Betsy says. "You know, the final scene where they discover the Statue of Liberty and realize they have stumbled into the future."

Floating a river is always a little like wading into another time, especially a river once as heavily settled as the Pacolet. At one time there were farms along these banks, and now we float through a forest of thirty-year-old poplars, oaks, and sycamores grown toward maturity in the grace period when the farms were abandoned and the mills closed down. The South Carolina Piedmont is a region in the midst of transition: once wilderness, then farmland, but now in an uneasy peace before the war of real estate consumes it all. The contrast between our daily lives—streets, cars, mechanical noise—and the quiet of the postindustrial river is appealing and fragile. As we float for an hour south toward our ride back to town, I think about the scarred yet somehow peaceful landscape this river drains.

I am a native of this place, not merely a visitor, a recreator. It is no water park where I pay admission. Though I was born in the coastal plain of North Carolina, my mother moved us back to Upstate South Carolina after my father's death in 1959; with the exceptions of a year out west, three in Virginia, and two in the mountains of North Carolina, I have lived the rest of my life in the drainage of the Pacolet River. Upon my father's death I was introduced to the rich flow of the Piedmont's declining mill culture, where my mother's family had worked in cotton mills for two generations. My mother's family's personal history (which is mine as well) was hardscrabble and stained by long hours and low pay. After migrating from the mountains, they moved in tightening geographic circles from mill to mill, pursuing jobs, working shifts, and living in company-owned mill houses in villages sprawled over hillsides right next to the river and its tributaries, the Buck, Chinquapin, and Lawson's Fork Creek.

Now the mills have all closed down, and in many places the forest has returned. I can see from the maps that the river meanders, in its final thirty miles below where we paddle, past four abandoned cotton mills—Converse, two mills at Clifton, and Pacolet—and on through miles of pine plantations, impressive stands of oak and poplar, and a few remaining farms. I do not pretend to know much more than the maps tell me about those lower stretches. The river, before it meets up with the Broad, is hard to see from roads (the river keeps to itself), and I've never paddled it.

"Is Pacolet a Native American word?" Betsy wants to know.

Yes, I explain. One of the theories as to the origin of the name "Pacolet" is that it is a Cherokee word meaning "running horse." Others say the river was named for a Frenchman who settled in the county early on. "No one seems to know which is true," I add.

"Why aren't there more rapids?" Russell asks.

I tell him there were once three impressive river-wide waterfalls in the mile-long trough of steep, erosion-resistant rock known as Trough Shoals about fifteen miles below the stretch we are paddling. The first town there was even named Trough, the river was dammed, and the steep drop of the river converted into power, enough to turn thousands of spindles. Later, when the town changed its name, the waterfalls were long forgotten beneath the waters of the impounded river. Russell, the lover of adrenaline, likes my story of the waterfalls. He asks if we can ever paddle them. I have to admit that there is something compelling about those waterfalls trapped beneath the waters backed up behind an inactive dam.

We stop and eat our lunch on a sharp bend where the physics of the river has created a sandbar on the inside curve. As the water sweeps downstream, the heavier sand held in suspension by the current drops out first as the river is pushed toward the outside of the curve. A few miles upstream from this spot was once a bend so wide and a sandbar so thick that locals called it "Cowpens Beach" until an enterprising sand-and-gravel company bought the site and mined it out for concrete production.

We eat our sandwiches in the sun on the small beach. All around the kayaks there are dark mollusk shells open like angel wings. I comment on their beauty, but Betsy reminds me they are a sign of how compromised the river really is. They are an intrusive Asian species that has driven out the native mussels.

After lunch we return to our kayaks, pack the trash into the empty dry bag, and head downstream. A few minutes later I realize we've floated along as quietly as a raft of ducks. Even Russell sees the beauty of such a gradient-free float so close to town. He seems reflective at moments, a rarity for a rambunctious ten-year-old. He has settled into the pace of our outing. Then suddenly he's singing at the top of his lungs. We pass the heavily wooded banks and they retreat behind us. As if in answer, a dusty blue kingfisher taunts the river from limb to limb with its shrill, cackling voice. The river offers a child's joy for unconstrained spaces where Russell can push the boundaries of what's acceptable in polite company, and he fills it with his whoops. It's only when Russell's vocalizations are answered by men on a high bluff above the river that some of the joy goes out of our journey. It looks (and sounds, with sporadic hammering filling the air) as if they are building a deer stand, though it is hard to tell, looking up through the woods. "You better duck," the men yell in accents as shrill and local as the kingfisher. "We might start shooting." Betsy quiets Russell, ushers him between us. We float on in silence with only the sound of the men's hammers following us downstream.

Soon after the hint of trouble, the Saturday river turns turbid and deepens. For a mile or more we paddle across the millpond I know is backed up behind the dam at Converse. Around one bend there are two men fishing in a bass boat, and someone has cleared a pasture down to the water and built a small dock. A Muscovy duck paddles along the muddy river edge. Russell's earlier screams of freedom now come out as moans of outrage at having to expend energy to move his boat. "Around the next bend," I keep telling him, not really knowing for sure when or where the dam will appear.

We pass a big bend in the river full of dredging equipment where a local concrete company has been mining sand for decades. In its weekend idleness, the dredge looks like some rusted industrial dinosaur. "Someone has gotten rich mining the river for sand," I explain to Betsy as we float past the spot. I find this ironic, how over the last half a century many of the concrete buildings downtown have been molded out of the river bottom itself. We drink its water, share its power, and we mine its sand. The river gives in all ways and ceaselessly.

I finally spot the mill. I have somehow paddled a few hundred yards ahead of Betsy and Russell. I turn my boat and look back upstream and can see them working toward me over the surface of the impounded river. I float a few moments without paddling, sit still on the surface of the pond. I can hear the falling water of the mill dam only a few hundred yards in the distance. The river forms a horizon line as it plunges in a perfect fall over the rock dam. Just downstream from every Pacolet River mill (Fingerville, the Clifton mills, Pacolet) there is a dam such as this one, which at one point may have produced electricity to power the manufacturing processes before the advent of the power grid.

The Piedmont mills always had "a village," a company-constructed community, a clutch of wooden houses, now often sided with vinyl and altered by ownership. And, of course, there is the river itself, channel and flow, which for years swept away effluvium of countless origin: sewage, process dyes, dead dogs and cows, garbage of settlement. There is that tough species, the catfish, still living in the impaired waters of the postindustrial stream. Now that the mills have almost all closed, one is more likely to see these fish pulled from the deep eddies below the dams. If a Piedmont river has a soul it is probably hidden in the swim bladders of these native bottom-feeders. Their genetic predisposition is toward making the best out of the current's changing conditions. They are well suited to life in the Piedmont.

There is beauty in such a cultural landscape for sure, but for a moment I find this a scene of unaccountable hardship and suffer through the darkest nostalgia when I see the bricked-up windows of the old mill. I get a vague ache, the way amputees have described the nerve memory of lost limbs, when I consider these Piedmont mills and their neighboring rivers. My family tree is like one of the surviving river birches along an up-country stream like this one, the roots undercut by the eroding flow of our particular regional economic history (King Cotton, king textiles, king development), the skinny limbs leaning out over the current, working hard for a place in the sun.

One element of this river's history I return to as I sit waiting for Betsy and Russell to catch up is the flood that roared out of the mountains on June 6th, 1903. Historic accounts describe how a gentle rain fell for almost five days, and then a cloudburst pushed the Pacolet to alarming levels. It was the single greatest catastrophe to ever befall the county. That morning, the slow music of the shoals turned into the cacophony of disaster. The waters swept away bridges, roads, and houses, leaving the small mill communities isolated from each other. Fifty people died as three cotton mills were carried downstream by the power of the waters.

My uncle Tommy's family worked in this same Converse mill, "long as the mill had been open," as my mama says. Uncle

Tommy worked here from 1942 to 1979, when it closed. His father had been the paymaster for the Clifton mills; his grandfather, born on April 13th, 1903, a few months before the flood, was later the RFD mail carrier for that corner of the county. Once, while visiting, I asked Uncle Tommy if he grew up hearing stories of the flood, and he said, "Didn't nobody talk about it very much." The memory was deep and painful. People moved away because of the damage, and almost every family in the village was affected by the death toll.

What had he been told happened to his father and grandfather? He said that the mill whistle blew that morning to warn everyone, but most thought it was simply a call to go to work. "When the flood came my grandpa hollered for my aunt Helen and picked up my father, Thomas. They came out of the house in knee-deep water." He waded with Helen under one arm and Thomas under the other, and headed for higher ground, watching as the house was washed downstream.

"You can't comprehend a piece of a river," says John Graves, talking of the Brazos in *Goodbye to a River*. "A whole river that is really a river is much to comprehend." He says all a human being comprehends if he spends his life navigating a really big river like the Mississippi is its "channels, topography, and perhaps the honky-tonk in the river towns." There are few honky-tonks on the Pacolet. This is the Bible Belt, the river was never plied by riverboats, and barge traffic in the nineteenth century was local, stifled by those shoals, those rocky ribs of gneiss.

I love rivers because they are real and not only metaphorical. In Upstate South Carolina many of the very real rivers (we have always been a place defined by swift-flowing water) were used first for power in the late nineteenth century by the growing textile industry; later, when power became more available, our rivers continued to be used as discharge channels for waste, human and industrial. I write about rivers because the ones I know best—those of the Carolinas—give me hope for the recovery of the land after great abuse. Even in the face of such abuse, a red-clay river like the Pacolet endures, and our relationships with it endure.

Betsy and Russell paddle up behind me. Russell releases one final whoop of arrival as our friend appears with his pickup to carry us back to our car. We pull the boats ashore safely upstream of the dam and step out on dry land. I drag my boat through brush willows, yellowing sumac, and saplings of volunteer hardwoods, poplar and birch.

I am not tied to the Pacolet the way my uncle, mother, and grandmother were, but I still drink its treated water. I know if it rains tonight the runoff from my city street will quickly find its way to a culvert and into the nearest "branch," and on down to the river in a day or two. Within two weeks that same water could be in the Atlantic Ocean. If the rain soaks in as groundwater it might take years before it flows into the nearest stream.

I do not watch the river stained by red clay to gauge its flow, to dream its flood, fish it for extra protein, but I float it to gain some time to reflect, to recreate. I do not really know the Pacolet, but my history is adrift on it as surely as today I have drifted on the surface of this living stream.

YOUGHIOGHENY

From the eddy above the Youghiogheny's Swallow Tail Falls, Chuck Stump, our guide, tells us about a boy some years before who had fallen into the swirling reversal of water below us at the bottom of the eight-foot ledge of rock. The boy's parents had watched in horror from the park overlook as their son disappeared below. Eighteen hours later, while his parents were treated for shock in a local hospital, divers found the boy shivering but safe on a shelf of rock behind the falls. He had sat there for almost a day staring through the falling water.

It's near the beginning of our adventure on the Youghiogheny, and I sit safely at the bottom of Swallow Tail Falls. I have avoided the fate of the little boy, skirting the crashing reversal of cold spring water. I've taken two strokes and dropped like a leaf over the lip of the falls. I felt the bottom drop away, and then as sudden as water down a drain, I was sitting safely in the calm eddy water below.

I look back upstream at the steady river as it pours over the limestone obstruction. My trip down the Youghiogheny is underway. In the next week, like the water, I will head downstream, covering fifty-nine white water miles of the Youghiogheny River's journey.

The day we arrived in the watershed it had been raining for eleven days. As we approached the Maryland panhandle there had been showers and occasional downpours. Along the roadside, tiny streams tumbled through cobbles. The leaves of oaks and maples sagged, sodden with rain.

As a young kayaker I'd prayed for rain. I was drawn, as all those of my watery tribe, to rapids, spots of resistant rock like this one. But now forty-six, the responsibilities of teaching, writing, and home had seriously eroded my time in a boat. In the late '80s and early '90s, when I was in my thirties and paddling difficult white water like this regularly, I lost two friends to paddling accidents. Something about attending funerals can change a middle-aged paddler's approach to adventure sports.

When National Geographic called to ask if I'd like to take an assignment to paddle the river for a book they were compiling called *Adventure America*, I hesitated. I'd never paddled the Yough, and I knew it was difficult. It had been several years since I'd attempted Class IV or V white water, though I'd been a regular on difficult rapids for two decades. "What's the worst that can happen?" my wife, Betsy, had asked.

"Death is unlikely," I admitted. "Only one or two kayakers have died in the difficult water of the top and upper Yough in thirty years."

"Injury?"

"Maybe I'll blow a shoulder," I said. "But I can recover from that."

"You should do it," she said. "How often do you get a chance for National Geographic to pay for a week of paddling?"

So I committed. My paddling partner on this kayaking adventure is Watts Hudgens, a younger colleague at Wofford. The term is over. The papers are graded. It's early June, and Watts, being a long-time boater, jumped at the chance to head for the hills of Maryland and Pennsylvania.

The Yough, as the locals call it, is one of four powerful Appalachian rivers—the Youghiogheny, the Monongahela, the Tygart, and the Cheat—that form the upper drainage for the Ohio River and ultimately, the Mississippi. Out of this wondrous marriage of Allegheny Mountains and water that shapes the corner of West Virginia, Maryland, and Pennsylvania also rise, just east, across the continental divide, the headwaters of the Potomac and the Savage Rivers, carrying water from Backbone Ridge to the Atlantic Ocean.

The Yough's headwaters form among bold springs and fern-studded seeps on the western slope of Backbone Ridge just above Silver Lake, an old resort a few hundred yards into West Virginia. near Silver Lake, the river is small enough to step across and is home to native trout. Below the lake, it quickly leaves West Virginia behind and flows into Maryland, where beavers block the Yough's flow as it meanders through alder and maple thickets. Neat farms are its neighbors in the first thirty miles as the river keeps to the fertile valley between Backbone Ridge and Chestnut Ridge.

Before the river leaves the Appalachians downstream at South Connellsville it has flowed through "the Tippy Top," "the Top," and the "Upper," three upper stretches of premier "advanced" white water; Lake Youghiogheny, a twenty-mile-long reservoir for recreation and power generation; "the Middle," a fast, isolated section; "the Lower," beginning in Ohiopyle, Pennsylvania, the most rafted section of river on the East coast; and "the Bottom," maybe the most beautiful of the river's reaches, a wide expanse of water and sky with long cobble shoals and occasional rapids as the river carves through Chestnut Ridge.

The human history of the Yough is as long and complex as one of the Upper Yough's rapids. Early Native peoples arrived around 8000 B.C. and by 1600 B.C.E. the Monongahelas lived in the river drainage. No one really knows when or why they disappeared, but they left their name for the river the Yough joins at McKeesport, just downstream from Pittsburgh. By 1737 the Youghiogheny had appeared on a map. By the middle of the century early white explorers were pushing to the west.

George Washington first journeyed into the headwaters in 1753 as a young colonial militia lieutenant, and in 1754 he returned to explore the river by canoe in hopes of finding a water route to the west to develop into a canal. The French claimed the Ohio Valley, a vital link between Canada and New Orleans, and Washington believed controlling the Youghiogheny was key to curtailing the French's access to the drainage. The French had successfully established Fort Duquesne at the site of present-day Pittsburgh, the confluence where the Monongahela and Allegheny form the Ohio.

In the opening battle of the French and Indian Wars, twenty-two-year-old Washington suffered his only military defeat when a detachment of colonial troops he commanded was defeated at tiny Fort Necessity in the "Great Meadow" in the Youghiogheny's watershed.

Settlers who followed Washington west settled in inviting valleys such as those found where Sang Run Bridge crosses the Youghiogheny. "Sang," or ginseng, a wild plant with a curative root, is said to have been common in the area. For the old-timers, hunting "sang" provided a steady cash crop—like vegetable gold. Today, white water outfitters have provided a new kind of gold for the hills of western Maryland.

I have arranged for two guides, Steve Strothers and Terry Peterson, to meet us on our second day paddling the Youghiogheny. We are to meet them at 11:00 A.M. out in front of Mountain Surf, a kayaking-gear shop in Friendsville, Maryland, the takeout for an eight mile section known as the "Upper."

The scene in Friendsville is youthful, thick, and electric, especially when the Upper Yough is running. Boaters who could just as easily be surfers or skateboarders hang out on the wall in front of Mountain Sports and watch for cars carrying kayaks. Everyone has a nickname. The chatter is relentlessly aquatic.

Steve and Terry lean against the wall in front of Mountain Surf. He works as a cartographer for the US Geological Survey in Washington, DC, but spends every weekend paddling the river three hours west of the capital. Terry offers a nice contrast to Steve. She floats the river full time, experiencing the Yough as both raft guide and kayaker. When we arrive they report the river is higher than normal, with two feet of natural flow plus water released from the dam upstream at Deep Creek Reservoir. To paddle or not? Steve suggests it is probably best to wait for the release from the Deep Creek Dam to pass.

We drive the ten miles upstream to Sang Run, where we stand on the bridge and wait for the water in the river to drop some. Steve places sticks at the water's edge so we can know when the water has dropped enough to paddle. As we stand watching the river flow past, Terry explains the complex politics of the Upper Yough, how the access has always been contested, and only in the last ten years—when river conservation groups such as the American Whitewater Association fought for the establishment of a Department of Natural Resources parking lot—has it become easy to leave a car at the top and put in on the river with ease.

For years the locals made recreational boating difficult. Gunfire was not uncommon on the Upper Yough. In the early days rafters would stop on the bridge, throw their rubber craft in the river, and climb down the bridge abutment as a friend drove the car away. "In the early days they'd bring me up here and show me the bullet holes," Terry says.

An hour later, when the sticks Steve had placed at the water's edge are high and dry, we know it is time to paddle. The extra water released from the dam had finally passed us. "That's about as low as it's going to get," Steve says.

A few miles below Sang Run Bridge, the Upper Yough takes on the character it is famous for—narrow, continuous, technical. The names of the rapids suggest the serious intent of the water: Bastard, Eddy of Death, Snaggle Tooth, Charlie's Choice and Triple Drop, Zinger, and Little Niagara, to name a few. "Exercise good judgment regarding your boating skills," one river guide urges—"Expertise, bravado, and life insurance."

"This is the most dangerous rapid on the river," Steve says as we enter a Class IV to V rapid called Heinzerling. I follow Steve and Terry as they slip through an impossibly narrow blind slot into a big eddy shaded with sycamores. "If you didn't know that slot was there, you'd head right into the worst of it," Steve says, relaxing in the eddy.

As I sit in the eddy I look over my shoulder and down comes a boater in a Kevlar wildwater boat with no paddle, only little black flippers on his hands. He is smiling as he goes straight through the forbidden passage Steve calls "the rifle barrel."

"That's Jeff Snyder," Steve says, smiling. "The father of squirt boating."

I know Snyder as one of the pioneers of paddling small kayaks through difficult white water. Steve does not seem surprised to see him in a boat that looks more like a huge cigar than a kayak.

"Does he do that often?" I ask in disbelief.

"Unprecedented," Steve smiles. "Probably the first person ever to have done it."

I look over my shoulder. Down below the rifle barrel Jeff has the fat wildwater boat standing on its end as he slams against the pillow rock and rides the current down to the left.

Steve follows Snyder downstream. I watch his route, how he too rides up on the rock pillowed with water that had stood Synder's boat vertical. I shake my head. "They're doing that on purpose," I mutter. I take several strokes and shoot down the rifle barrel too and drop into twenty yards of impossibly chaotic, slanted exploding water, "the death slot" on the left and the big pillow rock with a quarter of the river piling against it on the right. As I pop through the offset waves all I can see is the chaos below. I miss the pillow and somehow punch through the grabby hydraulics at the rapid's bottom.

It is in Class IV to V Heinzerling that I see most clearly how the dance of water and stone on a white water river speaks of danger. This slippery equation between challenge and risk is at the heart of adventure sports such as white water kayaking. When is a river too difficult? When is it best to stand on shore and admire a serious stretch of gradient? The lucky ones among us get to chase the answer down a wild rapid like Heinzerling and make it through.

Several miles downstream from the takeout for the Upper, the Yough disappears into twenty-mile-long Lake Youghiogheny, finished by the Army Corps of Engineers for flood control in 1943. The lake, the only major reservoir on the Youghiogheny, provides recreation of a different sort. On any summer day the whining of Jet Skis can be heard, and expensive powerboats leave tracks in the jade-green water.

Our third day on the river we stay just downstream from the Youghiogheny Lake Dam at the River's Edge, a bed-and-breakfast in Confluence, Maryland, that caters to the outdoor tourists drawn to town by the river and the bike trail that terminates at the base of the dam. Just off the main street in Confluence, the Casselman, the Yough's largest tributary, joins with Laurel Hill Creek and the Yough to form what Washington and the early explorers called "the turkey foot."

Early in the morning Watts and I switch boats, leaving our white water kayaks on the truck. We slip down the bank amid a din of indignant geese. Our blue and brown sea kayaks, longer and thinner than the white water boats, paddle straight with less effort on the flat water and still perform well in the five or six rapids we will descend.

Along the left bank of the Middle Yough runs the backbone of a contemporary recreational industry, a bike path stretching more than fifty miles downstream, a hard-packed limestone trail set on the bed of an abandoned railway that made Washington's idea of a canal obsolete in fewer than one hundred years. The Middle Yough also carries recreational canoe traffic, mostly fishermen and low-intensity paddlers who want an easy run and pastoral scenery downstream from the Upper and upstream from the Lower.

As we float past "the turkey foot" on the dam release from Lake Youghiogheny, I think about Washington's first canoe trip downstream. Unlike us, the "father of our country" had big industry on his mind—a trade route via water to the Ohio River— and he probably could never have imagined such a confluence of modern recreational desires as we can see from the Middle Yough.

Washington's early Wilderness Road, what became known as the Braddock Road, was improved and rerouted to later become, in 1818, the first federally funded highway. This highway, known as the National Road, ran from Cumberland, Maryland, to Wheeling, West Virginia. The road crossed the Youghiogheny just above the site of today's town of Confluence at an old ford called "the Great Crossings." The bridge that was built for the National Road across the Yough is now below the waters of Lake Youghiogheny. Sometimes in October, if the water has been dropped far enough, you can see the three-span stone bridge appear like a ghost from the nation's childhood just upstream of the present day Route 40 crossing.

Downstream is gorge country, with sharp Pennsylvania ridges descending a thousand feet to the river. If the Yough has a soul, it lingers in the broad peopleless floodplain within the horseshoe bend called Victoria Flats below Confluence where the coal mining town of Victoria once stood. Just past two islands we stop to look for the ruins of the old town. We find nothing.

Watts and I follow a tiny trail inland through dense spring wildflowers under sycamore and river birch. There are Jack in the Pulpit, and others. We climb the hill to a railroad and see five vultures take to the air from the fresh carcass of a white-tailed deer killed by a train. As we walk the tracks, we notice that this is not uncommon, this collision of train and deer. The bones of another deer—a young male with spikes for a rack—rest fewer than twenty yards up the tracks.

Soon we are back on the water. Halfway from Confluence to Ohiopyle we pass into Ohiopyle State Park, a 19,000-acre preserve. Within the state park's sanctuary, we drift downstream in our big boats. We look around more. I go deep inside and think about things—waves, trees, the shore, the mountains beyond. The woods beyond the river are mostly second growth, trees thirty or forty years old, though Watts points out one huge cedar in the woods that could have seen centuries of water passing downstream.

Five more miles of fast flat water broken by occasional Class II rapids, and we see the Ohiopyle railroad bridge ahead. We step out of our boats on river left with the eighteen-foot Ohiopyle Falls just below. We stand on the fescue corner of the state park's waterfront. Downstream, we can see nets across the river to catch any unaware boater who might float down from the Middle Yough toward the falls.

"There's no place like Ohiopyle, no place that even comes close," Tim Palmer wrote in his epic 1980s narrative *Youghiogheny: Appalachian River.* "All roads out of Ohiopyle are climbed in second gear. All roads into Ohiopyle burn the brakes." As we drag our boats up onto the grass, we can see what Palmer means. The green slopes of the Yough's formidable gorge slip down to the edge of the river on one side and on the other form the backdrop for parking lots and a few old buildings. There stands the old general store, now the Falls Store and Inn, several churches, a train station, and several dozen white clapboard houses.

Earlier in the week I had commented to Watts on the young Upper Yough boaters in Friendsville with their trendy short boats, dreadlocks, and their ritual of hanging out at the wall in front of the Mountain Surf shop. I'd called it "the grunge capital of kayaking."

"These are my people," I say today, laughing as we pull our boats onto the grass in Ohiopyle, pointing at the cars parked in the private boaters' parking lot. On the boat racks are ten-year-old kayaks, long Perception and Dagger boats in discontinued colors. The boaters mostly look like middle-aged professionals out to red-line their excitement meters on a day off.

Ohiopyle has been a recreational bonanza, the rafting capital of the East, since the early 1960s. Because of the regular releases of water from Lake Youghiogheny, the commercial rafting traffic can continue all summer when everything else in the mountains is dry. The power company regulates its release of water, and the state of Pennsylvania regulates the paddling in Ohiopyle. Five rafting companies operate there, with one hundred thousand tourists a year parceled out between them, each company floating them down the eight miles of the exciting, though not usually pushy, Lower Yough.

It is easy to see that the anarchy and alchemy of Friendsville is far behind. The dam upstream of Confluence provides predictable daily flow all summer. On the Lower Yough the private boaters must compete for several thousand permits, and launch times are assigned according to availability. Even "the shuttle" is complex and bureaucratic, a sharp contrast to the recently settled boating frontier just thirty miles upstream on the Upper. Private boaters in Ohiopyle must purchase a token to ride a bus back from the takeout to their vehicles parked a mile or so up the hill from the river.

The next day we hook up with Laurel Ridge Outfitters for the 11:00 A.M. commercial trip down the Lower Yough. The river is a good level, almost three feet. The dam is releasing more water because of all the rain. I ask the general manager of Laurel Ridge about our desire to paddle the last leg of the river down to South Connellsville, and he says, "You've got to go down with 'Cube,' a guide of ours who grew up on the river and fishes that stretch. I think he's got the day off."

He points to the staging area for the rafts. Cube is pumping up a raft. He has long grey hair pulled in a ponytail under his "Lawyers.com" cap. Cube agrees to meet us the next morning, saying he will paddle down with us in his Shredder, an inflatable catamaran, a popular craft of local design paddled often on the Upper and Lower Yough.

"What can I expect of that final stretch?" I ask Cube.

"You're gonna love it down there," he says, smiling. "No access except by river. It's bear and train country."

So, the next day, our final on the river, is shaping up to be an adventure, with Cube as our guide. But first, the famous Lower Yough still awaits us. The Laurel Ridge trip has three rafts, fifteen brave adventurers. During the July to August "high season" the outfitter might have eighty people on a trip. These guests are mostly British from the Royal Air Force. "They come over every year," Bo Harshyne, the trip leader explains. "We had a group of pilots come over one year," Bo says. "You know, face plants on mountain bikes. You couldn't stop those guys."

We put on with the commercial trip in the pool below Ohiopyle Falls. There's a big bubble of water at the fall's base, and we work against the strong current to paddle up on top of it, but the current pushes us downstream. I think about how every October many local boaters run the falls on Falls Race Day.

Chuck Stump, our guide on the Top Yough, had said that this past year he ran it nine times in one day, and he couldn't understand why it wasn't open for business all year. "Over a thousand runs on the Falls Race day and nothing bad happened. I saw Jeff Snyder go over it standing up in an inflatable kayak."

We follow Cube's safety boat and the other rafts through Entrance Rapid, the first of a series of rapids along the famous "loop," an oxbow where the Youghiogheny doubles back on itself. The peninsula in the middle is called Ferncliff, a nature preserve and National Natural Landmark.

One of the RAF rafts flips in a rapid called Cucumber, and we can see yellow helmets and paddles bobbing in the froth ahead of us. The vacationing pilots are laughing as they float past.

I laugh too. Though not as difficult or exhausting as the Upper Yough, the Lower offers pure recreation. It feels good to be on the water, breaking through the waves and into the swirling eddies.

The river is perfect for white water recreation. It drops twenty-seven feet per mile from the bottom of the falls to Bruner Run takeout, eight miles downstream. There are thirteen named rapids, many of them Class III, some even Class IV at higher water levels. Many of the best drops are in the first mile of the river, and often kayakers will put in, run the loop, and then walk their boats across the peninsula and back to the parking lot.

Downstream for six miles after the loop, we float through standing waves and past big slabs of limestone. One rapid, a Class III called Dimple, has claimed three lives in the last year, and I sit in an eddy impressed with the safety precautions Laurel Ridge Outfitters take with their trip. The trip leader stands on top of the rock with a whistle, moving rafts like a traffic cop. All the Laurel Ridge rafts make it through, the RAF troops slapping paddles in the fast, constricted channel below the deadly undercut rock. Other outfitters are not so lucky. Five rental rafts with no guide—what the outfitters call "unguided missiles"—flip, some dangerously close to the rock. The rafters float downstream, paralyzed with fear. We watch as kayaks rush into the current and pull the bobbing boaters ejected from the raft into the calmer side eddies. Some customers, with no kayak to rescue them, float passively fifty yards downstream until they lodge like litter among boulders. Finally, out of the current, they flop like exhausted trout on sidebars of gravel.

It is quite a show. In spite of Dimple Rapid and its deadly reputation, one hundred thousand people float the Lower Yough every year. All the way to River's End, the last rapid on the run before the takeout at Bruner's, I watch the faces of the British guests tilting their fun meters in Laurel Ridge's three rafts.

It is raining when the Laurel Ridge truck drops us off at the Bruner Run takeout for our final ten-mile float down the Bottom Yough to South Connellsville. This is where the Yough leaves the mountains behind. Just downstream from Bruner the high tourist energy of the Lower section recedes into memory and river miles.

"If you focus on the right things, and ignore the others," Rick Bass wrote in "River People," "you can find wildness and freedom anywhere, I'm convinced." Our final day on the river I focus on what Cube calls "the wildest, most beautiful section of the Yough."

I can see Cube is right from our first moment. The ridges on the Bottom Yough are high and green, constricting the river into a tight gorge. The water is swift and pure. It is as if the landscape, in its last ten miles of mountain wildness, is intent on holding the river for itself. There are not rapids as long or difficult as we have seen upstream on the Top, the Upper, or the Lower, but there is something—call it isolation or distance—that makes the Bottom Yough feel freer than any stretch above it.

As we drift downstream, Cube and Watts paddle the black shredder out in front of me in a band of soft mist. Cube has his fishing rod with him, and in a broad eddy he casts into the current. The river has always provided. "Once I was sitting in this eddy," Cube says. "It was midday and I was hungry. The fish weren't biting." Upstream, floating down from the Lower Yough like a tiny raft, was a bright red box, bobbing in the wave train. "The box floated into the eddy," he says. "It was a Tupperware container and inside was a full lunch just packed that morning."

By noon we have drifted through the last rapid before the industrial town of South Connellsville. We pull our boats out on a cobble beach where the local teenagers have positioned slabs of river-worn limestone to form a party bench, a Fred Flintstone sofa.

Upstream we can see the Youghiogheny carving through the mountain gorge the tourists frequented. Downstream, Cube points out a boulder the locals call "turtle rock." Generations of South Connellsville teenagers have painted the large boulder in a hundred different hues. It marks the head of a large island where Cube had once lived for more than a year.

Close by his boyhood home, Cube built a lean-to out of pallets, ate fish, and picked up firewood on the railroad right-of-way. "I was livin' like a Buddha monk," Cube explains, staring downstream at the site of his own personal Walden. He left that paradise to work on the river as a guide, to show other people the beauty of his home river.

A few miles downstream, the large industrial city of Connellsville diverts the river into a water-filtration plant. From turtle rock the Youghiogheny has forty-six miles before it disappears into the Monongahela just south of Pittsburgh. This is where the wild river ends, flowing around turtle rock and the cobble beach.

If the Youghiogheny has a wild heart, it pulses in the waterfalls, narrow rock jams, abundant forests, and turbulent white water all along its length. On my journey downriver I also found the heart of the river beating strongly in the chests of those like Cube. Before we haul our boats across the railroad tracks to my truck, the three of us sit on the bench and look out at the river. You can see that Cube loves all that flowing water coming down from West Virginia.

I follow Cube's eyes as they take in the river and watch it pass on toward Pittsburgh.

SOLS CREEK FALLS

On a Sunday in the Southern mountains I decide that rather than go to church I'll go searching for a waterfall with my friend Randy. Looking for just any waterfall in the southern Appalachians is a little like scouting trout in a pool in a mountain stream. You know they are there, it's just that you have to train your eye to stay focused spot-to-spot, and soon you'll see them flashing by. With waterfalls it's the opposite. Your eye's moving. It's the waterfall that stays still. Driving a curving mountain back road in the high country, you let your eye move along the ridgelines and creek draws, until sooner or later a waterfall will cross your vision.

But looking for a particular waterfall, like the one up Sols Creek, is a little harder. Many times the good ones (and I've been told this is one of the best) are high up in the deepest grooves of a crazy gorge, a place where even the trails lead into wildness and doubt, where you turn and look out and see something approaching the sublime.

The sublime doesn't exist down South. At least that's the argument. Whatever true wildness once found from Virginia to Georgia has been bleached out of the landscape, the sublime draining through the cracks of civilization and settlement. Maybe Mark Catesby or William Bartram wandered some true wilderness that would rival Wyoming, but today the southern Appalachian backcountry is checkerboarded with condominium developments, church camps, and patchy wood lots. So goes the argument.

"Sols Creek?" Randy asks when I mention a plan to go find the waterfall I'd been told is the wildest place in the South. Randy's an expert paddler, a river guide, an old friend from Spartanburg, and a classmate from the 1970s at Wofford College.

He's been to Sols Creek Falls once. He tells the story of clambering up on a little grassy knoll below the waterfall to drink some wine he'd hauled in, looking up only to see two goats with curving horns clambering along the cliffs next to the waterfall. Of course, they weren't mountain goats, only feral escapees from some mountain farm, but it was enough to make Randy think twice about time and space, to wonder whether he had slipped through some crevice into some real Western wilderness sublime.

On my map I can see how Sols Creek wanders eight miles off the high flank of Rich Mountain, its headwaters almost on the summit, just south of the highest stretch of the Blue Ridge Parkway, a country so far up in the air that it feels like Colorado or Montana even in the middle of a North Carolina July.

Right above Bear Creek Reservoir the creek crosses Highway 281, the only hardtop for ten miles, and drops three hundred feet a mile through contours suggesting a classic mountain-creek gorge. Randy assures me that less than a mile upstream from where Sols Creek turns turbid and green and disappears under the waters of Bear Creek Reservoir, it takes one of the most sublime plunges in North Carolina. There is a "rock amphitheater" where an ancient hemlock log is magically balanced between two boulders, a plunge pool deep enough to swim in, and standing tulip poplars ten feet thick at the base.

So, we head out on Sunday morning. Highway 281 crawls up out of the hamlet of Tuckaseegee and follows the river for four or five miles just to the north of Cedar Cliff Reservoir, where the state road begins to climb steadily into some of the highest, wildest country in the east. At one time prior to the 1930s, the Tuckaseegee was wild too, with rapids, moods, and a spring attitude like a mountain bear.

Circling on intuition, we miss the access road to Bear Creek and drive ten miles too far, all the way to the last of three lakes on the upper Tuckaseegee, Wolf Creek.

"I wanted to see this country anyway," Randy says, making me feel better for my lack of attention.

After we cross the high dam at Wolf Creek and see 281 turn to gravel, we stop a local man walking along the road and ask about Bear Creek. His gait is natural and prolonged. He is thin as a ghost, wearing a mountaineer's flop hat, and has milky-blue Celtic eyes straight out of the Iron Age. He listens, reluctantly gives directions, and we turn Randy's Trooper and head back down the mountain.

The access lot at Bear Creek Reservoir is full of 4x4s and empty boat trailers when we finally pull up. We have the only roof racks on the property. Paddle power has never had much clout, I'm sure, on Bear Creek.

Neither one of us is happy with the canoe we have been forced by timing to paddle across the lake, a tandem white water boat with a bow described by the manufacturer as a "bruise water." We have little hope of making much time pushing across, but Sols Creek is somewhere up the lake, and not very often on a pilgrimage do the pilgrims have everything they need or want. What would be the point? Part of the plan is finding your way at the appropriate speed. Chaucer knew all about this.

We take the canoe off the Trooper, load a little gear— paddles, life jackets, food, and a jug of water—and carry our vessel to the boat launch. My dog, Ellie Mae, follows, uncertain what we are up to with that long boat. I've never had her in a canoe before but figure I'll baptize her in Sols Creek, and she'll be a canoe dog forever.

After the obligatory rude powerboater entry into the lake (a bass boat nearly runs us over on the ramp as we are loading gear, as if the canoe did not qualify as a watercraft) we take our first few strokes and begin bobbing across the green water. We are sitting on paddling thwarts, not seats, and our knees are tucked under white water style. "I'm too old for this," Randy says. "My knees feel like rusty hinges."

Ellie Mae is riding fine and quiet in the small space between the two of us. We have to adjust our paddle strokes a little to avoid her nose, which she keeps ceaselessly to the gunnels as if to get a fix on her position by the smell of the lake's surface. A beagle-basset is not a water dog, but Ellie Mae accommodates to the slight embarrassment just fine. She looks much more comfortable when we spot a poodle on the bow of a passing bass boat.

After a thirty-minute paddle and one or two false starts up a wrong cove, Randy says, "Now this looks more like waterfall country." The walls of the valley are rising more abruptly, and there is visible rock among the trees, and even an occasionally sheer cliff of dark granite. We are following the course of the submerged riverbed, and I imagine the old wild river and the rapids below. I am haunted by the ghost of a drowned river below the surface of a reservoir; but down there, it comforts me to think the current's ancient flow is silted away for some future day of judgment when the temporal dam shows its age, and the river emerges again.

On Bear Creek Reservoir we are only ten miles west of the Tennessee Valley divide, but from there west to the Mississippi the saying from 1930 until the present has been, "If the flow's good, dam it." The government built dams at Thorpe Reservoir, Nantahala Lake, Fontana, Santeetlah, and the infamous Tellico with its ancient Cherokee burial grounds and snail darter. Almost everywhere there was gradient in these mountains, the hand of the Tennessee Valley Authority passed over a wild river and killed it dead in its ancient bed.

It seems the height of human greed and indecency to kill a wild river for political, recreational, and real estate purposes. I know it's mostly a "power" trip, pumping out the watts for North

Carolina's ten million summer air conditioners. TVA would say, "If God would had the money, he'da air conditioned the South."

But the Bear Creek impoundment is pretty, the way a poodle can be pretty. It has a few houses on it, and the fishermen are friendly in a general way as devoted users. It's only the Jet Skis, the horseflies of lake recreation, for which I can muster quite as much hate as I hold for professional river killers. Randy tells me that even white water rivers are not safe from the roar and slashing turns of a Jet Ski. "Out in Oregon they are taking them up Class II and III rivers," he explains. "They've already had to outlaw jet boats on the Colorado."

With each paddle stroke I hear the modern world closing in around me, and I feel powerless against it paddling my canoe. I remember arguing once about snowmobiles out West with a friend. "They should be banned in all but a few areas," I said.

"What's wrong with snowmobiles?" she asked. "They're fun, and people love them. Everyone loves them but you and your eco-nut friends."

"They pollute an entire area when they're there where you are cross-country skiing."

"They meet the government standards for emission."

"I mean noise. You can hear them for ten miles."

"Oh, noise! You think noise is pollution? That's a pretty extreme position."

"Of course noise is pollution."

"You've got a choice. Just don't listen."

Bear Lake is drawn down ten feet, and we stop on an exposed sand beach to stretch our legs and let the dog touch dry land. There is a fire ring of broken rock with a dozen beer cans bent, burnt, and abandoned. The beach sand is lousy with silver dollar-size scraps of mica, and I remember a tomb I've seen in a mound in Ohio, Adena culture, and how the corpses were interred with mica sheets big as pie plates as a ceremonial covering.

The mica was acquired in trade from tribes in the southern Appalachians. On the beach at Bear Creek each piece of mica mirrors my sadness for the drowned Tuckaseegee.

While we are stopped, Ellie runs along the water's edge where wave wash makes a strange noise she's never heard before, snapping at the incoming waves and barking. I see her as a canine Hamlet, taking arms against my lake of troubles.

Back in the canoes we pass an island in the channel where a houseboat is moored, and two dogs run the beach and bark as we make a sharp left. This is where we began a short paddle up the narrowing confluence of Sols Creek. The powerboat in front of us pulls in for an instant, pivots, and then throttles back out into the main lake.

"They're looking at something," Randy says. We drift, and at exactly the moment when our canoe lines up with the entering creek's last small cataract, we see the top of Sols Creek Falls, maybe a quarter mile up the rocky creek and one hundred feet above the lake's surface. "Yep, this is waterfall country."

We leave the boat and find the best way to approach Sols Creek Falls is to say a quick prayer to the god of free flow and wade upstream from the first tiny rapid though an enclosing snarl of blooming rhododendron, shattered slabs of granite, and cold creek water, boulders fallen into creases, fans, spouts, showers, and pools.

The space quickly grows charged with the ions of wildness with each hundred feet of falling water we put behind us. Sols Creek Falls is up there somewhere, maybe beyond the next cataract, and we are headed right for it. It is quiet in the way impossibly agitated water in a mountain stream is quiet. I slip once and scrape my calf on a rock and bleed a little. Randy has on his huge brimmed farmer's hat and is easy to spot in the shadows and mist. We both have on white water sandals and are wading in the deep fonts of cold creek water, sometimes up to our waists. The dog quickly has that wet-dog look, but she boulder-hops upstream toward whatever is pulling her dog's will over the boulders.

I know it's overdone, but the creek name alone (pronounced "souls") prods me to pull out the old cliché that deep mountain forests with wild water running through them can be compared to cathedrals. Well, it's true: that's why it is and remains a cliché. Clichés are in some essential way the truest truths our language has to offer. The forest in a place like the tiny gorge below Sols Creek Falls is awe-inspiring, like a cathedral, and strangely out of place and time. Who on this busy Sunday on a mountain lake would make the difficult pilgrimage up Sols Creek to see the waterfall? Everyone else within a square mile is fishing or sunning on their houseboat when paradise is less than an hour away.

We eat our sandwiches at the base of Sols Creek Falls, and, yes, there is that magic log. I'll come back sometime with another sandwich, navigating the next pilgrimage a little more on faith and less on the first-timer's intuition. As a famous Hindu scholar once said, "The best things cannot be spoken of, and the next best are misunderstood." Suffice it to say that Sols Creek Falls is sublime; it's out there, just off the path the bass boats motor along.

PADDLE TO THE SEA

Midwinter is the time for outdoor-adventure dreams. Since we moved into our Eastside Spartanburg house and I first saw the Lawson's Fork flowing through our backyard, I've dreamed of getting in my canoe and paddling to the coast. It's an urge I get every time I look out the window and see the ceaseless current passing by. Rivers all go somewhere, and I knew ours ends up in the Santee delta, two hundred miles east, twenty miles down the coast from Georgetown. I want to follow it there.

I-26 shadows the old river system all the way from the upcountry, and I've driven it a million times. On that highway we can get to Charleston in three hours. It probably takes the current I see out my window about two weeks after passing our house to flow down the Lawson's Fork to the Pacolet and then on to the Broad, the Congaree, through Lake Marion (which before becoming the Santee-Cooper system was the Santee River) and on down the old Santee to the Atlantic.

Last summer I talked five friends into dreaming too— "Paddle to the Sea" I started calling it. The plan was to take ten days and float to the distant Carolina coast over spring break in early April of '06. Cooler heads prevailed soon as Frank, one of my floating companions, took a string and actually traced the "river miles" from here to the sea and calculated a trip of 260 miles. Twenty-six miles a day in a canoe is not impossible, but with all that could go wrong—bad weather, low water, fatigue— we decided to only go from here to Columbia on the first leg, a comfortable distance half that long. Planning the expedition this way we'd leave a little something on our adventure plate and tackle the Columbia-to-the-coast leg another season.

Long-range river voyaging is a type of time travel. Floating the Santee system from the Piedmont to the coast was quite common in the eighteenth and even nineteenth centuries. Why not use gravity to get to Charleston or Georgetown? Back then the roads were bad, and river pace was once hardwired into our souls. Everybody who reads *Huckleberry Finn* longs to kick back and float a river. "Low bridge/everybody down/low bridge 'cause we're coming to a town," I remember singing in elementary school. "Fifteen weeks on the Eerie Canal." Does anyone sing that song anymore?

First the railroads killed river travel, and now the interstates are the new rivers, hauling freight from town to town, the old rivers flowing under them like ghosts at a hundred bridge crossings.

I paddle because I'm a self-propelled kind of guy, so I enjoy letting gravity do most of the work. Besides, every time I put a paddle stroke in the water, I like to think I'm countering the single stroke of an outboard engine somewhere on the planet. It's a sort of karma I've been working on for decades now—self-propelled river karma. If I hunted, I'd probably end up a bow hunter like Ed and Lewis in Dickey's river novel.

What else? On a not-so-personal level, our South Carolina river systems are some of our most important recreational assets and they're underutilized. Charleston still draws the tourists. What about our rivers?

Planners are just beginning to realize that every mile of navigable free-flowing stream is a moving personal resort if you've got the right gear. The largest kayak manufacturer in the US is over in Easily. When those engineers and professors start flocking into Greenville and Spartanburg, I'm betting they'll be surprised no one has of yet filled our local rivers with canoes and kayaks.

We aren't pioneering this river route. In the nineteenth century the Broad and Pacolet formed a highway system as reliable and familiar as I-26. It's only with the advent of good roads in the twentieth century that the rivers took a backseat to pavement. I'm recovering a noble pioneer pastime—watching the river flow, heading downstream to the next town and the one beyond that.

Ours will not even be the first "Paddle to the Sea" from Spartanburg. I've heard the late Sam Manning, local legend and former legislator, paddled alone in the 1940s from here to the coast as a little vacation before being shipped overseas. In January of 1969 Wofford's athletic trainer Dwane "Doc" Stober took seventeen students down the river from Pacolet to Charleston. Finally, in June of 1999 David Taylor, former Converse professor, floated from Glendale to Columbia in a blue kayak and wrote an account of the trip in the first (and only) issue of *The Upcountry Review*. I'm sure there have been other trips, but these are the only ones I've heard about.

Steve Patton, who will float with me in April, also paddled to the coast from Spartanburg in late April and early May of 1981. That time he was alone in a wood canoe and says he looks forward to the company on this trip. Last weekend, as a little warm-up, we drove south into Newberry County and put Steve's canoe in the water on Parr Reservoir. Steve wanted to paddle down to the Parr Dam to see if there is a decent portage route to get us back into the river channel.

RIVER TIME

We're camping on a small island in the middle of the Broad River, twenty-two miles downstream after our launch last Thursday from behind my house in Spartanburg. It rained last night, and off the eastern tip of the island there's a rainbow, a good sign for the five days to come on the river.

There are six of us who paddled here in three canoes to this small island. I sip my coffee and think about how we were supposed to camp on a friend's land downstream, but we were late setting up camp, and how could we turn down sleeping on an island. It was good enough for Huck and Jim in *The Adventures of Huckleberry Finn*, so it should be good enough for us.

There's also a thin mist on the Broad, and two geese are making quite a racket over near the York County shore. The geese are watching me as I watch Frank and Ken stoking the fire for breakfast. Steve is just getting up, and both of Ken's boys, Dunk and Grady, are still asleep in the tent.

This is our second morning out. The Lawson's Fork and Pacolet, full of fallen trees but beautiful in their small, intimate ways, are now behind us, smaller veins in this living circulatory system we call a river. Yesterday when we left Spartanburg, we miscalculated how much light we had, and it was deep dark by the time we reached our first campsite downstream from Pacolet Mills. As we floated in the dark, beavers slapped the water, and once, a turkey flew overhead like a stealth missile headed for the other bank. The frogs formed a chorus in the low spots.

All day Friday we paddled down the Pacolet until we stopped at Skull Shoals to pick up the last of our crew, Ken's son Dunk, who had class to attend on Friday. His mother dropped him off with a resupply, a homemade coffee cake we plan to eat this morning.

It could be the nineteenth century here and I could be Huck Finn if I am willing to ignore the nylon tents, the plastic and Kevlar canoes, and the aluminum pans Ken will cook with. The Broad was used for a few decades to move goods up and down from the coast. Less than three miles from where we're camped an extensive canal system moved barges around the shoals at Lockhart. In the early mist I can almost see the boatmen poling their barges upstream.

It's easy to get caught in a fantasy like this on a river. When you're paddling a canoe it feels like time, as I've known it back home, loosens up—minutes, hours, don't seem to hold as much sway. Instead, it's the length of the daylight and the way the light rises in the morning that matters most, that give the trip its borders. River Time I call it.

Though we have only been here overnight, this sandbar has probably occupied this spot for centuries, a function of geology, hydrology, and weather. It changes from each flood, sometimes one way, and others some other shape. Sand has always been a symbol for time, and it's no different here, slipping slowly through my fingers as I sit and wait for breakfast. We're operating on River Time here, away from it all and slowed down to river speed, a couple of miles per hour.

Not everybody's relaxed like we are. The rest of the world goes on with other occupations as we cook breakfast on our island. Turkey season opened this morning and already we've heard the gobbling, and every now and then somebody takes a shot from one of the two shores. Last night we heard owls and I thought for a moment there was an owl convention on the river until Frank and Ken, both occasional turkey hunters, pointed out that these were weak imitations of owls meant to get the toms to gobble and give up their roosting sites.

But enough talk about turkeys and turkey hunting. There's bacon frying over an open fire—and soon Ken will have another pot of coffee brewing. I tell Ken's son Grady, now up for breakfast, that I'm writing a column and he might have to help me get out of it. He thinks for a moment and accepts the challenge.

"My English teacher says you can end any story with 'it truly was,' and add the title," Grady says, mixing up his first water bottle of Gatorade for the day. "You know, like, 'It truly was...a heart of Darkness.'" I think about the way the day has slipped past us. And so I give it a try: "It truly was...River Time."

$35 MILLION RIVER

Since the Nashville Agrarians took their stand in the 1930s against the industrialization sweeping the South, the region has been pulled between two minds: one, an entrepreneurial grab-all-you-can New South, maybe best exemplified by Atlanta and Charlotte; the other, a sort of stay-with-the-land Wendell Berry ruralism of small communities, farms, hunt clubs, and family timber plots that looks skeptically (even threateningly) at sprawl and jobs reliant on a manufacturing and distribution-center world economy.

The former endures in literature, song, and the new local food and farmer's market movement. The latter is also flourishing, and it is spreading at an alarming rate. The South is criss-crossed with interstates. At every exit the ganglia of feeder roads reach into Fast Food Nation, Lube Nation, Strip Mall Nation, and Payday Loan Nation. Concerning this mind, the South is just like anywhere else in America. It trusts in investment and abides in commerce. Harken back to natural history and there are still some differences. A botanist can detect something indigenous in the woods. Native hardwoods persist against the onslaught of nursery stock: crape myrtles, plane trees, and Bradford pears.

Patches of the region's iconographic landscapes have endured as well against industrial logging, mining, tourism, and agriculture: coastal salt marsh, bayou swamp, rounded Blue Ridge mountain peaks, Piedmont red-clay hills, bottomland cornfield, and higher up, roaring rivers bounded by laurel hells. Yet for many (most?) the iconographic places, the vacation and recreation havens, have morphed through capital investment into tourist destinations: Disney World, Dollywood, Six Flags, the casino beaches of the Gulf Coast, even Pedro's industrial rest stop, South of the Border on I-95.

Up the interstate from where I live in South Carolina is a $35 million recirculating river. It's in a white water park called the US National Whitewater Center, and at the center of it are two ponds between which twelve million gallons of treated Charlotte city water is pumped, creating the largest artificial white water recreation course in the world. Every minute, 536,000 gallons of water return from lower to upper pond. They flow down three shallow channels of varying difficulty. The water gathers in the lower pond after its twenty-one-foot loss in gradient, where it's sucked once again by seven giant pumps weighing in at more than twelve thousand pounds each. After descending the river, a boater can ride a conveyer belt 180 feet in length back to the top pond. Paddlers stay seated in their boats as they ascend two stories to once again run one of the artificial channels. Heraclitus be damned, the paddlers descend over and over to the bottom.

I cut my white water-paddling teeth in the 1970s on ancient time-carved Southern streams with American Indian names like Chattooga, Ocoee, Nolichucky, Nantahala. In the decades since then, I've pushed my passion outward and kayaked and rafted natural rivers in more than a dozen states and five foreign countries. How could I not be intrigued with the Charlotte park in spite of its New South industrial sheen?

In Charlotte, Olympic-hopeful kayak and canoe athletes train and compete in North Carolina's mild four-season climate and hone their slalom skills against the man-made course challenging enough to ensure fast times in international competition. An answered prayer for the sport of white water is how Cathy Hearn, a paddling coach and former Olympian, describes the training center.

If you're like me and have left your Walter Mitty Olympic hopes far behind, twenty-five dollars grants you as many descents as you can pack into a day. If you don't paddle a kayak or canoe then you can sign on for an hour-and-a-half guided raft trip. You can strap on the helmet and the PFD (personal flotation device) and scream when your craft smashes through M-wave or the last rapid on the course someone named "Biscuits and Gravy." You can ride the escalator from the calm bottom pond back to the top and do it again until you're ready for a beer and your guide paddles you ashore and tells you your time has expired.

Some brag that Charlotte's US National Whitewater Center is one of the wonders of contemporary recreation. Many love it. It's quickly becoming the dream destination all the Charlotte Chamber of Commerce-types hoped for. Thousands wander the grounds and watch the fun. People come mostly for the falling water. The concrete course is a riot, a narrow trough full of real rocks anchored in placed, one by one, in constricted flow and augmented with artificial barriers and adjustable gates around and over which water sluices almost like a real river. Proponents of "active living" mountain bike free trails crisscrossing the facility. There's a forty-six-foot-high climbing wall for the boulder bandits. You can get a sandwich at the café or drink a beer. There's talk of a planned residential neighborhood next door called Whitewater Glen.

But there are also purists, white water fundamentalists, who are critical of the new park and its purposes. They say since it's not a real river, it's turned wild water into a commodity like soap or beer or tennis shoes. They call it "a ski mountain with water on it." They snipe about how it's really no better than a glorified waterslide. They claim that when the pumps are operating, the park is one of the largest electricity users in the region. These critics point to electricity consumption as the primary reason to steer clear since this recreation complex has, they say, a carbon footprint the size of Godzilla.

I'm sympathetic to both sides. The critics are partially right. There are undeniable costs to running the longest purely recreational river in the world. There's the cost of building the resort-

style conference center and choosing not to pursue LEED Certi-
fication, of constructing something from nothing along the
shores of the very real Catawba River. There's the cost of sewage,
of supplies and provisions for the outfitters shop, restaurant, and
bar. There's beer and boats and sunscreen and hummus for the
California wraps. And there are those energy costs that only
grow. One friend reminded me that with every pulse of the M-
wave at the white water center in Charlotte, a carload of West
Virginia coal goes up in flames at one of Duke Energy's coal-
powered plants.

But there's nothing more fun, as the Water Rat claimed,
than "messing about in boats," and the proponents of the white
water parks claim they're keeping the boaters local, thereby reducing the carbon footprint of a tribe that is known to drive
hundreds of miles to spend three hours on a white water run.
Sure, Charlotte's an expensive park, but it's a park just the same.
How much did Central Park cost in real dollars when Frederick
Law Olmsted conceived and constructed it in the nineteenth
century? Nobody wants to take it back to the dales and woods it
replaced.

Artificial white water courses and park are nothing new.
The Munich Olympics in '72 used an artificial course in Augs-
burg, so the concept of running competition slalom in artificial
channels is as old as *Deliverance* itself. Opened twenty years later
for the '96 Atlanta Olympic games, the Ocoee course was laid
out by engineers and hydrologists in a "real" river channel. The
water is released from a lake above, flooding the old channel
with the new artificial rapids. It's exciting and challenging. You
can still purchase a ticket and float down it in a raft.

The *Charlotte Observer* has reported that the Nantahala
Outdoor Center, one of the East's largest adventure outfitters,
plans to modify the half-mile section of the Nantahala at their
historic NOC outpost for freestyle kayak competition. "The
white water park, which would be free and open to the public,"
the *Observer* reported, "could draw up to 10,000 spectators.

NOC will pursue state and federal development money for the estimated $5 million park planned for 2009."

I worked for NOC for ten years from 1983 until 1992. During that decade I don't think it would have occurred to anyone that someday the Nantahala waterfront past the old gas station and rustic restaurant would be called a "white water park." It was a river to us. We understood that it could be turned on and off at will up at the power plant at Lake Nantahala, but it was still a river. If we'd been there long enough (and I had), we'd seen it rage out of its banks in flood, making the dam irrelevant.

But now the gas-station-turned-outfitter's-shop and the old hippy restaurant have been replaced by large resort-style retail. Last year eighty-two thousand people floated down the river in rafts rented by the NOC. The company's value topped $15 million. Rocks have been moved around below the store in the riverbed to make for better slalom and play-boat competition.

The numbers of "guests," though, are unsteady, and the corporate number crunchers are worried. Now it seems people want a destination, a place they can go and get a meal, buy a T-shirt, and watch a few trained professionals challenge a difficult course. Sutton Bacon, the new CEO of the NOC, is a twenty-seven-year-old businessman, and he understands the challenges and risks of the old-time adventure business and marketing to aging baby boomers like myself: "We want to stay relevant with our guests," Bacon said in the Charlotte Observer article. "They might want to watch their grandkids paddle around while they want to have an upscale meal (and stay in upscale lodging). You're out there to have fun, not be cool and look cool, but to have fun with your family."

I guess I was having fun thirty-five years ago when I first paddled the Nantahala River, but Bacon's right—I thought I was cool too. I was part of a fairly small tribe—the skilled white water kayakers of the Southeast. I knew practically every paddler in the region who could safely descend Section IV of the Chattooga.

There's a hardness scale to white water boating, rafting being the softest with no real learning curve. You just strap on a helmet, grab a paddle, listen to a safety talk, practice a few strokes, and head down. Kayaking is different. The learning curve is steep. The boat's tippy. You're in it alone. There's that sexy spray skirt keeping you in. It's the hardest boat to learn to paddle.

We were definitely cooler and more elite than the unskilled rafters who could plop down their twenty dollars and bump their way down the river, the touroids, the bubbas in big black boats. We kayakers wore special gear and performed our ritual rolls like Samurai warriors.

If white water boaters had their equivalent of the back-to-the-land crowd, the Agrarians, the anti-industrialists, it was the tribe of kayakers and canoeists who paddled the South's rivers every weekend before the age of short boats and concrete rivers. "River people," Rick Bass calls those friends of his who drive from Mississippi to North Carolina to paddle the North Carolina mountain rivers, in *Wild to the Heart*.

Recently Christopher Dickey was in Spartanburg. He was here in his role as war correspondent and Paris bureau chief of *Newsweek* to speak at the college about the war in Iraq, but our conversations when he was offstage turned often to his ancestral South and the wild and free Chattooga, a free-flowing river he loves and one that we both on more than a few occasions described and pondered in print.

The son of the famed poet was on the set for the filming of his father's novel *Deliverance* in 1971. He followed the crew downstream on the Chattooga and worked as a production assistant. He even served as a stand-in for Ned Beatty draped over the log in the infamous rape scene. His only on-camera appearance was as the body of dead adventurer Drew Ballenger pulled from the river and displayed on a stretcher under a sheet. This scene, unfortunately, was lost on the cutting room floor.

Even though we now often associate *Deliverance* with the Chattooga River, the younger Dickey thinks about *Deliverance* in a context few have explored. For Christopher Dickey, his father's novel and the John Boorman film made from it are time, not space specific. The novel and the film are about a slippery place—the mythic Cahulawassee River, a made-up North Georgia river, but the time of the novel is crystal clear and easier to pin down. It's the early 1960s at the end of the old South, a world Christopher Dickey's father came to maturity as an artist in. James Dickey's first novel is one balanced between the rural-subsistence South and the emerging 1960s Sunbelt South. It points directly in the direction of places like the US National Whitewater Center (USNWC), a place where the old South has been replaced by a tourist economy.

Before James Dickey wrote mythically about death and heroism in canoes there was little to draw the masses to rivers. Now, decades later, millions raft, airboat, canoe, and kayak through most every difficult stretch of white water in the world. Chris Dickey likes to wear the T-shirt that still, thirty-five years later, proves most marketable with all of America's white water river rafters: "Paddle harder. I think I hear banjo music."

There is a wildness in the old South, a violence embodied in James Dickey's mountain men, but also a beauty as seen through the wild, free-flowing river he evokes. With the fictional damming of the wild Cahulawassee, Christopher Dickey likes to say that the South is "denatured" a little. James Dickey's mythical wild Southern river is trapped under a lake, and the dam fulfills Lewis Medlock's prophecy "to push a little more power into Atlanta."

The South may have been the first American landscape to be denatured through plantation agriculture and industrial logging, but it could be argued the South has persisted in its idea of living in nature as long as other regions with more wild land.

Southerners have a high percentage of hunters among its population, and the persistence of "sense of place" as some sort of deep abiding value has haunted the Southern landscape as long as it's been settled.

When we discuss the USNWC, Christopher Dickey likes to deepen the irony even more. He tells the story of the movie's waterfall scene filmed in Tallulah Gorge in 1971. The Tallulah River gorge, in North Georgia, was known in the early nineteenth century as "the Niagara of the South." Its two miles of dramatic waterfalls and appeal to nineteenth-century travelers and artists did not save it from going dry when the river was dammed in 1913 to provide electricity to Atlanta. The gorge is now operated as a Georgia state park, and water is released for recreational kayaking several times during the fall and spring. The five major falls evoke their romantic past with their names—Hurricane, Ladore, Bridal Veil, Tempesta, and Oceana. Christopher Dickey says that for shooting the canoe crack-up scene and Ed Gentry's ascent of the cliff the crew turned the raging river on and off as needed at the power station upstream. "How weird was that? That's Hollywood, and now in Charlotte it's everyday."

It never occurred to me when we worked at the NOC outpost that we paddlers were already tools of empire, reliant on the power company to release the water we needed into the natural river channel of the Nantahala. We made little money at our work and the company made even less. Profit is a word I never heard at NOC. We were more like a small communist country, maybe called "Kayakastan," than a business. Our meals and housing cost a pittance. We could buy anything we could afford in the company store for cost—clothing, boats, bikes, Ben & Jerry's ice cream bars.

It never crossed my mind that in the future I would be perceived by someone twenty-five years younger as an aging baby boomer whose primary desire is to have fun, to watch, to consume, to settle into clean sheets and eat a good meal rather than that hippy food I enjoyed when I was younger.

A few months after the park opened in the summer of '06 I finally let my curiosity get the best of me, and I headed up with a paddling buddy to Charlotte. It was September. Mackay and I drove in off the interstate, took a turn or two, and found ourselves on McCorkle Road, a narrow country lane. It quickly showed the effects of the collision of the new Southern leisure and good old working classes in the Piedmont of North Carolina. Along McCorkle Road there were big fenced country lots with goats and chickens in the yard, but the farm fences and pickup trucks now have a sheen of red clay dust covering them from the recreational traffic. There was a big sign that explained how the rural neighborhood and the new park reached an agreement about access, but there were strict rules for legal transit: speed bumps were the outward sign. A little further down the road the agreement sign was contrasted with the "Hey, asshole slow down you killed my dog," sign one resident had scrawled on an old piece of siding and propped up in their yard.

After we reached the end of McCorkle Road, a gravel entrance drive takes you into the park. Around the last curve, past a wide power right-of-way, the US National Whitewater Center rose like a recreational Oz. There were a dozen acres of gravel parking lots on a ridge above the Catawba River, and behind them the center lodge stood like something straight from Aspen or Vail. The big building was all angles, big timber, metal roof, and glass. One route in feeds straight into an outfitters shop, raft check-in, and restaurant, terrace, and climbing wall; another leads "hard boaters" like us (canoeists and kayakers) to their sign-up hut near the upper pond.

We took the second. When we arrived we were assigned red jerseys to slip over our personal flotation devices. A few minutes after arrival we carried our boats to the solid curb of the pond and entered the red-clay waters of the course. It was a weekday and there weren't many people on the course. I paddled out and tested my roll. When I popped back to the surface I noted, though the early morning air was cool, I was overdressed for the water's temperature—bathtub warm.

I took stock of what was around me, as I would upon entering a river. To my right, there were rafters getting a safety talk on a concrete beach studded with river rocks Just to their right, water from the pond disappeared down "the competition channel," the most difficult of Charlotte's three runs. Across the pond the pump house flushed thousands of gallons of recirculated water back into the basin from below. The sound of the pumps and the conveyor belt next to them cranking like a cannery was not so inviting. It sounded like a factory, but if I tried I could hear it as something different, maybe a fair, with mechanical rides.

Mackay paddled toward one of the two easier channels on far left and I followed. The white water fun awaiting refocused me on the matter at hand—my first descent of a concrete river. The horizon line on the first "play feature" of the far-left channel looked inviting, and that's where we headed.

We slipped through the first small channel-wide wave and eddied on river right. We spent five minutes getting our boats under us by playing on the wave. Down at water level lost in the play it's hard to separate the experience at Charlotte from the hydraulics of a natural river. The engineering is just that good. A wave's a wave, whether nature made it or it came out of somebody's head. It's only when you look around and see the smooth concrete walls or the people strolling past on a sidewalk with their dogs that you realize you're not on a river.

The intensity picks up the rest of the way down and I enjoyed it. We played for two hours in two artificial channels of trapped, surging current, and before we left Mackay even paddled the short, explosive "competition channel" where the Olympic boaters practice their refined craft. I watched from the lip of the concrete channel as he made it down upright, a cork bobbing along on an engineered Class IV tumult. I took photos, secure in my knowledge that at my age it's sometimes best to leave a little adventure on the plate for future visits.

A year later my relationship to this new "river" only an hour up the interstate remains complex and lasting. I want to find fault with it, yet each time I paddle the park I like it more and more, and I find myself feeling guilty. "Think of all the carbon offset credit you could get because this river is an hour closer than the Chattooga," one friend argued unconvincingly, trying to make me feel better. "Multiply that by all the recreational paddlers and you get real savings on gas for recreation."

Like the river, everything in Charlotte comes back around to business. "We're not selling kayaking," Jeff Wise, director of the white water center has said in the business magazine *Water-world*. "We're selling a lifestyle." Wise predicted the nonprofit center would break even in its first year, but the numbers aren't so good as they hoped. "Our goal is to keep you out long enough to eat, drink, and spend a little money."

The name of the 307-acre North Carolina park on the banks of the Catawba River—the US National Whitewater Center—gives the place a real professional feel. At least they didn't call it "Thunder River." Instead of a Disney theme-ride, the USNWC sounds more like a recreation destination—and it is.

Unlike a real river there are no headwaters, no confluence with larger rivers downstream. Downstream on this circular river is a continuous liquid state headed nowhere. On the artificial Charlotte river there's simply start and stop when your time runs out.

The folks in Charlotte aren't embarrassed about their desire to make as much money as possible off falling water, but the business model is part of what still keeps me uncomfortable. When I think about becoming a paddling regular at the white water center the word consumption comes to mind. I'd be part of the recreational sports machine in a way I'd only experienced in glancing blows over the past thirty years. I've always bought my boats and gear from the industrial white water machine, but the water itself was always "natural" river water tumbling over authentic rocks in a riverbed. Already over fifty and cast pretty solidly in my white water ways, should I share my river time with a concrete trench?

When I look at the white water center's website, I have to admit it's not my entertainment dollars the park is chasing. "Take It Outside," the site proclaims. In other words, "All your young couch-bound video game addicts need to come out and throw down at our water park." They're pursuing a different demographic. Wise sees the park as one of many "gateway projects" nationwide introducing thousands of younger paddlers to rafting and kayaking in a controlled environment.

Another disturbing aspect of the white water center for me is how layered just below the competition hype is a pay-per-float experience not far removed from a Disney World ride. On a busy Saturday or Sunday hundreds of rafts ping-pong down the three channels and ride the escalator back to the top pond. This is the profit center of the business model. The US National Whitewater Center's hired boats are full of screaming, paddle-slapping tourists, and the guides are trained to entertain them. "Hey, Julie," one supervisor yelled at a raft departing from upper pond on my first visit. "Your parole officer just called and it's okay if you check in after the run."

On another visit I took a friend from California, a kayaker who has written a book about a wild western river. He enjoyed himself but came up right away with what he thought was the primary difference between paddling in Charlotte and on a natural river: "I'm critical of such an engineered experience in a way I never am on a wild river," he said. "This paddling experience has been designed as a service rendered. Paddling a wild river is always a gift. You take what it gives you."

Another paddling friend I took to the park compared paddling the engineered course to rock climbing: "In climbing it takes skill to get into a situation where you might kill yourself. On a wild river you can just sit down in a boat and float into a place you might die. In a white water park the risk is gone, and it teaches paddlers to drop their guard."

Demographics are one thing, profit's another, but what about the cost in river karma, one of my religious river-runner friends asked me a few weeks ago after we'd paddled the Chattooga. She'd heard I'd visited the white water center and acted like I'd been boating with the devil. Who, she mused, are the local gods of the concrete channels? Are they appeased in the same way as the spirits on a wild river like the Chattooga?

When I put in on a wild river, I feel I'm in communion with a deep and abiding state I've always called "river time," something spanning millions of years of flow and erosion. I even say a small prayer as I snap my spray skirt in place. Up in Charlotte it doesn't occur to me to ask permission to descend. I've had my ticket punched and pulled on the jersey that tells those working the ticket booth I've paid their fee to float their private river.

But because the river has been secularized doesn't mean it's pointless to paddle in a concrete trough. Does this "denatured" river open up other possibilities? Will people who visit the Charlotte park see white water recreation as a possibility for their leisure dollars and then paddle with a rafting company down a truly wild river like the Chattooga someday? Will this contact with "nature" lead to a deeper understanding of the challenges of conservation of our iconographic landscapes?

Here's an anecdote that's hard for me to process: One day in Charlotte I was hanging around the ticket office before putting on, and an African American family stood quizzing the attendant. They'd rafted the park that day, but their two young boys wanted more—they wanted to learn to kayak. "How much are the lessons," the father asked. "How much is the equipment?"

My first response was, "Another satisfied customer pulled in by the hype." Yet digging deeper I remembered how I had been brought to river running: through a club at a small college and the instruction of a professor. I'd learned to roll a kayak in a municipal pool and paddled my first time on the Nantahala, even in 1977 not far removed from a Six Flags ride on a busy summer day.

Does the concrete nature of the Charlotte park negate what paddling joy comes naturally from putting a boat on moving water? What new perspective would these young Black men bring to an activity (river running) that has always been mostly white? Would their Blackness add any new and surprising perspectives to the conversation? It's unlikely we'll find out without places like Charlotte. Parks open up the scene. They make white water a suburban sport like soccer. Is that bad? It's a long way from the ancient "grail quest" of Lewis Medlock and his hell-bound aluminum canoe in *Deliverance*, but it's always good to remember that just off the interstate in the South there's still plenty of religion to go around.

Over the next few months I went back two or three times and each visit tried to work out the problem of natural and unnatural resources, and how amazing it is a society like ours can afford to build a $35 million recreational river and create an "ecotourism" destination out of concrete and imagination in the Carolina Piedmont. Each time I paddled I reminded myself that someday I would continue to ponder the difference between real and artificial, raw and cooked, wild and tame, but usually the pure fun of white water directed me in other directions. Paddling, like meditation, has a way of settling my mind, even if the channel is man-made.

FOUR

RIVER POEMS DOWNSTREAM

No Water in the River

River, where do you live
When the weather turns
And the rain stops?

Where my ribs show.
Where dry moss scabs my rocky shins.

If You See the River

at its thickest you see land
whittled by the knife of every inch
of rain. Mud is the last testament
to sediment, and sediment, every
field's red tongue. Land preaches
when the rain falls, run clean
down every drain. Rain tilts continents
builds shelves in the basement
of oceans, like the preacher
with a secret hobby beneath the steps.

First Spring Flood

What floats is all we've discarded.

Water has a way of pure dispensation,
from each field by the laws of erosion;
to each stream according to its flow.

The river curves in the willows.
Red current roils past the roots.

Gospel truth: tomorrow frogs
will spawn in new mud.

An old tee shirt, a baby's beach ball, two shoes, unmatched,
a bald tire, foam in the eddies, limbs, leaves, a dead duck.

The water drops
over night.

Water bugs gondolier
back and forth

on the clearing stream.

Teaching the River

My student asks why the river
Bends left and right as it flows
Downhill. She says that all
Things fall if given time
And distance, and turns the question
Into a physics problem she's learned
Before in school. I say it's like
Your own life, the way
Meanders form when dreams
Are left behind. And she says,
Dreams and rivers are not
The same, one is a long muddy
Drainage connected to some
Source far in the mountains,
The other never there really,
Always just beyond the next
Desire—or delusion.
"You can step in a dream twice,"
she jokes, twisting an old adage
to the needs of the class.
"Yes," I answer, but "In rivers
Responsibilities begin."

Ridge Music

For Mike Delp

Ours were two familiar voices—crusty
With years, thick with the sediment
Of beer. And then two crows overhead
Danced as you'd never seen before.
You wondered if they mate in air—
Their calls another dark punctuation.

There were fish in the Boardman River—
You knew their habits and watched
The glassy edges of eddies for feeding
Signs—most evenings you wade there,
Your line and reel sounding a familiar
Note in the breeze—we sat and watched
The river flow soundlessly past just off
Your little dock. No music like that
Of silence, no sound like that of absence.

That is your home water and like
Most familiarity you settle in its presence
Like a fog and flow outward through
Your senses until you've covered it.

Later, when you'd left me in the dark
With only the river for company, I heard
Coyotes on the ridge top—a counter chorus
Full of longing—break into unfamiliar sounds.
I looked out at the river to make sure
Its flowing had not ceased—assured by
Its action I went inside your cabin
And slept surrounded by the song.

The Half-Finished House

for Betsy

More statement than investment, more Frank Lloyd Wright
than Martha Stewart, we dreamed our house as mostly glass
and abstract comforts.
No lawn, we left the lot lousy
with underbrush and saplings most would cut and haul away.
The driveway's down slope turn hides it, our angular gray
ghost—

a modern gesture emerging from that wooded space.

We invest in photosynthesis.
Our return, paw paws by the creek,
the sweep of swamp oaks rising.

Place:
this slab of concrete, no foundation
feature wall rising for no clear utility. Instead, our defining gesture,
a very-real wood-framed forest filling every window.

***

It was on the hardwood hillside where the outside wall now
stands that we found past evidence of occupation: small

fractured atlatl point. Around it lay scattered quartz chips,
the refuse of archaic labor.
I picked it up, pocketed it, talisman
securing this continued settlement.

A ruined river road forms our southern property line,
risks flood when Lawson's Fork rises.
Yesterday I walked down
slope, slipped off my shoes and waded the orphan current,
glimpsed upstream

a flowing, a future, the run-off moving through.

FIVE

RIPPLES OUTWARD AND INWARD

REGENESIS:
SEEKING WILDNESS IN A DAMAGED
SOUTHERN LANDSCAPE

Mixing pleasure with curiosity I set out on a Sunday morning in late October with some friends to paddle a three-mile stretch of Fairforest Creek just outside the city limits of Spartanburg. Four of us will put in on South Liberty Street in Arkwright, an old mill village, and take out a few hours later downstream on 295-Bypass. This will be urban boating at its best. Fairforest Creek is not a wilderness: it drains most of Spartanburg's south-side industrial zones—small-time machine shops, distribution plants, even a large petroleum-tank farm just downstream from where we'll take out. The Fairforest is not blue-ribbon water for anything—fish, recreation, or scenery. It's a working class creek and the Department of Health and Environmental Control (DHEC), South Carolina's regulatory agency, classifies it "impaired," a word a friend once pointed out tells us little about the stream but loads about our relationship with it.

In spite of the less-than-pristine nature of the creek I've convinced my companions, G. R., his teenage son Phillip, and Gerald, that a morning on the water—any water—is worth it. Paddling pleasure is not hard to come by once the boat's in the current, even on the Fairforest, though the water's low, the result of a record-dry fall many are quick to blame on global warming. Pleasure aside, the curiosity is easier to explain and appreciate. As we're loading the boats, I tell my friends that what I'm really interested in is claiming what may be "a first descent" through the territory of "ReGenesis," Spartanburg's national poster child for environmental justice, an EPA-cited brownfield and two Superfund sites, what ReGenesis founder and local environmental activist Harold Mitchell called "the Devil's Triangle" when he brought attention to this industrial neighborhood in the late 1990s. Arkwright, primarily a low-income African American community, has fought for almost a decade now to clean up the horrors of an abandoned fertilizer factory, an old textile mill with leaking chemical storage tanks, and a thirty-acre city dump full of industrial and medical wastes. ReGenesis was formed for this struggle. Its story, and the story of Harold Mitchell, its founder, is so compelling that in 2002 the EPA gave Mitchell its National Citizens Involvement Award, known informally as the "Erin Brockovich award." Since then ReGenesis has become a national model program for cleaning up low-income communities all over the country.

Several weeks before, Harold Mitchell had visited the humanities/biology learning community I coteach with a toxicologist, so I'm still full of the ReGenesis story. Mitchell, fresh off a victory in a Democratic primary for the South Carolina House of Representatives, had lunch with us, visited class, and then drove us around the ReGenesis Project site in a van, giving me perspective on the story that Gerald, G. R., and Phillip don't have. Though they live just up the hill in the middle-class neighborhood called Duncan Park, the nearby ReGenesis Project is still unknown to them. I'll fill everyone in on what else I know about the project as we make our way downstream.

Before we launch, I reveal one more wrinkle in the Sunday-morning story. I lived in Arkwright for a year in the early 1960s, when the village was still mostly white mill workers. I was seven years old when my mother moved us there, and I have a few clear memories: eating figs off a fig tree in our backyard, which sloped down to Fairforest Creek, and going with my uncles to the nearby phantom dump to shoot rats spotlighted amidst the rubble. When we turn down the street near where I'd lived, the creek is at the bottom of the hill. "It's so quiet here," Gerald says.

At 9:45 A.M. we unload the boats from G. R.'s old green pickup next to the mill site. I've emailed Harold to warn him that if he gets reports of white guys in a fleet of old canoes headed southeast into terra incognito, he'll know it's us. When we had visited the site earlier Harold had explained how by the middle '90s the old mill had become crime central, with drugs and prostitution, and the only alternative seemed to be to clear it out and start anew. A few houses and families would stay, but mostly the Re-Genesis vision was one of "renewal," a word that mostly white people had used to level the African American community further north on Liberty Street in the 1970s. I could only hope we had learned a great deal more about renewal since then and could get it right this time.

On a literal level, something clearly needed to be done to clean up this corner of Spartanburg. We drag the boats through busted bottles, old wire, and loose trash and put in at a little bold tributary running from under the old mill outflow pipe, rusted and unused for decades. Behind us on the hilltop loom several huge piles of old wood from the teardown of the mill. ReGenesis now owns the property, and Mitchell told our class that bricks and timbers are stored at the back of the site in hopes they can be reused to build a project headquarters or an ecology center someday. DHEC has approved a huge bonfire, a controlled burn, for later in the year to get rid of all the old ruined timber, the lumber with paint painstakingly sorted from the raw wood to make sure ReGenesis doesn't add more toxic waste to the air and water of Arkwright.

Finally we're on the water. Soon there are three canoes and a small kayak mirrored on the dark surface, a flotilla that almost overwhelms the narrow waters of the silted-in Arkwright mill-pond. Gerald and young Phillip head downstream, and I paddle with G. R. a little ways upstream under the bridge. I want to commune for a moment with the epicenter of Arkwright, a community that makes up one of the most complex strands of my place-based DNA. I know from a class discussion of Lake Conestee, a similar old textile site in Greenville, that the toxic industrial chemicals trapped below me in the millpond sediment could fill a graduate toxicology seminar, and so instead I prefer to focus on what's around me. I fix on some of Spartanburg's old granite curbstones, now pressed into service to keep the shore from washing out under the bridge. I point them out to G. R. and note that they are an adaptive reuse of a local resource from quarry stone to curbstone, to riprap, to historic curiosity in a hundred years. G. R., a nature photographer when he's not teaching physiology at the college, is more interested in the way the early morning light bounces off the greasy surface of the water and settles on the bottom side of the concrete bridge in interesting patterns. As G. R. gets his camera out, I'm reminded there is beauty around us in the world, in spite of what we do to extinguish it.

We head downstream to catch up with Gerald and Phillip. There's a large kudzu field on river left and the eroded, littered slope of the mill site on our right. Gerald's already birding. Sociology professor by day, writer and naturalist by evening, he has his binoculars out, and his true passion for the natural world is on full display. He's left the ugliness of Arkwright behind him in the rearview mirror. We've only been on the water five minutes but by sight and call Gerald's already identified ten species. He repeats the names and I write them all down—eastern phoebe, song sparrow, white-throated sparrow, great blue heron, crows, blue jays, kinglet, rufous-sided towhee, kingfisher, and mallards. "The mallard is the only duck that quacks," Gerald says, and I tell him he sounds a little too much like a science teacher, but I write that fun fact down anyway. For a moment Gerald's ornithological fact serves as a finger in the dike of ugliness surrounding me as we float through the endless tunnel of kudzu.

We round another bend, and a strong odor of sewage enve-
lopes us. I decide it's coming from a tributary entering the mill-
pond from our left. I know that this small creek, unnamed on
our topo, if explored to its headwaters, rises only a few hundred
yards off of Spartanburg's Main Street, parallels Liberty Street,
and empties here amidst the tires and kudzu. In its short two-
mile run it drains some of the poorest areas of the Southside—
government housing, shotgun shacks that have somehow survived into the twenty-first century, mean streets, and vacant lots
full of abandoned needles and malt liquor cans. This morning
there's no denying the elements that lead to what academics and
government pundits have come to call "environmental justice"
issues as I look up the small stream—poverty, racism, ignorance,
denial, and outright criminal neglect by the community's rich
and powerful. It all drains into Fairforest Creek. I turn my face
to avoid the smell.

We paddle on around another bend. The creek looks dead, a
green fur coat of algae on everything hidden just below the surface—railroad ties, an old shopping cart, a City of Spartanburg
plastic garbage can, a quarter of aluminum siding. "Gerald can
have the birds," G. R. jokes as we head on downstream. "I'll keep
the fish list today."

Old tires are everywhere. Downstream the half circles of
four upright radials sunk in sediment look like a headless river
monster in the glare. As the horizon line comes into sight where
the creek drops eight feet over the concrete dam, four wood
ducks shoot overhead like cruise missiles. "Oh, look," I say.
"We've already had our 'wood duck moment.'"

Nobody knows what I mean, so as we beach our boats to
figure out a way around the dam I explain my nature joke, how a
few years ago in an environmental literature class I'd asked my
students to come up with a master list of what elements every
nature essay has to contain. "At least one profound wood-duck

moment," one smart-ass student had suggested after reading Annie Dillard's *Pilgrim at Tinker Creek* and Franklin Burroughs' *The River Home.*

Smart-ass or not, my student had been right on. There's something about the flight overhead of wood ducks that seems to fit our idea of a nature essay so much better than the slow ghostly dance of blue-green algae on a twisted shopping cart thrown off a south Spartanburg bridge years before. A heavily impacted urban creek like the Fairforest has about as much in common with Tinker Creek as a wolf would to a pit bull chained to a trailer. So why not write about nature with the brief (in geologic time) brutal pageant of human use as the backdrop rather than the contested history of wildness and beauty?

This struggle of wild and tame, raw and baked, green and paved is all around us in nature writing, and not until recently did urban nature began to show up as a protagonist in the story. As I drag my boat through the kudzu and broken bottles to portage the dam, I notice "wild" native river birch and box elder reaching for sun out over what's not silted of the pond. "See, there's even wildness here," I say to Gerald. "Isn't it strange that just upstream from a government-certified toxic wasteland, I'm pulled toward dreams of wild restoration?" Gerald brings up ecocritic William Cronan, who would dismiss my hopes of wildness as the myth of some untransformed landscape that exists somewhere else.

But I'm unwilling to give up on wildness and beauty and such. Surely there's hope here for what's wild to creep upward through the poor Southside toward the inner reaches of the city, like fingers of green clutching at the urban heart.

Gerald's more bothered, as we portage our canoes around the dam, by what I've told him of Harold Mitchell's dream. Mitchell wants to "renew" the community partially by turning the floodplain below the mill site into a golf course or tidy green space with paved trails and landscaping provided by the University of Virginia's renowned landscape architecture department.

We clear the dam, and I comment on how the old settlement of Arkwright will remain upstream of us now all the way to
295-Bypass. From our topo we can see what's left is wooded
country with no houses, maybe a thousand acres or more of raw
land, much of it in a one-hundred-year flood zone. Renew or
restore? With the terrible truth of Arkwright's history behind us
and the vision of a golf course clouding our ideas of wilderness
restoration for this floodplain, we get back into our canoes and
head downstream, bumping over a few exposed rocks and rubble
of construction debris left below the dam. I haven't done a very
good job of explaining ReGenesis to my friends, and so I take
the next mile or so to bring them up to speed.

The headwaters of the ReGenesis story is Harold Mitchell, who
grew up "across the tracks" from where we are now paddling, just
south of the old Arkwright mill village. The day I met Mitchell
at Wofford he walked toward us from the visitors parking lot.
Mitchell looked to be in his early forties, of medium build, nicely
dressed in a tie and striped shirt, black pointy shoes, silver-and-
black glasses, sporting a neatly trimmed beard. As he approached, I noticed Mitchell had his cell phone in his left hand
and an earpiece in his right ear. "You wouldn't believe who he
gets calls from," a friend who knows him well had told me. Was
he talking to someone out there in his global environmental-
justice network?

At lunch Mitchell told a story that illustrated the opportunities his success with ReGenesis has opened to him and how
much political savvy he's developed running in environmental-
justice circles. He'd been invited to serve on the US delegation at
the World Sustainable Development Conference in Johannes-
burg, South Africa, in September 2002, and he was at a cocktail
party with all the big shots—Hillary Clinton among others. The
anti-American sentiment was high, and Harold picked it up
right away. He said he'd turned his nametag around in order to

avoid detection as a member of the US delegation. When the Africans came up to ask him where he was from, he said in a very brusque tone with the hint of an accent, "I am from Arkwright." Where? "Arkwright. I am from Arkwright!"

So what about Mitchell's Arkwright has made it what several sources call a worldwide model for environmental justice? It's a complex and intriguing story, part *A Civil Action*, part *To Kill a Mockingbird*. Back home after college in 1991, Mitchell contracted a mysterious illness. He lost a great deal of weight, and the doctors considered kidney, colon, or prostate cancer. After a series of tests, the doctors couldn't find out what was wrong, and Mitchell wanted answers. "Just tell me I'm dying of something," he told them.

During the same period Mitchell was sick, his father died from a mysterious ailment. One day, looking out the window of the family home, Mitchell began to wonder if the illnesses in his household could be connected to the abandoned fertilizer plant that had operated across the street from 1910 to 1986. The fertilizer company that owned it is the largest producer and supplier of concentrated phosphate and potash fertilizer in the world. They'd sold the old plant site to a businessman in Gaffney, South Carolina, after they shut it down in '86, and in the middle '90s it was still being used for storing textile supplies.

Mitchell wondered if living so close to a fertilizer factory could make you sick. He knew his street had stayed on well water because city water was too expensive to bring in from across the tracks. Could that be a problem? He also began to ask neighbors about their medical histories and discovered quickly there was a very high incidence of cancer in his neighborhood—sixteen cases on his street alone. There were only five or six families, so it made the survey quite easy. At this point Mitchell didn't know anything about "cancer clusters," but so much illness in one community seemed odd.

In the late '90s Mitchell recovered his heath and was living in nearby Greer, working as a teacher, but he was still looking into the neighborhood fertilizer plant back home. Oddly enough, South Carolina DHEC had certified the plant clean when it closed in '86, but what Mitchell was hearing from the plant's neighbors did not jibe with what was appearing in DHEC's files. On one of Mitchell's visits to the DHEC office a clerk mistakenly handed him a fat file to take home, and it confirmed his worst fears of what sort of chemicals and potential waste had accumulated at the plant for almost a hundred years. He began to read, ask questions of government officials, and explore all the possible ways the plant could be contaminating the area he'd grown up in.

In 1997 a DHEC survey of the neighborhood did not put Mitchell's fears to rest, though once again the agency found no contaminates. Mitchell was relentless. What we now call "environmental justice" meant little to him then, but he pushed forward simply because he wanted to find out if there was some reason why he and his neighbors were so sick.

In 1998 Mitchell tired of going it alone. It was the beginning of his remarkable ability to build partnerships and consensus. He formed a small grassroots group in Arkwright to begin to organize the information the neighbors were gathering. Mitchell began to get threatening phone calls, many suggesting he didn't need to be asking all these questions.

What could possibly be the matter with asking questions about the closed fertilizer factory? In South Carolina's "pro-business environment," low or lax government regulation had always been—along with a strong anti-union past that guaranteed low wages for workers and higher profit margins for stockholders—the honey that drew out-of-state development. Mitchell began to realize that industrial pollution, dumping, and the siting of the dirtiest of the industries in Black and poor neighborhoods was one of South Carolina's dark secrets many felt better left undisturbed.

One morning Mitchell had an unexpected visit from a representative of the South Carolina militia. The man stood on

Harold Mitchell's porch and calmly told him that the questions the budding investigator was asking were very dangerous, and that he should consider driving various routes to and from Greer when going to Arkwright to do his research.

The man seemed to know everything about him. The militia member said the Arkwright inquiry could challenge the very business establishment of the state. "Don't trust anything from the state level," he said. "Go straight to the feds." Was this guy friend or foe? It was a little confusing. When Mitchell thought of the militia, he imagined those skinheads in Montana. Then he gave Mitchell the 800 number to call the EPA. Before he left, the man pulled a handgun out of a holster behind his back. "He's told me all this, and now he's going to shoot me," Mitchell had told my class he thought as the gun appeared. "Do you have a permit to carry one of these?" the man asked. "If you don't, you need to get one."

Mitchell called the EPA and on the day before the agency was supposed to inspect the fertilizer plant, the owner brought in bulldozers and caved the building in, making it impossible to do an easy inspection. Mitchell filmed the demolition with his video camera, part of a long record of the project he has assembled on tape. In '99 Harold presented all the information he'd gathered at a community meeting. DHEC stopped the owner from destroying any more of the evidence as a result.

The EPA then sent an inspector from the Atlanta office, and he walked around the site as Mitchell followed him with the video camera. The inspector dismissed everything, downplayed it all. Undaunted by this roadblock at the regional level, Mitchell used a high school connection to convince US Senator Fritz Hollings to get involved in the Arkwright case. Hollings's chief of staff was Joey Lesesne, Mitchell's former center on the Spartanburg High School football team in the mid-'80s. Mitchell called Lesesne, and Hollings became interested in the Arkwright case and requested an EPA investigation of the fertilizer site.

The third EPA inspection revealed that sulfur had been dumped over the back fence of the fertilizer company. There was a small visible yellow pile of it on the slope going down to the creek. Once the area was explored extensively, inspectors discovered there were twenty tons of sulfur in the area. There was also an abandoned acid factory underneath it as well. How had the state agency missed all this?

"With seepage velocity of forty-six feet per year there was no doubt all this was affecting the creek," Harold had explained to us when I visited the site with my class. The inspection also revealed an abandoned waste pond on the site where the EPA estimated 1.3 million gallons of toxic liquid had been drained along a ditch dug with a backhoe right into the creek. When the EPA started to inspect the abandoned factory the agency found forty-eight tons of abandoned super-phosphate fertilizer. The walls were saturated with it. "Tim McVee blew up the federal building in Oklahoma City with two tons," Mitchell had said, explaining how volatile the whole situation was. There was a homeless man living in the plant and burning scrap wood for fire. Arkwright was a time bomb waiting to blow. Also, the whole site was overrun with rats and the snakes that eat them. "You could have filmed *Anaconda* in that old factory," Harold said. Once the EPA got involved in the inspection that would lead to the Arkwright site gaining Superfund designation, the feds kicked state agency DHEC off-site, the first time that had ever happened in South Carolina.

The discovery of the Arkwright dump, located by the EPA while the inspectors were on-site to deal with the fertilizer company's assessment, was the second point on Mitchell's "Devil's Triangle." The dump had operated from 1958, when the city incinerator closed, until 1972, when a new city dump opened. It was a thirty-acre landfill that DHEC didn't have records for, though it was on the city's land. "They dug a two-hundred-foot hole and filled it up—everything—trash, bulk oil, medical waste," Mitchell explained.

The site was not fenced, and excavations and EPA depositions from the neighborhood show that the local hospital was
dumping there, along with much of the industry in the area. The
depositions given by neighbors tell of boxes of human fetuses
and amputated arms and legs that dogs dragged into neighboring
yards from the dump during those years.

In 1998 the Arkwright community addressed the landfill
with the Spartanburg City Council. At the first meeting, 120
people showed up in council chambers. There were people there
from three communities surrounding Arkwright—lower-income
Black families, lower-income white families, and middle-income
Black families.

The third point of "the Devil's Triangle" of environmental
justice was the old Arkwright mill site where we had launched
our boats, and where contaminants exist as well—old leaking
petroleum tanks on-site. In 1999 the EPA designated the ferti-
lizer-plant/dump/Arkwright-mill site part of the Superfund program, and Spartanburg officially had its own little Love Canal.
IMC bought the site back that year and put a tent over the plant
property, installed monitoring wells, and began the costly complex cleanup.

When it was clear how extensive the problems in Arkwright
were, the neighbors decided to organize the whole lower
Southside area and create a "regenesis." The name has a religious
ring to it, and soon events took on revival proportions. Six hundred people were at the first organizational meeting to discuss
the rebuilding and revitalization of the neighborhoods—Black,
white, poor, and middle class. The EPA held workshops to ad-
dress cleanup, educating the community concerning its plight.
Soon the number of community members signing on to the Re-
Genesis vision grew to 1,400.

In the past five years ReGenesis has grown into a communi-
ty-revitalization organization with 124 partners—public, private,
government, nonprofits. About $134 million has come into the
venture to date. Out of the ReGenesis has grown the model that

is being repeated all over the country at similar brownfield and Superfund sites. The ReGenesis model addresses environmental questions, pollution and blight, crime, housing issues, healthcare issues. Why has Harold followed through now for almost ten years? What drove him through all this? "The voices of the dead tend to ring loud in my mind as I press forward," he said in his acceptance speech after winning the Ford Foundation's prestigious Leadership for a Changing World Award in 2002.

It's after noon now, and we're strung out along a quarter mile of shallow water, paddling our three separate boats, setting our own pace. Phillip leads the way, his youthful spirit of adventure pushing him downstream in front of the old farts. I'm next. As I float down Fairforest Creek I keep watching the western shore, looking for signs of the mysterious abandoned city dump in Arkwright's back reaches. I know it's somewhere in the woods. I don't want to paddle past a Superfund site and not see it. But all I see is trees.

"Look, the whole creek's a landfill," G. R. says, pointing in his canoe when I tell him what I'm looking for. All the way downstream he's been picking up the brightly colored bottoms of a hundred broken bottles. He'd found them washed up on sandbars and collected them as we passed, a prospector for beauty along the creek's sandy bottom. When I ask him what he plans to do with the bounty of glass, he doesn't know.

"It looks like somebody threw every plastic bag in Spartanburg County in this creek," Gerald says, catching up, pointing to the high-water line in the river birches fifteen feet above us.

"They look like prayer flags when the wind blows a little," G. R. says, paddling his old black canoe forward toward more broken bottles.

I look downstream. There's beauty to be seen in the garbage, though even here, a mile or so below the old mill site and the crumbling dam, the creek valley is not a wilderness. It's not

"Little House on the Prairie" rural either. There's no patchwork of farm fields and sleepy homesteads with wood smoke drifting from the chimneys. It's nothing but a flat expanse of creek bottom, just like a hundred others, grown up for forty years in privet, kudzu, and spindly hardwoods. It's not even desirable real estate down here. There's no developer out there—except Harold Mitchell—who looks at this floodplain and thinks golf course or anything else. "What would all this mean to a developer?" I ask Gerald as we rest on a sandbar. "Do the developers worry over the idea of development the way we worry over wilderness?"

"I don't think developers sit around and think about what anything means," Gerald says. "They don't do self-critiques or soul-searching when it comes to buying property. They run the numbers. I don't think Roderick Nash has to worry much about his intellectual market share for *Wilderness and the American Mind*. You won't see a book anytime soon called 'Development and the American Mind.'"

We had enough talking, and we get back in the boats. Our trip is drawing to a close. I can hear 295-Bypass a few hundred yards downstream. Gerald quickly falls a little behind, birding along an opening in the power line that follows the creek all the way, hoping to prolong his day on the creek as long as possible. So, what has ReGenesis not addressed so far in its remarkable community revitalization?

Though it calls itself an environmental organization, it doesn't seem from the story that ReGenesis has much to do with traditional environmental issues—species diversity, wilderness, habitat destruction. How much discussion goes on among the partners about what's best for the creek, for all the wildlife, great and small? ReGenesis is a powerful people organization with high hopes for cleaning up and revitalizing the community. I can only hope that they see their community as both the human and nonhuman world.

There's a plan on the books, with national and state money committed, for cutting a road all the way from South Liberty Street to 295-Bypass, crossing the creek somewhere downstream from the dam, and "opening up" the entire area for that golf course and a mixed-use village along 295. It seems so remarkable to think that the densely wooded dirty reaches we've paddled through for hours could someday look like any new subdivision with a freshly graded avenue through it.

I can see G. R. has stopped ahead of me at the outlet for a small clear stream feeding Fairforest from the east. I stop too and ask about Phillip. G. R. says not to worry—Phillip is already ahead of us at the takeout. He's won the race and now he has to wait a few more minutes while the old guys catch up. I get out of my canoe to stretch my legs.

We haven't seen one human track on our paddle, though Gerald points out an interstate highway of deer prints when he lands on the sandbar. "I hope Mr. Mitchell knows this qualifies as a major urban deer sanctuary," he says. "They probably hide in here and go out and eat people's yards in Duncan Park at night."

I'm still concerned with the question of where is the environment in environmental justice? In the "EJ" movement does environmental concern always get relegated to funding people-friendly hiking trails and planning for "green space" as the money rolls in after cleanup? Once, when I brought up more passive green space for Spartanburg, a former mayor asked, "But how will we afford to mow it?"

I tell Gerald we should file our own vision for this place we've paddled through. "I'd like to see at least a hundred acres of this big Fairforest floodplain cleaned up and left wooded," I say. "I'd sure hope they plan to leave at least a one-hundred-foot riparian buffer along the creek."

Will ReGenesis recognize untended land as sensible stewardship? It's possible. Harold Mitchell is a man who has made a career on listening to all comers with good ideas, even ideas from old conservationists like us. One thing about rich developers, it's hard to get in on the ground floor with their plans, but a community consensus builder like Harold Mitchell is different. The motive for ReGenesis was not profit. It was justice. Maybe the redevelopment of the lower Southside will not be profit driven either.

At my feet, the season's last yellow jackets work the sandbar. In a clear, shallow pool I watch a school of tiny fish feeding, the hopeful signs of the creek's health I've been watching for all along the way. There is plenty of life down here a few miles downstream from Arkwright, where one small bold creek feeds another. It's mostly small or fragile life, though, overlooked or undervalued by those who occasionally take notice. I lose focus for a moment, think how I can't wait to get home to take a shower. Then I focus again at the new life earning a living at my feet.

A WEEK OF MEXICAN WATERFALLS

Just before Christmas my family is on a bus rolling west across thirty dusty miles of coastal plain between Mexico's Tampico and Ciudad Valles. It was straight, flat, potholed two-lane highway lined on both sides with sugarcane. The pace of contemporary Mexican bus travel was staccato. We were either barreling along at one hundred kilometers per hour or slowed to a near stop behind a donkey cart. The drivers have evolved an intricate system of communication between buses, hand signals that look like a baseball umpire signing to a batter. It's either a language to stave off disaster or simply amuse each other as they pass.

We four sat across the front of the bus—Betsy and me in one double seat, both sons, Rob and Russell, in the other. As we rolled along, the boys listened to American music on CD players. I daydreamed how it might have been to drive between American cities in the 1930s—but with modern bus and truck traffic mixed in with transportation that goes back to the Spanish conquest.

I've been to Mexico a half a dozen times, mostly on wildlife study, working as a research assistant to scientist friends. My visits have often served as a screen on which I project my nostalgia for a better, earlier America, a strange pastime that I was initiating my new family into for the first time on this trip. This was the first time since a trip to England we'd been on an extended vacation together. "Let's to Mexico," I said to Betsy. She was game. She was happy to get out of the country over Christmas, to go somewhere warm, and the boys liked the idea of an adventure vacation and adding a few challenging foreign rivers to their short life-list.

I'll admit I was looking forward to the paddling as well. For fifteen years my life was centered in rivers. Seasons revolved around water levels and weekend paddling road trips. Most recently I'd spent more time writing about rivers than paddling them. Mexico was a chance to get back to "river time" for a week.

Mostly, though, this trip was about Mexico, the full-body immersion of it. I wanted to put the country back on like a body stocking. The bus ride to Ciudad Valles gave me plenty of time to think about Mexico. Before Cortez arrived, no one in the western hemisphere had the wheel except for those found on toys, so if there were ancient hand signals on this old Meso-American "Camino Real" (Royal Road), they were between Indian couriers running up from the coast with fresh seafood for the king. The first conquistadors, led by Cortez, landed south of here in 1518 and marched inland to take on the Aztec empire. In a few years he'd conquered the whole country, and what poet William Carlos Williams called "the Flower World" was gone. The cultural loss was staggering, and only now through archeology and genetics is the story coming into focus. Increasingly, the scholars are making clear how throughout the hemisphere languages vanished, styles of art, music, ceramics all disappeared under the onslaught of the European invasion, and what we have now is one consumer culture that has eaten old Tampico since I was last there almost more than a decade before.

Driving from the airport our first night in Mexico I noted the spread of fast food along the highway into town—Wendy's, Burger King, even a Taco Bell. CNN is available on every TV. Everyone has a cell phone. Having passed through Tampico I couldn't wait to get further inland and fool myself into believing everyone in the world is not becoming us. Driving west, I could see the mountains in the distance out the big bus windshield, and I turned and told the boys that there were rivers blue as swimming pools falling through them that we would paddle. They flipped their headphones down for a moment and listened. I was talking about adventure, and that's what we'd promised them.

Estimates now say there could have been as many as twenty-five million native people in central Mexico when the Spanish arrived on the coast, and one hundred years later there were only seven hundred thousand left. It wasn't until 1968 that the modern Mexican population density reached similar percentages again. Mostly the Indians were killed off by the invisible invaders from Europe—smallpox, measles, plague, hantavirus. Our mission on our Mexican vacation was less dramatic and hopefully not destructive, a weeklong foreign beachhead upgraded to the twenty-first century. It was a family vacation right out of *Outside*'s list of "one hundred things you should do before you die"— a week paddling rapids and travertine waterfalls ranging in height from eight feet to more than twenty feet on three separate rivers—the Micos, Tiburon, and Salto.

At the bus station in Valles we were met by Grant Amorial, the tall, rangy American proprietor of Agua Azul Whitewater, a company I'd found with a simple internet search. When we walked into the dusty station someone yelled "John," and we turned and Grant was there, sitting on the shoeshine stand with a cell phone to his ear. "The tall skinny gringo" is how he'd said we'd know him. The shoeshine was perfect. He leaned back, and a Mexican boy shined his old boots. The only resident American in Valles, Grant liked to play it up.

Grant stood, shook hands all around, wearing seventeen years of Mexican white water adventure (he pioneered many of these Sierra rivers) on his tanned, lined face. He seemed a little impatient to get out of town and said that his Mexican guide Pollo was out looking for us, so he hustled us out of the station. When I looked at Grant I was struck right away with how old I have become in the last ten years. Approaching fifty, I'm out of paddling shape. Grant was ten years younger, but his life was still rigged to keep him lean and active. Twenty years ago I believed that I, too, would end up like Grant, living in a tropical country pushing white water adventure on tourists from the north. Instead I became a college professor, writer, and more recently, a step-father and husband, and now most of my adventure was in my head, a Class-IV imagination accompanying me to my desk each morning.

Pollo, our young guide and driver, soon hustled up, loaded us in the big red-and-black Agua Azul Suburban, a shuttle vehicle he called "Pepe" with a kayak cage on top for carrying gear. Grant said he'd see us at camp and vanished into Valles to run errands. We rolled through the busy streets of Valles, a bustling farming city of almost one hundred thousand, packed in between two slow valley rivers with mountains rising to the west. Pepe the Suburban was quite a rig and looked like it had one hundred thousand Mexican miles on it. Pollo's English was good but broken, and he talked nonstop. He was from a middle-class Mexican family in St. Luis Potosi, east of the mountains. He was a climber, mountain biker, and kayak guide. When I said to Pollo that Grant seemed upset we were late arriving from Tampico, Pollo laughed and said, deepening his Mexican accent for affect, "Grant? Et ees part of the show, no?"

I laughed too. You could find a thousand young people just like Pollo working the rivers of North Carolina or Colorado, outdoor migrants who follow the tourists from white water to snow and back to white water again the next year. They are young adventurers, and I knew our boys found this attractive. Pollo's part of an industry and a lifestyle only available to the upper classes until well into the twentieth century—outdoor adventure—poorly paid to do what they love with water, wind, or snow. I envied his freedom and youth but realized I am now one of the tourists he was staging the show for and settled back in the seat for the ride. We were in Mexico, and I would let it wash over me.

We drove out of town, and Pollo stopped the Suburban on a rise and pointed out a dramatic gash in the mountain front still ten miles west where the Rio Micos pours out—"the canyon." We drove toward it for fifteen minutes, first on a paved highway lined with sugarcane, and then finally onto a two track road that descended a mile to the river past huts with thatch roofs, pigs, goats, and outdoor cooking sheds. Pollo said Grant's encampment is called "the Ranch," and it is on banks of the Micos, at the mouth of the canyon we could see from outside of Valles.

As we descended to the river, Pollo explained how the ranch was built on top of a Huastec ceremonial site. As we drove in, we could see the mounds in the milpas all around. Pollo said the ground is littered with pot shards, bones, and basalt blade fragments, though, of course, we aren't allowed to keep any since this pre-Columbian litter is part of the cultural heritage of Mexico and taken very seriously by the government.

As we unloaded, Pollo described with great pride how the Huastecs "kicked Cortez's butt" in 1520 and lived an extra fifty years without Spanish domination. I looked around and could see on Betsy, Rob, and Russell's faces that they knew as well that it was a pretty remarkable place we'd wandered into via the internet. A pyramid mound was next to the cook hut and served as the site of a red radio tower, and the stones that line the pyramid had become stepping stones, retaining walls, and foundations for Grant's outpost. Adaptive reuse, the archeologists call it. Grant had a ragtag group of locals working for him—Pedro the driver, Pollo the guide, Margarita the cook, and three or four others who work the yard crew, most of them, Pollo explained, paid four or five dollars a day. He said everyone wants to work for Grant because it beats the heck out of cutting sugarcane.

Soon after we settled in, Pollo gathered gear together, and Pedro drove us upstream to the Cascadas de Micos, a section of limestone travertine ledges ("teacup falls," they call them) and deep-blue, slow pools—only two miles upstream from the ranch. As we "geared up" on the road above, Pollo explained how we'd walk a hundred stone steps with our boats down the wall of the canyon then paddle back to "the Ranch" for supper—two miles below. Sugarcane trucks rattled past, "Rasta trucks," Rob called them, the cane sticking out from all sides.

We followed Pollo down the long steep stone stairway as Betsy watched. We looked like a line of brightly colored beasts with the kayaks balanced on our shoulders. I rested on a small overlook as the boys and Pollo descended, and below I saw for the first time the initial waterfall we'd run on the Micos, an eighteen-foot drop into a blue pool. At the water's edge we slipped into our boats at the top of the falls, and Pollo floated up to the sharp horizon line and dropped off backward. Part of the show.

And so we followed Pollo all that first afternoon into adventure—Rob, Russell, then me. What was it like running a waterfall? It was like a parachute jump into a rushing faucet. It was a Tinker Bell flight with a blue pool at the bottom. It was one of the greatest acts of release I've ever experienced—paddle, let go, and whoosh, one second, two seconds, water all around you sparkling, then you're down below, bobbing back to the surface with a smile and some serious perspective on gravity.

Downstream on the Micos there were ten travertine falls over eight feet before the cascades quieted down in a small regional park and pool where the locals swam. From the park the last few ledges were amazing to look at—vegetation growing all over them—green ferns, blooming flowers, caves thick with a plant that looked like a philodendron. The Micos is the river Walt Disney would have built if he had the money. There were spots on it where you could sit in a pool and look back upstream and see three or four travertine falls lined up, a green-and-blue stairway to tropical heaven.

That night Russell convinced Grant to drive us all back into Valles to find the Carolina Panthers football game showing somewhere in a bar. We found one place willing to switch from soccer to American football and sat there all night watching the game in Spanish. The game went into overtime, and we left before it was decided, much to Russell's frustration.

We slept that night in thatch huts made of mud and bamboo beside the remarkably blue water of the Rio Micos. The next morning Pollo asked Betsy if she had heard "the carrots," meaning the green parrots that were flying up and down the river. On our second day Rob and Russell went with Grant to paddle the Rio Salto with more waterfalls, including a twenty-three footer. Betsy and I drove with Pollo two hours deeper into the mountains to see the "eccentric gardens" of Edward James in the little mountain town of Xilitla. All the way Pollo told us stories about the mountains we were driving through and talked about the native people who survive there. He had a deep respect for these mountain people. "This is the heart of Mexico," he said with pride as we passed more and more people who were obviously of Indian descent. He tuned the radio to an indigenous station, and we listened to a scratching fiddle tune that went on forever, all the way up the mountains. Pollo became very excited when the announcer spoke Huastec: "Listen, no Spanish!"

The garden in Xilitla, called Los Pozos ("The Pools"), was inspired by Edward James's friend Salvador Dali and was built in the '50s and '60s. Pollo had hired a guide. The guide arrived on a moped, got off, and gave us a good long tour. There were concrete flowers, optical illusions, long stairways that disappeared into the jungle, a wild waterfall and creek, all falling slowly back into the Mexican jungle. It was market day in Xilitla, and so we wandered around and saw the sixteenth-century mission church and "the indigenous ones," as Pollo called them, the ones who come to town and sell their pottery and their tamales.

Next day was a long one on a more traditional drop-pool river, much like the Chattooga through a deep canyon—the Rio Tampion. Betsy floated down in a raft. I had a bad swim in the worst rapid, but Rob and Russell rescued me just fine. Pollo paddled up beside me, smiling, saying, "Part of the show!"

After the swim the rest of the day had a little edge to it, but it was grand down in that deep Mexican canyon. The river had carved the limestone so it looked like a pipe organ. Where the

Rio Tampion emptied out of the canyon it disappeared completely underground. This portage, about twenty yards, is called Puente de Dios, the Bridge of the Gods, and since it was the winter solstice (December 21st) Grant explained how the sun would later line up perfectly with a Huastec ceremonial site to the east and set on the natural bridge. The site was where we would take out for the drive home. We would be lined up in our own way with the pre-Colombian past.

The next day we all went back to the Rio Salto so I could paddle it, and we took Betsy along. The boys ran the twenty-three-foot waterfall again, and Betsy and I watched from a downstream eddy where we would join them for the rest of the river. Grant had borrowed a long yellow sit-on-top kayak for Betsy. It looked like she was paddling a banana. We headed downstream. In this boat Grant was able to slip Betsy through the easiest routes, and twice she had to throw her kayak down and then jump fifteen feet or so into a plunge pool below. She ran two waterfalls close to eight feet and somehow stayed on her boat. The Salto is a beautiful, wild river, with cane, cedar, and, of course, all those ferns like we'd seen on the Micos. My two favorite waterfalls on the trip were on this section—each dropping about fifteen feet into a blue pool.

On the Salto we took out just above a ninety-foot falls with our hearts thumping. There were Mexicans watching from the overlook, and two young girls got an instant big crush on Rob and wouldn't leave him alone. They hooted and whistled as he took off his paddling clothes. On the way back we stopped at a *tacoria* in a small town and ate a plate of soft tacos—beef, onion, cilantro, and salsa verde washed down with "brown" Coronas, the local beer and Cokes in glass bottles made with real cane sugar.

And so it went. We remained adventure tourists for our first few days in Mexico, suspended outside of the local, but on the way back from the Rio Salto, something changed. The change fell over us all like light or weather. For an hour we cruised in Pepe the Suburban with our boats on top through endless sugarcane fields, and they somehow rose in my mind in importance. We'd hopped from the drainage of the Salto into the upper watershed of the Micos, Grant's "home river." We were an hour above where the clear Micos falls through the cascades of the canyon. It was not only the rivers and the perfect blue waterfalls we were experiencing on this trip. It was those endless fields as well.

On the way back, Grant and the driver discussed which ruined and abandoned power poles along the route they could "salvage" in order to push electricity a mile downhill to the ranch, the next big project for Agua Azul. Grant said we were the probably the last group to experience the ranch "off the grid," a distinction I hold dear. Once we began to talk about electricity Grant began to tell stories of how it only came to this area in the 1970s and how there are still shop owners who will sell power to many low-wage campesinos, whom they allow to illegally tap into their line, and how these shop owners will sometimes owe thousands of dollars on bills that go back all the way to the installation of the original lines, and the national electric company will just let them slide. "Coming into the twentieth century hasn't been an easy transition in the countryside," Grant laughed.

Later, at my insistence, Grant gave us all a brief history of the sugarcane industry. Cane is a grass originally from New Guinea but brought to Mexico soon after the conquest, he explained. After it's planted it grows back for eleven years. "It's got a six-month growing season, then they burn it," Grant said. "They burn the fields at night so that nobody sees the smoke, the visual evidence of the pollution." The burning gets rid of the dry leaves, clears the fields of snakes, and also causes the water to be sucked out of the roots, making the stalks heavier. After the fields are burned, only the cane is left, and then it's cut by hundreds of hands holding machetes, as it's always been. "The burning's called 'cortar,' and the harvest, 'cafra.'"

After burning and harvest, the long cut cane is loaded on big open-sided trucks and hauled to the refinery. There are seven refineries dotted throughout the region. The cane comes in, is dropped off, chopped again, and boiled down in huge vats. The dirty smoke from the refining fills the upper valley of the Micos. The cane waste is burned to fuel the refining. As we passed the local refinery on the way back from the Salto, we saw the huge smokestacks billowing black smoke, and Grant pointed out a big settling pond out back for water. "At least they have a pond," Grant said, "and don't release it directly to the river."

As we passed through the miles of sugarcane fields, Grant explained how big changes were underway in the "cane culture," whose tradition stretched all the way back to colonial times. There are ten thousand who still follow the way of the cane in the region west of Tampico. An American in the valley has introduced mechanical harvesting—Grant pointed out the trucks with solid sides and how the cane is cut into small pieces by the machines. These were the trucks filled by the mechanical harvesters.

"How will these ten thousand people in the region make what little living they have if not cutting cane?" Betsy asked. "If that work disappears as an economic force, where will they go?"

"They'll probably head for Mexico City to join the other thirty million poor people there. Mexico has one hundred million people and only five million live above the poverty line. It's hopeless here. No chance to move up, to improve. The elite and middle class are fixed, and at the bottom, the campesino is fixed. If you're born campesino you die campesino."

"What about the Mexicans working in the north? There are thousands around Spartanburg where we're from," Rob asked.

"It's the only way to move up—to go north. Oil used to be Mexico's number one industry. Now it's money from the north coming back into the country from those working legally and illegally there. It's a complex story you're driving through here. It's something not on most of the tourist trails."

The next day, our last, we paddled the Micos again, and Betsy was supposed to meet us at the little public park below the waterfalls and paddle the last mile of river with us back to camp in her yellow sit-on-top. When we arrived at the park Betsy wasn't there, and we headed downstream assuming she'd decided not to go. After a mile we saw her floating ahead of us on her yellow banana. She turned, thrilled to see us since she'd gotten confused and gone down by herself. She said Pedro, the shuttle driver, spoke no English and so she didn't really know where to wait for us. She'd had a solitary adventure running a mile of river alone. It was all in all the biggest adventure of the trip for her, she agreed as we pulled up to Grant's "ranch" downstream. "All the way down I kept waiting for the poison darts to come zinging out," she said.

So ended our week of Mexican adventure. The next guests at the ranch would have electricity as Grant and his crew pushed grid power down the hill to his huts on scavenged power poles. If we ever come back, Russell might not have to drive into town to watch his beloved Panthers play American football in the wilds of Mexico. Eric Leed, in *The Mind of the Traveler*, says the modern tourist often carries a nostalgia for the time "when travel was truly travel, when there were boundaries between the known and unknown, civilized and uncivilized, when escape was still possible."

Escape is not an option anymore. Tourists arrive more easily. The grid is now nearby—phone service, internet, TV, paved roads. Our bus ride back to Tampico was uneventful—from Pepe the Suburban we loaded our gear on a first-class bus in Valles complete with American video. I remember it was an American comedy full of cheap jokes and recycled humor. An hour later we were in Tampico, and soon after we were winging our way back toward "El Norte." The boys mostly slept through their easy transition from Mexico to Texas to South Carolina. Did they dream of Mexico, of waterfalls and breaking the surfaces of a hundred blue pools in a week? Or did they dream of cutting cane?

MEET THE CREEK

The yellow public school buses will pull through the gate at White's Mill at nine A.M. and disgorge sixty fifth graders from Chapman Elementary School. It has been raining for days, but finally it's clear. Our four learning stations are almost set up for "Meet the Creek," and sixteen freshman college students are busy spreading green and gray tarps on the ground and finalizing their plans to introduce four pods of wild kids to our learning landscape, the Lawson's Fork Creek.

The Lawson's Fork is a tributary of the Pacolet River and one of the headwater streams in the Broad River Basin. Here at White's Mill in Spartanburg, South Carolina, the stream is thirty feet wide and two feet at its deepest point, though the water level is up a bit today. The sound of the water falling over the dam just upstream is constant and soothing. The old dam, where a gristmill once ground meal for flour, was built from stone cut from the shoals now invisible beneath the pond. This old mill site is one of the most scenic spots on the thirty-mile creek, the only significant stream contained entirely within the political boundaries of Spartanburg County. Few citizens know of the stream's existence, let alone understand its role in the local ecology, perceiving it instead as a drainage ditch for urban runoff. Through "Meet the Creek" we introduce a new generation to this place we've come to love, a living stream on the path to recovery from an abusive past.

This stream, like the others of the South Carolina Piedmont, has felt the strain of "progress." Nearly all the rivers and creeks in the region are classified as impaired by the South Carolina Department of Health and Environmental Control (DHEC). All are unsafe to drink, and most aren't fit for swimming. A few still can't support aquatic life decades after the Clean Water Act took effect.

The floodplain downstream looks the way an outdoor classroom should look. We're surrounded by big tulip poplars and sycamores, and we know the children will enjoy digging their hands in the tons of sand that were deposited across the plain last week by high water. Where the old mill stood there's a rustic clubhouse used by the affluent subdivision now surrounding the property. Every year the homeowners are kind enough to let us bring the kids in for this day of discovery and excitement.

We know from the teachers that many of the kids have older siblings who were with us for this event during one of our three prior years, and their stories have set high expectations in the minds of today's visitors. Unlike our first year, when we worried over the outcome, we're confident that this "Meet the Creek" will be as compelling as the others. Our college students will feel humbled and empowered, and the children will feel inspired to learn in this setting where they are free to be wild.

"Meet the Creek" has become a symbolic highlight of our work together during each of the last four years of place-based collaboration. We've been reflecting this year on the beginnings of this undertaking, which has so enriched our professional lives and had a broad impact on our institution and beyond. In many ways, our collaboration was born from frustration as much as inspiration. An English professor by title and a poet and nature writer by avocation, I often feel trapped by the four walls of a typical college classroom. A toxicologist in a prior incarnation, Ellen Goldey is a biology professor whose teaching load is weighted toward the premedical-minded students in her anatomy and introductory biology classes. Although we have been friends for years, prior to 2001 we had never worked together in the classroom, as the disciplinary divide between the sciences and humanities is wide and deep.

Wofford College has a strong academic reputation and our students are bright eighteen- to twenty-one-year-olds, mostly from the Southeast, but increasingly from around the country. The college's academic calendar reserves the month of January for a compacted term called Interim. This is when the faculty is encouraged to be creative, to accept the risk of failure, even to step out of our disciplines and develop learning opportunities for our students that engage them deeply—whether in some great work of fiction or through some shared experience abroad.

In January of 2000, Ellen offered a course titled "Science: What Should Everybody Know?," in which she asked the twenty-one students (mostly freshmen and sophomores) to accept a challenge: "If you partner with me to research and design a new general education course for our non-science majors that addresses the title's question, I'll seek the funding to implement it." For the first time she found herself teaching without a "script" of well-prepared lectures. The students were tentative at first, awkward in this role of partnering with a professor to develop curriculum. It was new territory for all. The interim team researched the undergraduate science education literature, developed pedagogical goals, brainstormed ideas for course content, benchmarked courses at other institutions, and interviewed administrators, family members, and faculty members for their ideas.

The day I visited the class, however, the students began to sense the possibilities that lay waiting in a different approach. "Why does the question 'What should everyone know about science?' have to be so narrow?" he asked. "It's too confined within disciplinary boundaries. What if, for example, Ellen and I were to blend our freshman courses around some environmental topic broad enough to cross the disciplinary divide? Ellen would bring her knowledge and training as a scientist, a toxicologist, and I would bring my writer's eye and my knowledge of the natural history of the South Carolina Piedmont." It was immediately clear to all of us that in such a setting both students and professors could benefit from a deeper understanding of information that different disciplines would bring to a topic. The students were soon buzzing with ideas about other faculty members that they would like to see similarly partnered around a rapidly expanding list of topics.

These ideas for interdisciplinary teaching became the basis for a successful grant application to the National Science Foundation (NSF) titled "Seeing the Big Picture: Linking the Sciences and Humanities." What began as one professor's desire to collaborate with students on developing a new course evolved into an institution-wide initiative to create fully integrated, team-taught, two-course learning communities (LC) serving freshmen in their first semester. The NSF approved its maximum funding ($200,000) to launch the initiative, much of which paid summer stipends for each team of two faculty members (one from sciences and one from humanities) and two students (called preceptors) to work together to develop their LC. The titles of a few LCs suggest the range of topics that emerged, such as "Madness, Creativity, and Literature," "Cosmology and Ultimate Questions," and "Science and Science Fiction."

While awaiting NSF funding, we launched our pilot learning community in 2001, "The Nature and Culture of Water," for which sixteen freshman students were enrolled. Financial backing for our work came from a unique source, the Spartanburg Water System and Sanitary Sewer District (SWSSSD), whose visionary general manager, Graham Rich, saw our work as directly supporting the utility's public education initiative. Each year, Graham and Ed Neal, the plant manager, give our students a remarkable behind-the-scenes tour of Spartanburg's sewage treatment plant, and the students learn of the plant's codependency with the Lawson's Fork that receives the plant's effluent and its operators' commitment to keep it clean. "The guys that run this plant are unrecognized heroes," one of our students wrote just weeks after 9/11, but that's another story.

Working with local schoolchildren allows our students to apply what they have been learning in a way that serves the larger community. We prepare for "Meet the Creek" through the first month of the semester. A montage of readings on the library's electronic reserve supplements our fieldwork—there is no text-book for the work we're doing. We begin by introducing the students to our collaborative teaching initiative by invoking C. P. Snow's *Two Cultures*. In the discussion that ensues, students recognize that the two cultures at Wofford College are embodied in the "science" (BS) and "non-science" (BA) tracks. We ask them to give us contrasting adjectives for scientists and literary humanists; "Male vs. female," a student says, and we laugh with them about how Ellen and I reverse that stereotype. We discuss how rhetoric functions in the writings of scientists and humanists, and after their close reading of "Rivers of Death," a chapter of *Silent Spring*, the students begin to see how Rachel Carson's deep understanding of science informs her passion for saving the planet.

By the time "Meet the Creek" comes around in October, our freshmen have studied the stream's ecology and geology, sampled macroinvertebrates as indicators of water quality, and learned the science behind the treatment of urban sewage and maintenance of a safe drinking water supply. At the same time, they have learned about the stream's natural history as well as human uses of the stream over the last eight thousand years. They have written about the stream, considering issues such as its aesthetic value, human impact, and whether or not they have any responsibility in protecting and restoring it. In their frustrated struggle to sort the notes in their field notebooks by discipline, students sometimes complain that they don't know when they're learning "science" and when they're learning "humanities." As professors, we're pleased with this indication that we've achieved a true integration of our courses. "Wow," we say to each other with a grin, "it's working!" In another few weeks we'll hear them criticizing the unnatural disciplinary separation that exists in their other courses.

A couple of the elementary school teachers spend several hours with us in September teaching our freshmen about South Carolina's fifth-grade educational standards, and they warn the group that the lessons of "Meet the Creek" must purposely ad-dress those standards. They also stress safety issues and the need for regular "potty breaks." Their underlying message is clear: "We are entrusting our jobs and these children to you for the day, so don't screw up." They also inspire the group by telling us that they often refer back to "Meet the Creek" as they introduce related topics throughout the year, that children continue to talk about the experience weeks later, and that at the end of the year the kids identify their day at the Lawson's Fork as the "best thing they did all year."

After the teachers' visit, we share the pictures of scenes from prior years. Then our freshmen get down to business by forming four teams, each of which begins two weeks of brainstorming, planning, and practicing their highly interactive learning station along the stream.

It's now 8:45 A.M., and the freshmen are working to make sure their stations are ready. At one station there will be a scav-enger hunt, in which children will find different objects and clas-sify them as biotic or abiotic. Charles, one of the Wofford stu-dents, has actually dressed up like a white-tailed deer, with a tanned-hide cape on his back and antlers on his head, to make "biotic" more fun.

At another station freshmen will lead the children to identi-fy different tree species in the riparian zone, and then help each child use paint and rollers to stencil real leaf patterns onto a new white T-shirt that the children take home. In final preparation, two of our freshmen are sorting the shirts into stacks by size (each child's name tag will have their requested size on the back), while the other two gather leaves from nearby sycamores, mimo-sas, and water oaks. The tarps are laid out, and the plastic bottles of paint are lined up next to the roller trays. They're ready.

At a third station the children will write nature-inspired po-etry. The freshmen in this group are testing out their props and practicing their opening "lecture" one more time. They're hold-ing up their posters with funny pictures and glued-on objects that define personification, metaphors, and similes: "The tree's arms reach to the sky"; "A magnolia leaf is like an umbrella." They've set up dozens of colored markers, and the paper they found for the children's compositions is colored like grass. Initially, this will be the least popular station, but it will become a favorite when the poems are read aloud, with much fanfare, by the college students.

The most popular station of all is the macroinvertebrate sampling station, where, every forty minutes, fifteen more kids will get to wade into the Lawson's Fork and catch, sort, and identify creatures they didn't know they shared the planet with. Several Wofford football players happen to be manning the sampling station this year, and they've squeezed into their waders and are fiddling with their gear—kick nets, buckets, ice trays, tweezers, and plastic spoons. We've watched this day unfold for three years now, and we know that at the end of the day there will be sixty wet and happy fifth graders. We also know how exhausted our own students will be—especially this last group, whose physical activity will have equaled a day of football conditioning.

It would not be completely honest to say that our experiment with outdoor education and disciplinary integration has been universally praised or accepted by all our colleagues. The resistance, often subtle, has sometimes surprised or disheartened us. One humanities professor was opposed to us calling our all-day Thursday outings "field trips," as if such a term would erode the rigor of the Wofford curriculum, suggesting more fun than education; so we adopted the term "field experiences" and continue to unabashedly support combining fun with learning. Another colleague in the sciences worried openly that the freshmen would not learn enough about the scientific method, so we attempted to ease that concern through extensive internal and external assessment of the program.

But in other ways we've been inspired by the widespread support that the learning communities have received. The students are the most outspoken advocates for the program; for example, a formal presentation to the board of trustees by the LCs' preceptors gained a line item of funding to continue the program. We've presented our "Nature and Culture of Water" model at various national conferences and conducted workshops on campuses all around the country. The message seems to resonate widely. People are struck by the common sense of it all: if we respect each other's disciplines, work to integrate our courses, and model for our students a desire to learn from each other, we can't help but transform our students and become better teachers ourselves. And if we empower our students with place-based knowledge and the responsibility to share that knowledge through service-learning projects such as "Meet the Creek," not only are they more cognizant of the natural world that surrounds them, but they are also more responsible toward the human community that exists outside the walls of Wofford.

The yellow school bus finally pulls into the drive a little after nine o'clock, and Ellen yells to all, "They're here!" Bea Bruce, the Chapman Elementary librarian, steps out of her car, which precedes the bus. Bea has been our contact at Chapman all these years; today she laughs, admitting that someone forgot to reserve the buses in advance, but she scrambled to find a driver and squeezed all the kids onto one bus. Somehow, they still managed to show up on time. Our freshmen swallow their trepidation and greet the excited kids as they spill out of the bus. Each child is wearing a name tag in one of four shapes—blue dolphins, green frogs, red leaves, or yellow butterflies—so that we can keep them sorted into four equal groups.

Ellen, the pied piper of the day, welcomes everyone, toots her famous air horn, and guides the group to the lawn behind the clubhouse to begin the day. She leads them in a call-and-response to get their blood moving: "Which is the BEST elementary school in Spartanburg?" "Chapman!" they scream, louder and louder as Ellen repeats the question several times. "What's the name of our college?" "Wofford!" they yell, and we break off into the four groups.

Throughout the morning, each jostling, silly group of kids rotates between stations—the dolphins go first to the leaf/T-shirt station, the frogs to the scavenger hunt, the red leaves to poetry, and the butterflies head off to get wet. It is a noisy swirl of joy and learning that rotates through the different stops every forty minutes as the air horn blows. The teachers watch, helping out if needed, but glad to have a well-deserved day off from instructing. The Wofford students take pride in their teaching, and the elementary teachers are surprised to see many of their most problematic charges become stars in this setting. Last year after "Meet the Creek," one boy "who had never written more than two sentences," filled up two pages with his excited description of the day. His teacher was so amazed that she sent it to us to share with the class.

The kids learn that leaves have veins like we do, and they stencil those same leaves onto their new white T-shirts. They scramble and dig around in the sand chanting "biotic" or "abiotic" as they pick up scraps of wood or debris left behind by last week's flood. The young poets wave their poems in the air to ensure that they are read aloud by their new heroes from Wofford College. The football players in waders lead another group into the creek's cold October water, and the kids squeal as water and sand fill their shoes. The young men hold the kick nets on the stream bottom as the kids dance in front of them to dislodge the critters and send them into the net. Then the net is held up and little heads excitedly crowd around and peer in. With each exclamation of "there's one," a child eagerly dips in with a plastic spoon for a prize: another dragonfly or mayfly larva. "Lobster!" they yell with each crayfish that is caught, and they're particularly thrilled with one small catfish (not an invertebrate, we have to point out to them over and over). If they'd netted a shark they wouldn't be any more excited.

The cool morning gives way to a warmer midday, and we have lunch. The kids sit with the Wofford students, and laugh and tell stories from the three stations they've been through this morning. The one dry group is now glad that they will get to go into the stream last. After one more round, the happy, tired, dirty, and wet kids collect their T-shirts from the hangers suspended on a temporary clothes' line. We expect them to head straight to the bus, but a request from one child for the football players' autographs turns into a chaotic assembly line where our young men patiently sign their names on shirts. Finally satisfied, the children pile back onto the bus and head away from us, and ultimately back home to where some have their own creeks. "I'm going home today and look at the creek behind my house," one little boy says. "I'll bet there's something living in there, too."

Once again, we've done what we came to do—give sixty local kids the chance to, as environmental artist Andy Goldsworthy describes it, "shake hands" with this place we call Lawson's Fork. From the look of their clothes, some have hugged it and sat in its lap! Now we can pack up and go, too, but first we all make our own leaf-stenciled T-shirts, and it gives us a chance to share the day's highlights. Our college women laugh about the number of young boys who asked them out on dates, and several of us recount favorite phrases from the children's poetry. "The mosquitoes are like my sister and brother" generates a chuckle. One entire poem is embedded in our memories:

The waterfall is like a child crying over a piece of candy.
The smell is like a clear summer day when the wind blows.
When the water hits the rocks it goes splash, splash, kapow.
It sounds like milk splashing down in the cheerio bowl.

We're all filled with pride at what we've accomplished today, and the bonds developed from this shared experience will hold us close for the rest of the semester and beyond. "Meet the Creek" symbolizes the reason why the two of us added this work to already heavy teaching loads, and once again a deep feeling of fulfillment washes over us.

WATERSHED THINKING

When I take my students out to Glendale, South Carolina, to teach them about watersheds, I walk them out on the old rusted, steel-beamed bridge over the creek and I ask them to look around for a moment. Get oriented. What I mean by this request is I want them to get oriented in space. How does the air smell? Where's the light coming from? Are there any sounds besides the water falling over the rocks? If so, what are they and where do they come from? Where is north? South? East? West? Which way is Lawson's Fork flowing? Is that a surprise, or is it what you would expect?

We call Lawson's Fork a creek, but some old maps call it "the Lawson's Fork of the Pacolet River." We think it was named in the late eighteenth century for an early settler who had a large grant of land near the creek's confluence with the Pacolet River a few miles below Glendale.

Once we're oriented, I tell my students about watersheds and how the whole country is made up of rivers, creeks, runs, streams, and branches and how every square inch of dry land drains into them. I point downstream and tell them that I've paddled right past Glendale and five days later ended up in Columbia. I point upstream and explain how twenty miles up near Inman, in the shadow of Hogback Mountain, Lawson's Fork begins.

I work as a teacher to make rivers real for my students. I want them to be what I call "watershed thinkers," to be able to look at a map and think their way outward from the center line of every creek to the ridge tops defining the next drainage. I want them to drive over bridges and chart the flow of the water beneath them. I want them to conjure the natural and human history of a stream's banks and calculate the health of its floodplains and the cost of the development along its meandering trail to the Atlantic Ocean.

I want them to have experienced a watershed's life, both great and small. I want them to care what happens to our water, and when they graduate from college, I want them to influence law and policy that protects our watersheds.

Most of my students start out like the majority of South Carolinians today. Almost all could get in a car and drive to Charleston without a map, but few of them know which river system in our state would take them there. They know bridges ice before roads, but they know little about creeks or rivers below those bridges. They don't think much about where the water flows through their neighborhoods or cities. They suffer inconvenience when roads jam up with traffic, but not when someone pollutes or dams a local river. South Carolina rivers and creeks are abstractions, like peace, honor, truth, and beauty.

I like to think that after they've met Lawson's Fork, and by extension, the Pacolet River, they see it all in a different way. They're watershed thinkers from that moment forward, and roads, as important as they are for our busy, modern way of life, take their proper place as secondary systems in the primary web of our watersheds. Aldo Leopold talked about how important it is for people to "think like a mountain." I want my students to think like rivers.

ON THE CHATTOOGA

I.

On my fiftieth birthday I'm floating down Section III of the Chattooga River with four of my paddling friends. The Chattooga is James Dickey country and will always be associated with the poet and his 1970 novel *Deliverance*. The actual setting of Dickey's story, though, is the mythic Cahulawassee, a remote Southeastern river assembled from his experiences on several North Georgia rivers. Many scenes from the 1972 film were shot on the Chattooga, so there is a "real world" connection to this wild place. Here, in Dickey country, it's hard to disconnect the imagined river and the real river. As we float along, I reflect, as I always do, on the blurry lines between imagination and reality.

Our plan is to float thirteen miles and camp tonight at Sandy Ford around a fire ring I've shared with countless friends through my twenty years on this very real river. We range in age from thirty-five to seventy-eight, and between us we have more than one hundred years' worth of descents into this section of the Chattooga. I guess you could call at least four of us—Watts Hudgins (thirty-five), John Pilley (seventy-eight), Alliston Reid (fifty-two), and me—"advanced" paddlers well within our range of skill to enjoy a late October day on "the Deliverance River." Most of Dickey's canoe experience on rivers came in his thirties, and so we're mostly all well past the sort of early-middle-age angst that he describes in his novel. There's little angst on this trip. It's a celebration instead. It's where, for the past decade or so, I've imagined spending my fiftieth birthday, floating my favorite river.

My fifth friend, Wes Cooler, who is fifty-two, is an expert on the river in other ways—he's been coming over here to fish since the early 1950s, and he knows the weather, wildlife, ridges, and rises of this landscape much better than any of us. His watercraft of choice, a sit-on-top Perception Torrent, has drawn his dedication to the craft of paddling white water into question, though. He confesses he's walked the banks along this section many times but has only seen it from the water once, from the overblown middle tube of a black rubber raft in the early 1970s.

As we glide through Warwoman, the first rapid of consequence downstream from our Earl's Ford put in, Wes falls off his boat in the big eddy at the rapid's top but quickly climbs back on and shoots on down through the standing waves. He's retired army and, if anything, is not about to be undone by cold water. At the rapid's bottom we kid him about his yellow plastic barge, though he knows enough about river kayaking today to note that all four of us "advanced" paddlers are floating in old kayaks true Chattooga paddling experts would consider out of date. All our white water kayaks are discontinued models from the '70s and '80s, faded plastic antiques, too long for the modern world of eight-foot kayaks known as "play boats." What's cutting edge is hard to keep up with when you get past thirty, though the passion for floating the river stays high, even if not sustained.

It's misting rain today, as I would expect from my history with the Chattooga, though the temperature is in the high 60s, strangely tropical for the smoldering end of the last week in October. Wes cites global warming as the culprit and suggests we should hog-tie any politician not in agreement and leave them for the trout to nibble in an eddy. We all agree and begin a litany of the usual suspects—starting at the top. It's a few days before election day, and so it's hard to separate politics from recreation on this wild and scenic river. What we see around us is threatened on all sides by a marauding administration with what could be the worst environmental record since William Howard Taft. The air above us, the water below us, the forest around us—all threatened by the yard sale mentality of George W. Bush. Or so we all think. We laugh and admit we have brought along no dissenting opinions, and we'll have to wait until we get back to civilization to find one. We are of one political mind, and the only other voice we hear is the river roaring its watery joy in the rapids.

I'm glad to be back on the river in my own boat with no outward responsibilities except getting safely downstream. I've spent too much time in the Chattooga watershed the last year talking and not kayaking. My own book about the Chattooga came out seven months ago in April 2004, and for me, it has created many opportunities to come to the river to raft and hike with classes, talk to book groups, even once, in early September, to revisit the river with the whole Dickey clan at the close of James Dickey celebrations down the road at Clemson University, with sons Christopher and Kevin and daughter Bronwen. That day we stood with our backs to Woodall Shoals and had our picture taken in the rain, the river relentlessly falling behind us. It was a sort of family photo—the three children of James Dickey, plus me, a family friend, a wife, and, of course, the river. The portrait shows a joyful group of humans who love the Chattooga and who want it to survive politically and spiritually.

Dickey's children understand how their father's memory will forever be associated with this landscape, much as Mark Twain is tied to the Mississippi. The Chattooga is an intimate landscape, unlike the Mississippi, so when the Dickey kids visited the river, they expressed a desire to celebrate its wildness. For now, a few newspaper articles and a picture or two will have to do.

I am grateful for all of these opportunities, though each of them has made it impossible to put my own boat in the water and commune with the river and its current. It's not quite the same to see the river, maybe stick a hand in, or wade out into an eddy. You need to enter a river to understand it, to gauge its moods and mystery. "The urge to merge," that's what literary critic and Dickey-celebration participant Casey Clabough calls James Dickey's love of rivers, as expressed through *Deliverance.* I think I understand what Clabough means on days like this when I float on the Chattooga. I want to be the river, not just be on it. I carry downstream not only my lunch, my foul-weather gear, but also James Dickey's concept of merging.

I'd thought about merging a great deal on early mornings reading Dickey's poetry on my screened porch many miles from the river. One morning I read "On the Coosawattee," his long three-part canoeing poem from the 1963 collection *Helmets*. I missed being on the river, and Dickey's poem is full of river reality—how the light feels falling through fir branches, the sounds, the smells—but it's also full of angels and flight and escape from reality. It's a poem of failed entry where the speaker wants to merge with the river but is repelled first by his own imagination, then further along by the ways that a town has used the water for chicken processing, and in the poem's final section, how a retreat from the river to higher ground after a canoeing spill distances the speaker from it.

For Dickey, the world—the very real, wild world—is always repelling the human ego, and maybe it's only through art we can enter it. But in that zone of possible entry—canoeing being that zone here—there is a space (art?) where the magic of entry can happen. The magic happens when you are riding into a place "that cannot be told," as Dickey describes it. The merging for Dickey is always just beyond words.

Today I'm thinking about Dickey's merging as we approach the bigger rapids where, on a bad day, something tragic could happen, as it does to the speaker and his friend Braselton in the final section of "On the Coosawattee." These two canoeists survive their encounter with the rapids on the Coosa, what Dickey describes as "the leaping shore where I almost died." "On the Coosawattee" is a beginner's experience on white water. After a paddler learns to control his craft, he learns you cannot go successfully, as Dickey put it, "into the stone." That spill at the end of the poem has always bothered me. Would the poem even have been written by someone with a higher skill level as a paddler?

Maybe James Dickey had an expert level imagination, but it was trapped in the body of a novice canoeist. Maybe it's only the "beginner's mind" that allows for such merging. Merging with water and stone is what you want to get a beginning paddler past very quickly.

II.

So, this merging thing continues to haunt me as we float on downstream. It's a difficult rapid, like the Narrows, where merging really becomes an issue for a kayaker. As I pointed out to Casey Clabough at the Dickey conference at Clemson, merging is a fine literary concept to think about, but in white water paddling, when you merge with the river you're dead. In a difficult rapid the goal is to get downstream upright and above the water. You hope that death is a distant factor, not a goal for transcendence. I've always found it odd that, if Clabough is right, Dickey wanted so badly to merge with water, wind, other animals. This merging seems to me a need that gets pushed further off the more intimate you become with landscapes. Commune yes, but merge? Most kayakers are happy with the thin plastic line that separates boat from water, it from us.

Wes seems the one most intent on merging today. In the eddy at the top of the rapid he falls off the Torrent again, but he's dressed for it, shorty wet suit, so he just laughs and crawls back up on the open cockpit and lurches the big boat back into the rapid

We make it through the Narrows without serious incident and eddy at the bottom. Looking back upstream, I'm taken once again by the spot's beauty. It's a dark primordial landscape, pure gorge. When I'm paddling down through the offset hydraulics and standing waves of the Narrows. I'm reminded of the wild country described in *Deliverance*, a haunted lonely place. What would it be to merge with such ancient stone and river channel? "The bones of the earth," another poet calls rock. There's nothing lethargic about the river here. It's all action, all scour. A knickpoint geologists call a waterfall, or a shoals, a place where water nicks at rock, moment by ceaseless moment, over time. It's here that a river merges with the deepest processes of geology and gravity.

On the calm water below the Narrows I don't tell Wes of my interest in Dickey's literary themes and how his antics on the Torrent prompt me to think more about merging; instead, I pay attention as Wes paddles up beside me and draws me off into the very real forest along the river's banks, explaining the threat of the hemlock wooly adelgid, its life cycle, and how the whole population of trees in the corridor could be doomed by the infestation. When I researched my book five years ago the wooly adelgid threat was real but just beginning. "In the Shenandoahs it has killed 95 percent of the trees," Wes says. I try to imagine anew the Chattooga without its graceful dark-green hemlocks, a species lost to a foreign pest. Dickey. The wooly adelgid. Our own history with the river. They all merge into one as we float down through shoal after shoal, the fall color brilliant around us.

III.

Now, we are halfway through the trip. The Narrows and our lunch stop are behind us, and I decide that I'm way overdressed for this birthday party, so I stop to take off some gear and let the others float ahead beyond the next foggy bend. It's midday and clear. All that's left of the morning's moisture is some fog on the river, bend by bend. I stop in the shallows and climb out of the boat, strip to the waist. I'm standing in the river, working to secure my wet gear in the kayak. The current pushes against my legs and the boat, lodged against one of the river's shin bones. It's a ridge of banded gray bedrock emerging from the surface near the shore. There's a swirl of sand in the current near the bottom, and suddenly my feet disappear. I look down through the clear current of the river, but I can't see them. The sand is all the way up to my ankles.

If I stand here long enough, I will be planted deep in the Chattooga River sand, and I will have to accept a certain level of merging. I will, over time, become a human geology experiment—transportation, deposition—and the results of that experiment will be harsher than anything bad that could possibly happen to me as I float downstream to the next bridge, where the Forest Service takeout awaits. It's a funny thought, letting the river's current cover me completely with sand.

I realize I'm alone with the river. It's maybe only the second or third time in twenty years of paddling on the Chattooga I've been left like this. Paddling is mostly a buddy sport, even kayaking. It's a little unnerving, seeing my feet lodged deeply in sand, and the boats of my companions beyond my line of sight, somewhere on the water ahead of me beyond the next bend. The river offers the only sounds—the rapids downstream, upstream, and the creep of current along the shore.

In "Inside the River," another poem about the power of water to transform, Dickey commands, "Let flowing create/A new, inner being," and I try, thinking I understand finally what the poet means by merging. The imagination somehow holds the outer world at bay and is able to go deep "inside the river." That's why Dickey sees angels on the surface of a river and tries to mate with stones. I dip my hands in the river and pick it up, reaching for the "heart of the current," and let the river and the sand pour through my fingers. For a moment I feel the river moving over me and even through me, "gone/Into purposeful grains/That stream like dust/In a holy hallway." And then the moment's gone, and I'm back with the boat and my fifty-year-old responsibilities—friends, poetry, Wes's story of the hemlocks dying along the shore, all downstream, waiting for me.

I turn from the river, climb back in my boat, and paddle downstream to rejoin my friends. Dickey's lesson is that life is a dance between the imagination and the forces of nature. So quietly the earth fills in the empty spaces.

SIX

THE MAD KAYAKER POEMS

Hears the River Flood

His boat sits dusty beneath the house
But the mad kayaker wakes to hear knocking
Like a sailboat against the racks.
The water has risen overnight and taken the backyard,
The oak trees, the gravel he carefully spread
For walks to the river. There is nothing
He knows to do but paddle, so he crawls
Into the boat's narrow cockpit, snaps on the skirt,
And floats into the monster flood.
He leaves his wife behind, even his two
Sons still snug in their beds.
They too know the ways of water
But he will let them find their own
Path toward the river's roiling heart.
This morning he must go alone
Into this acre of falling water
Where a small rippling stream used
To meander through their suburb.
He keeps his craft tracking true
As he finds a line through down trees,
Surging pressure waves, and washed-out bends.
Sand is his dance partner as he floats to the sea.
He passes over the old banks and the mouths
Of feeder streams. He watches backyards
Become flood plain and flood plain fill
From ridge-to-ridge. He tries his old roll
In the current and finds it waiting
To twirl him back to the surface.
He catches the only eddy on the river's
Clogged hurtle toward the sea and stops there—
He watches as the world turned liquid in the storm
Passes by. He moves back out into the flow.

Teaches His Wife to Roll

She hangs upside down in the current
And the Mad Kayaker waits for her head
To pop up. He's taught her how to place
Her paddle, snap her hips, and appear
Like Houdini from the flowing world
Once more into air.
All he sees now is the plastic bottom
Of the boat. What's she doing down there
Among the trout and boulders?
In the pool she had it down—and the boat
Twirled like a top. Now he waits a second longer
Than is natural for his wife's body
To appear and float toward him.
He doesn't think she's scared—
The boat hasn't moved or bucked like a pony.
Could she like it, this reverse image
Of the world—all water and shadow?
Finally, she surfaces. The move performed
With grace and no rush. As she rights herself
He sees the smile as the water drains
From her helmet's ear holes. She's touched
By what he knows—what's down is up,
And what's up is down—
And the art's in moving in between.

SURVEYS HIS GEAR

He descends to the basement and flips
On the bare bulb at the foot of the steps
And enters the kingdom of floating.
The cinderblock walls and the raftered ceiling
Are a testament to his worship of things
That keep him safe in falling water—

Four kayaks stacked like missiles
In a wooden rack, a red tandem canoe
Suspended from above, helmets
Like severed heads on corner posts,
Lifejackets hung to dry like body armor,
Paddles standing like Trojan spears
In the corners. It's his armory against
The everyday he has assembled
In his basement, and even on those days
When the river flows without him
He stands here and surveys it all.

Upstairs his wife, reading in a chair,
Wonders what he does down there
Below her in the dark and mold.
She's seen the grounded kayaks
Like torpedoes waiting in their bins.
With him she's taken the canoe,
Like a Viking galley and swamped
It in the drink, then beached it high
And dry on some sand bar for lunch.

She knows that in the dark night
Her husband slips off in pajamas
And looks over his gear, but does
Not suspect that on nights like this
He descends the stairs and rummages
Through the gear and finds his
Favorite moldy spray skirt
And spray top and pulls them on,
Then locates the oldest helmet,
The one he's worn like a warrior
On distant noisy rivers, and then
Snaps on the cracking vinyl strap.

Then he positions the nose clips
And tugs on the back rubber booties
Then drags his kayak down and sits.
He stretches forward to flex,
Before he leans into invisible current

And rocks the boat from side to side

The concrete floor gives way to stones
And waves. If there is a river here,
It is only in his head where the roaring
Never ceases, where he always sits
At the top of another stair step of rapids,
The water soundless in the silent house.

Dreams of Waterfalls

In the Mad Kayaker's dream he stands high above
The world's last wild river and the mist
Climbs like steam from a kettle out of the gorge.
In the plunge pool below are other kayakers,
And he knows one is him, already somehow
At the bottom of the world's final waterfall.

Somehow the vast watershed of his dream
Is home to magic, and the conjured hopes of place.
He knows if he woke up this landscape
Would fail and flood with the demands of reality
And he would be left without this last demand—
To slip in his kayak and join the boaters at the bottom.

The falls before him is like a story ready to plunge,
Forever into telling. He joins his twin below
In the mist, and stands with his boat on his shoulder
For this brief moment below the rocks and river roar.

First Psalm of the Mad Kayaker

Though I walk all day on asphalt,
Concrete, and milled hardwood,
My feet abide and long for flow.

Though the streets span rivers
On bridges, I stop at the crossings
And look downstream with longing.

Though electric companies
Build dams and choke the narrows
With utilities, I dream them free.

Though the valley has deep shadow
Where the river takes a hard bend,
I fear no evil there.

I dwell in the roaring house
Of water and strap my boat to the truck
When the holy water rises.

I walk the scouting rock
And it is that promenade which
Restores my bony dry soul.

On the river I fear no evil—except
The evil of encroaching suburbs,
run-off, parking lots, and oily streets.

For though I go to the river
For strength, there are those
Who see it as a blankness to fill—

Dump seepage, drainage ditch,
Poison sluice, effluent valve, dye vat,
Silt slurry, waste channel, sewage leak.

For these are the voices of doom,
For these are the shrill notes
Of the out-of-touch and wandering

In the desert of commerce.
For these are the product of staring
Too long into human stillness.

Though my days among humans
Are numbered, I will dwell forever
In the country of wild rivers and cut-banks,

Of eddies, and riffle gardens.
I will lie down in the shallows.
They will restore my soul.

Votes His Values

He casts a vote for the senator of roaring streams,
The representative of scree and marmots
Attending the high springs; for the alderman
Of many ripples following outward on still pools
Beside a flood-prone creek; for the poll master
Of plunging waters through a gorge; for the president
Of abandoned dams, flood plains, and migratory trout;
For the councilman outside of something human,
Who pauses on bridges and looks both ways;
For the precinct chief waist deep in current
Who feels at home in the last district of the wild,
The clear, the distant, the flowing free.

Watches His Sons on the River

Their boats are the size of teacups
And colored like rainbows.
The Mad Kayaker watches as the two boys
Buck and spin on a wave just offshore.
They stay in one spot to perform—with so much
River to go. They are young and excited
By the perfect movement of the river in this
Perfect spot, one pulsing wave. It's so perfect
It draws a crowd. They've told him the names
Of the moves they practice—the triple axle,
The throwdown, the squirt—and he knows
They are having more fun with the flow
Then he's ever managed. It all makes him
Feel old and a little more mad than usual.

He stares at the water downstream.
He's anxious to get back to paddling.
Surely, they can see that moment
Around the bend is what the river is waiting
On, them on it, the current under them.
So he sits in the eddy and waits—
Cartwheel, three-sixty, ender—
A rebel against these new things
A hobo in a world of watery highways.

The Drought

He sits on his back porch and sizes up
The river barely visible from his chair—
A tiny dark stream too weak to float
His kayak much less a canoe.
How long has it been—a month or more—
Since the last gully washer sluiced past
The put-in, salving his need for flow?

There's power in waiting but the Mad Kayaker
Can see the sky offers no possibility of rain.
His wife offers a glass of water too tiny
To float in, so he drinks it, each cell
A river of its own needing replenishment.
He goes to the yard and unfurls the hose
And fills the sloping path behind the house
With runoff and pushes a tiny twig into
The pipe's artificial flow. He watches
As it turns and eddies behind a flower bed
And then bobs back into the current.

Inside he turns on the bathtub
And fills it up, then pulls the plug.
The drain sounds like a whirlpool
In a wild river. There is nothing
He will not do to fill the empty space
Where the river would flow if a downpour
Suddenly filled the land with water.

Plants a Garden

For Bill Aylor

His old Noah Jeti has been in the yard for years.
The old boat has faded in the sun and once
Brighter than the blue June sky, it's now a shade
He knows does not exist in nature's spectrum.
The Mad Kayaker walks down and looks inside
And sees it's full of oak leaves fallen through all
Those autumns he should have spun in his boat,
Looked up, and watched the multi-colored world
Above kaleidoscope through sunlight and shade.
Now it's dirt as dirt does, rotting leaves compacting
Downward an inch a year in rich, dense masses
Of dark worm-eaten loam and spongy compost.
Maybe, he thinks, he should plant heirloom tomatoes
This year in the cockpit. Maybe he should use
The pick in the garage to puncture the plastic hull
So the roots can reach the firm warm earth below.
Soon the old boat fading in the sun won't look
Much different from what refuse he's spotted
In his county neighbor's yard—old toilets twined
With climbing hydrangea, two truck tires painted
White and sunk halfway, filled with pansies,
A red wheelbarrow no longer in service, housing
Parsley, sage, creeping rosemary, and thyme.
If the Mad Kayaker lives long enough he'll see
His whole world recycled, the old drytop settled
Into a soft pile off-gassing a half-life of chemicals,
The wooden paddle, dust already around the edges,
The helmet's plastic brittle and finely cracked,
His head turned to gray granite he used to avoid.

THE OLD WET SUIT

He finds it on a shelf in the basement.
His black full body suit with the zipper
Lowered looks like the shed skin of a snake,
But the Mad Kayaker is determined
To give his old full-body wet suit a try.

He takes it down and it's turned a ghostly grey
After years in the dark and the rubber looks
Like it will not hold. His stomach
Is the biggest obstacle to closing
The old plastic zipper. He remembers.

SEVEN

MOSTLY FLAT WATER

KEOWEE

It's the middle of May, almost 224 years to the day after William Bartram left Augusta, Georgia, and journeyed west and north up the Georgia side of the Savannah River in what becomes "Part Three" of his *Travels*. In the third section, Bartram ventures deep into the southern Appalachians, what were then known then as "the Cherokee Mountains." A few days after he left Augusta, he rode forty-five miles through an "uninhabited wilderness" and arrived in the evening at the rebuilt Cherokee town of "Senica" (Seneca, South Carolina), a town so devastated by decades of frontier war and strife Bartram speculated it would only be "able to muster about a hundred warriors."

The next day Bartram rode sixteen more miles to old Fort Prince George on the Keowee River in the mountainous northwestern corner of South Carolina. Fort Prince George had once been the principal military outpost against the Cherokee Lower Towns. For a decade between 1753 and 1768 the palisaded fort guarded the western flank of South Carolina's colonial frontier.

Bartram had a sinking moment upon his arrival at the old fort deep in Cherokee territory. In the *Travels*, Bartram says he was "somewhat dejected and unharmonized: all alone in a wild Indian Country, a thousand miles from my native land...some hundred miles yet to travel."

By the time Bartram arrives in the Keowee Valley in 1775, "old fort Prince George...bears no marks of a fortress but serves for a trading house." Francis Harper, the author of the naturalist's edition of *Travels*, went looking for it in 1950s, and there was nothing to mark the old fort's location but a huge mulberry tree a farmer pointed out to Harper in a cornfield beside the river. There are artifacts in the South Carolina Institute of Archaeology and Anthropology that were recovered in a hurried archaeological dig in 1967–1968, and there's a wooden scale model of the fort at the nuclear plant visitor's center. But the excavated outline of the real Fort Prince George is far below the turquoise waters of the Lake Keowee. Contemporary writers like me are left to patch that spot together through scientific reports, literature, interviews, and local lore.

It's Bartram's literary rendering of Keowee I'm interested in today, though the Keowee/Fort Prince George passage of Bartram's *Travels* does not rank as one of Billy B's greatest hits. It's not the bellowing Florida alligators, his frolic with the Cherokee "nymphs," or his oft-cited scene later in "Part Three" where, deep in the Cherokee Mountains, the Pennsylvanian naturalist meets the entourage of Cherokee "emperor" Attakullakulla near what is now the Nantahala River.

Keowee may not be a household name, but a day trip up there from my home in Spartanburg will get me on the water and triangulate my contemporary corporeal presence with an exact Bartram literary location where I can ponder the human change that two centuries of "progress" can bring to one corner of the landscape we've shared through time.

I've picked up a little of Bartram's mood. I'm melancholy and maybe even a little "unharmonized" about my planned daylong research assignment to kayak down South Carolina's vast Lake Keowee and ponder the site of Fort Prince George, the vanished frontier outpost William Bartram visited.

What's agitated me is that the old colonial fort has been lost below two hundred feet of reservoir water for forty years. I'm prepared to pause in elegiac sadness above the site in my kayak and spin in a 360-degree circle and mourn the vanished valley. I know I'll still be able to see Bartram's storied mountains beyond through my own twentieth-century nature-writer's eyes, but the view won't be enough, sullied as it probably will be by the present lake. It's my hope I can forget the present and recover through a poet's act of imagination what the famous naturalist had seen around him more than two hundred years in the past.

Since my assignment is to write about Bartram, I've been thinking my essay will touch, as always, on some venerable environmental themes of the past forty years, "green" chestnuts taken up often and at length by David Brower, Edward Abbey, and the like: dams are bad and lakes that back up behind them aren't much better, and we environmentalists must look at the high-dollar real estate that is sold on their shores as not much better than opening up Africa to ivory hunting in the nineteenth century.

It will be hard not to be critical of what's happened to the Keowee. There is now no beautiful river in Bartram's Keowee vale. Duke Power (now Duke Energy) dammed it in 1968, filled the valley as a cooling tank for their nuclear power plant, and then sold the land around it to real estate speculators, who for three decades have built gated communities along its riprapped shore.

You don't have to read between the lines to see that I've already prejudged modern-day Lake Keowee before I get there. I've privileged the past over the present. After all, isn't Lake Keowee a typical engineered/manufactured reservoir that's drowned a good river for utility, boondoggle, profit, or all three?

My nature-writer's sentiments are complicated, though, because this time out it's soon obvious that it will be impossible for me to remain a stand-alone eco-warrior for some past Eden. Riding shotgun in my truck is one of my English department colleagues from Wofford College, John Miles, and we will launch this research mission from the boat dock of John's in-laws, the owners of a lake house deep in a gated community on the shores of contemporary Lake Keowee, a place he calls beautiful, where he has spent many a lovely day kayaking with his six-year-old daughter.

On the drive over I outline my latent river-rat dam-hater position for my English department colleague—that those who remember it say the natural Keowee River flowed through what was possibly the most beautiful river valley in the South; that try as I might it's difficult for me to ever see a power company lake as beautiful; that as far as I'm concerned the lake we'll visit is a sad diminishment of Bartram's paradisiacal "vale;" that if the social and ecological critics of modern utility lakes are right, then Duke Power's damming of the Keowee is morally equivalent to the loss of the Hetch Hetchy Valley in California in the early twentieth century; that if this river had been out West rather than in South Carolina, a state desperate for economic development of any sort, there would have been a furious fight to save it.

John can't wait to get to the lake to paddle. He's tall and slim, thoughtful, but holding on as well to his youthful athleticism. He listens intently and then tells me that he, too, has some of the same qualms about dams and lakes and high-dollar developments along their shores, but that he's always balancing those qualms with the actual time he's spent (lots of it) on Lake Keowee with his in-laws and his wife, daughter, and son, and that he back burners these issues the moment he drops a kayak into the lake and looks around and sees where he and his daughter are privileged to explore.

Then John quickly ratchets up the discussion and darts from the tropes of environmentalism into the deep waters of his favorite "ism," postmodernism. John, a just-out-of-graduate-school literary critic twenty years younger than I, understands what I want to put my faith in: a beautiful place as it had been more than two hundred years ago, a river valley filled with Bartram's "fragrant strawberries" and "high hills and mountains...rising boldly almost upright" that could be summoned anew through the time-travel of a literary essay. John just can't quite buy into it all, and he presents an intellectual alternative about a real lake that he has grown to love—a beautiful lake at the foot of the Blue Ridge Mountains. As we approach Pickens, John Miles explains the modern mountain landscape we are heading into in terms of the ideas of one of his mentors, Native American critic, poet, and cultural historian Gerald Vizenor.

"Vizenor calls how you're thinking 'terminal nostalgia,'" John says with a wry smile. "You want to recapture Bartram's valley, a past that no longer exists."

We spot a box turtle crossing the road, and its reptile rumble to make the other side becomes a plot point in our story. I'm compelled as always to stop and do my part to alter the future genetics of that corner of Pickens County's turtle population, and so we pull over to the shoulder, and John jumps out and grabs the struggling creature and carries it across two lanes of traffic.

A truck passes and I think how that truck would have made turtle hash, and I say, "I suppose that turtle doesn't exist either."

"That turtle is real," John says. "No arguing otherwise. But the stories we tell about saving the turtle are already part of a past that no longer exists."

The guard at the gatehouse is military serious, as if there is an undeclared war between the outside world and his gated protectorate. He's dressed in a brown starched uniform and has lieutenant's bars on his shoulders. We tell him we're visiting John's mother-in-law, but he looks my dirty truck up and down and hands us a "worker" pass to display on the dash.

After the indignity of the gatehouse, we pass under a high-tension power line with mountain laurel blooming in the clearing below, and I think of beauty side by side with utility and a power plant feeding the lines for almost forty years. We pass a trimmed and inviting muscadine vineyard that John's in-law's development is named for, and their "equestrian center," and up the hill, their championship golf course, and I reflect for a moment on how several decades ago, visiting here I would have been smack dab in the middle of the "belly of the beast." But something's changed. Call it compromise or simply call it that moderate turn toward the conservative that even radicals like me often take as they age. With all my understanding and admiration for environmental battles, I'm unwilling to stick my neck out quite so far anymore. I'm feeling a little like our box turtle crossing the highway on a wet morning, and now I'm just hoping I can get through the traffic before some Mack Truck of modernity bears down on me.

We soon arrive at John's in-law's house. They're retired and living the good life. I take in the view and begin to draw my writer's conclusions. It's a certain form of twenty-first-century paradise John's in-laws have carved out of Bartram's wilderness—immaculate, mulched yard thick with native hardwoods, practice putting green, large comfortable lodge-style house overlooking a cove of the upper lake. It's not that much different from the house I live in—sans the putting green—and I'm caught off guard by how comfortable I feel with the landscape once I'm inside the gates. Carol is excited that we've come all this way (after all, Pickens County, South Carolina, might not be the eighteenth-century "back country," but it's still off the beaten track) and she offers good advice—maybe we should paddle down to the fort from here rather than them depositing us down there to paddle back since the wind is from the north. I feel a little like Billy Bartram relying on the kindness of strangers.

Within a few minutes Carol has also shown us on the map how to get down to Keowee Town Landing, the closest lake access to the site of Fort Prince George, where she'll pick us up in a few hours. The lake is a familiar landscape to her. They've lived there for almost a decade. Carol recounts the route downstream and warns about confusing spots where we might get lost among islands and coves. The logistics settled, we're soon on the water and headed down the lake toward our rendezvous with Bartram and my deeply imagined "vale."

"My mother-in-law is an amazing woman," John says as we paddle away from the dock. "She's the type who always knows which way the wind is blowing."

John and I talk as we paddle but I can't remember much of what we say—breezy stuff, mostly about his first year of teaching at Wofford, his trips with his daughter on the lake (how she loved to sit with him and occasionally walk out to the nose of the kayak and jump in, using the boat as a big yellow diving board), nothing as heady or deep along the way as John's earlier brief foray into Vizenor and postmodernism.

I have to admit that I like the lightness of our float down the lake, and I'm almost to the point where I might call it beautiful. The water is clear and calm at first and there are few boats to trouble us. Then I look back upstream before we pass under Highway 11 and take in all the houses either built or under construction. The styles are consistent, all from one period mostly, and very few houses that fall outside the conventional million-dollar lake-house look I'm so used to seeing in these gated developments of the boom years—stone accents, big tinted windows, shingles, high-pitched roofs. It's all sort of Adirondack lodge meets Hilton Head. There's heavy mulch on the hillsides and big rocks accenting all landscaping. It's a nice look, but the resource footprint is enormous.

As we approach the Highway 11 bridge, I point out to John how on our right is the late-1800s James Alexander Robertson House, one of the few original structures left standing when the lake was cleared. The restored white, two-story farmhouse stands out like a rustic sore thumb among the resort development.

Then I tell John another story I've heard: on the left, in the steep woods across from the Robertson House, is the site of a little ruined rock house where a USC history professor named Meriwether died a decade before the lake was built. I know about the rock house because the site is on former Wofford president Joe Lesesne's land. We paddle over toward the shore and see the Lesesne house on a large lot tucked back into a grove of big hardwoods. It's an old-timey lake house from the 1980s, a rare survivor on the high-dollar lakeshore. The Lesesne house was built years before gated communities became the standard for developments on the lake. In many ways the Lesesne lake house has more in common with the old farmhouse isolated on the peninsula across from it.

After we pass under Highway 11 I'm not paying attention, and soon we somehow get crossed up and turn up a cove and paddle an extra mile or so before we dead-end among more mansions and hillsides prepped for construction. By the time we extract ourselves from the wrong-turn cove, it's near lunch and we stop to eat. We're so turned around we can't even figure out which way is downstream, and which is up. "It's the ghosts of the vanquished Native Americans screwing with us," I say.

John decides to call Carol and she gets him oriented by cell phone when he spots one of his favorite recreational destinations in their trips around the lake directly ahead of us—Red Neck Rock, a twenty-foot perch with lots of teenagers jumping into the lake below. John says he too loves to jump from Red Neck Rock and asks if I want to get in a quick plunge. "I bet we could get a cold beer over there," John says, laughing.

Directions clear, we paddle on. We're both tiring a little as it sinks in that what would have been a six-mile paddle is really going to be eight. Just when I've synched with the May sun, the wind, and clear water, and I'm about to give in to the beauty of Lake Keowee, a gray-haired guy in a huge cigarette boat straight out of *Miami Vice* buzzes past us, and the presence of our tiny kayaks doesn't slow him down. I turn my bow into the wake to keep from swamping. The speed boat makes more noise than I can believe. "If I were dictator of the world that guy would be illegal," I say. My disapproval doesn't slow him down. The boat disappears around an island and then appears again, and the old man guns the boat up the lake right past us again.

"My in-laws would agree," John says. "They hate those boats too."

That's one of the problems with a vacation community full of wealth. Even the residents hate some things about it—like this old guy with his late-life crisis boat. But with as much disposable income as circulates around Lake Keowee, it's hard to predict much less control what toys will appear in the next wave of purchases. Monster Jet Skis, pontoon boats, ski boats, cigar boats—they all pass us by as we paddle along. Some slow down

and nod, and some pass us without a glance at full speed, as if by
paddling kayaks we have not bought a ticket to their show.

An hour later we finally approach the site of Fort Prince
George. I can see the Keowee Dam a mile or so in the distance.
The valley here is flat and wide, not as dramatic as I thought it
would be, but then I remember that two hundred feet of vertical
elevation is lost to the lake. Two Jet Skis zip back and forth
across where I think the fort is hidden. They make an X and
mark the spot for me.

I paddle out to where the infernal Jet Skis have crossed and
pull Bartram's *Travels* from my dry bag and read to John as we
sit over the spot the naturalist has written about so beautifully. I
look back upstream and the Blue Ridge Mountains are laid out
just as he described them two hundred years in the past. In the
passage I choose, Bartram describes the Keowee "vale" he approached in his long-ago mid-May as "a most charming situation...through which the beautiful river meanders, sometimes
gently flowing, but more frequently agitated." The mountains
beyond Bartram's gaze are "lofty, superb, misty, and blue."

With the lost fort finally below us and the mountains in the
distance, I'd planned to sit for a while and ponder the past, the
present, and the future of rivers, but instead I'm drawn to shore.
Partially it's the responsibility I feel toward John's mother-in-
law, whom we can see is already waiting at the boat landing.
She's already spent more of her afternoon than she'd planned to
wait our adventure out. "Stay as long as you need," John's says,
though I know he wants to get back and make his wife Alfredo
sauce tonight. There's nothing postmodern about that basic desire to return to hearth and home. I write one brief note in my
journal, that none of us are so free as Bartram was years ago here
on the edge of the wild land.

A few days later I'm visiting with writer Philip Lee Williams and
his father, Woody Williams, in Phil's house deep in the Georgia

woods. Phil and I are sitting cross-legged on the living room floor, and Mr. Williams is comfortably settled on the couch. I'm here because I know Phil Williams, his dad, and his brother Mark spent plenty of time in the Keowee Valley before it was dammed. They worked the archaeological dig at Fort Prince George from beginning to end, and Phil's dad went on to write the only extensive report on the work. Mr. Williams also built the intricate scale model of the fort that thousands have seen in the Oconee visitor's center out of real Keowee Valley dirt and stone. From their experience in the valley in the 1960s Mark developed his interest in archaeology that led to his profession, and Phil became a novelist, essayist, and poet with the human and natural world of the Southern mountains and Piedmont at the center of it.

"I was the one with the more literary/creative angle," Phil says. "I saw the world a little differently. Mark's the scientist and dad's the historian, and I'm the creative writer with the abiding interest in science. I spent lots of time up there sitting at the ford listening to birds."

Phil continues by telling me about his latest project, a three-hundred-page poem about William Bartram, *The Flower Gatherer*: "I first read Bartram when I was twelve. My poems in three parts—Bartram as an old man, Bartram during his traveling years, and then a section about the time I spent up in Keowee with my family in the 1960s. It's what I've done to remember. There were wild strawberries the spring we were digging, just like Bartram described it. He says his horses' hooves were red with them."

Mr. Williams listens quietly as his son talks of poetry, then opens his briefcase and pulls out the journal he kept during the excavation of Fort Prince George during 1967 and '68 and follows it with the one-hundred-page Fort Prince George archaeological memoir/report he wrote thirty years later.

Mr. Williams had grown up in Seneca, and so he'd known the valley all his life. He probably saw it for the first time in the

1930s. Now retired and in his middle eighties, Mr. Williams recalls vividly how in the early 1960s he'd been reading *The Simms History of South Carolina* and saw a reference to Fort Prince George on the Keowee River and decided to take his two young sons up the valley to find it.

"Phil was nine and Mark was eleven," Mr. Williams said. "We already had a big interest in Native American history. On one trip we'd been up to find Chief Blue, one of the last of the native Catawba speakers. When we got there, some researchers were in the middle of a field recording for the Smithsonian."

Mr. Williams and the boys poked around the valley a bit before they heard about the plan for the lake. "There was a town hall meeting in Clemson, and Dr. William Edwards talked about the state doing perspective archaeology work up there on Fort Prince George. That was 1965."

Thanksgiving Day 1966, Mr. Williams drove into the valley and met John Combes, the South Carolina archaeologist who would carry out the excavation. "Combes had moved into the old Isaac Few House and had opened up a trench on the site of the fort. I walked up and ask if he needed any help with his dig. He was indifferent in the beginning. Finally he said yes, and I worked every weekend and Christmas holidays in '67." They worked fast and there was virtually no money for the dig. Thanksgiving of '66 John Combes had just started his first trenches and by May 12, 1968, the site was under water.

While his father fills me in on the family's history with the valley, Phil turns a tape recorder on that's sitting between us. I lean close and hear the unmistakable sounds of water rushing over stone. Phil cranks up the volume. "It's a recording of the shoals on the Keowee Bartram would have crossed. To our knowledge this is the only recording of the Keowee River." Phil's brother Mark has transferred it from the original reel-to-reel to CD, and it accompanies every copy of *The Flower Gatherer* in a little glued-in sleeve.

"This tape's the first thing I play when I teach nature writing," Phil says. "It gets their heads into the real eco-aspects of writing. When they hear it, they're often stunned and muted at the very idea that this is the sound of a river that's been destroyed. It's an amazing aural artifact."

Mr. Williams listens, but he's intent on trying to recall whether the recording was made in '67 or '68. "I think the water was too high by '68, so it must have been '67."

I, too, want to be stunned or muted by the sound of the Keowee. It's moving and important—possibly the only recording of a vanished Southern river, but I think I expected too much. Phil had told me of the existence of the tape in an email, and so I was prepared, and, to tell the truth, I'd been thinking about the moment for weeks. How ironic that I'd sat on the real lake in a kayak and yet I hoped that a recorded sound from forty years in the past would sum it all up for me. Before I arrived at Phil's I'd formulated the idea that sound of the lost river was to be my essay's climax, my true Bartram moment, a supreme relic of relics. I realize now that it's their moment—a Williams family moment, one that translates well to classes of beginning nature writers—but I find it hard to make it entirely mine. I never saw the remnant Keowee Valley and the vanished river was nothing but stories for me. In my lifetime, it never will be anything else.

By the time I'm ready to leave I'm back to Bartram's feelings of dejection and "unharmony" when Mr. Williams reaches in the briefcase for one final relic of the Keowee Valley. He hands me a vitamin bottle with "Fort Prince George Pit Dirt" written on the side in blue ink. I shake it and it sounds just like a Native American rattle for a moment. Mr. Williams says he's got two buckets of it that he took off the site in 1968: "This is from the early powder magazine floor, east side of the fort. It's probably dirt Bartram walked on, so you can have a séance with him when you get home."

As I drive back to Spartanburg, I try to pull the two scenes together. The Cherokee and Bartram and the Williams family and Philip Lee Williams's three-hundred-page poem about it all form one reality, and everything else post-1968—the dam, the lake, the development, my discussion with John about postmodernism, our paddle through the flooded Keowee Valley, are all on the other side of a cultural divide.

I decide my melancholy comes from knowing I fall on the other side of that divide too. I'm no longer so Romantic as I used to be. Maybe I've moved from innocence to experience, and I'm not so often terminally sad about what's been lost. Like Bartram, I am on the edge of wild Indian country, but the "Indians" who have troubled my certainty are postmodernists and developers.

I didn't know the Keowee Valley as that first-level paradise Phil Williams remembers and writes about. I only know the lake as a place I'm uncomfortable on. The nuclear power, the high-dollar developments with guards at the entrances, the cell phone service from midstream islands—these are all things I live with but can't quite square with a lost "flower world" that William Bartram described in 1775. What's more, if I listen to the stories and the tape of the lost river, I'm almost convinced again that paradise existed up to the butt end of the twentieth century, and it was taken away by an ill-conceived utility project that stole a wealth of agricultural land, biodiversity, and the historical center of history for the up country—what Phil Williams calls "the bottom end of the empire of the Cherokees."

As I drive home, I find my comfort is not in thinking about the lost Keowee Valley, but about the eternal paradise of literature. After all, William Bartram was a lousy farmer, a wayward son, a great botanist, but that's not why we literary types still read him more than two hundred years later. The botany and the history are not why Coleridge read him or Wordsworth or a hundred other poets like Phil Williams and me. We all read him because his prose so often sings. There's beauty everywhere in the book, and Bartram takes us to places even more beautiful than valleys that can be lost to the next power broker with a good real estate agent for clearing the locals out when he wants to make money from a dam.

I read Bartram because in my personal canon, the *Travels* is great literature. I'll have fun thinking and writing about my time lost in modernity among the gated mansions of Pickens County and my little vitamin bottle of Keowee Valley dirt, but then I'll pull Bartram's *Travels* off the shelf and read about the flower-haunted world again and remember why I keep trying to do what I do.

THE UPPER BROAD RIVER:
A PASTORAL

Every time I drive I-85 north toward Charlotte and cross the Broad River near Gaffney, I look downstream and think, "Cherokee Ford and 99 Islands." Before Duke Power dammed the Broad in the early part of the twentieth century, the river was storied territory, and I've always wanted to paddle it. There was an ancient river crossing at Cherokee Ford where Revolutionary War soldiers waded back and forth before two of the great battles of the war. Gold miners roamed the ridges and creek valleys looking for riches. An ironworks even operated at Cherokee Ford in the early nineteenth century. Then an early industrialist captured the falling water for power and made a textile fortune doing so.

Over spring break several years ago I finally took a three-day canoe trip down that section of the Broad with my friend Venable Vermont. Venable, Spartanburg born and raised, has lived in Alaska since 1983. Before he retired from his day job, he was an attorney, but weekends and summer vacations he's always paddled, hunted, hiked, and climbed over as much wild country as he could get his arms around.

He hasn't forgotten his roots. Once a year Venable flies back to the South and turkey hunts with his brother John. He still misses the southern river swamps, and so a few years ago he brought back an acorn from a South Carolina swamp chestnut and planted it in his greenhouse. It grew to over six feet tall and pushed against the roof, reaching for northern sky.

Once while I visited Venable in Alaska, he and his wife, Kim, drove my wife and me downtown. The city of Anchorage sits in a bowl. In a state twice the size of Texas, Anchorage accounts for almost half the population, two hundred thousand souls, with a sprawl of buildings surrounded by a profound uplift of peaks. Look around and it's a 360-degree feast: the Alaska Range to the north, the Chugach Mountains to our east, and the mountains of the Kenai Peninsula to the south.

We discovered Anchorage is a study in contrasts. The highway leading downtown is wall-to-wall contemporary Americana: Blockbuster Video, Home Depot, fast food and fast retail. But then something jars you back four thousand miles north and you realize you're not "outside" (what the locals call the Lower 48) anymore. A few blocks from the central city we saw a cabin where someone still lives with moose skulls covering the roof.

Once in the central city, Kim pointed out a line of ugly buildings along Third Avenue, a main drag hit very hard by the '64 earthquake: "You know, up here there's a ban on architecture. If you're an architect, you can't come to Alaska."

If I lived in Alaska, I'd probably choose Anchorage. It's a place, unlike most cities, that encourages you to believe the human world is puny and temporary. That's a lesson we need more in the world today. Being Southern we tend to think in terms of established human patterns. Not always so in Alaska. The dew's still on the world up there, even a city like Anchorage.

The dew's not on the Broad River, but it didn't dry long ago. We started in North Carolina in the shadow of White Oak Mountain. The first day we paddled the Green River, camped there, and then the second day floated toward South Carolina and spent the second night camped just above the state line. Venable had paddled part of the Green and the upper Broad with Scouts in the 1960s, but it was all new river for me. The best I could claim was that I had scouted some of the stretches from bridges.

The weekend was perfect for paddling. But what is perfection on a river? Silence and pace of the journey have something to do with it, as does the way your eyes adjust to the little things—a hatch of small dark flies on the river's surface, or a silver stick bobbing in the current, a mottled trillium ready to open on the sandy bank, or the way the gray ghosts of gneiss outcrops on wooded slopes appear suddenly from the shadows and disappear again into the creases of the landscape as you pass. Perfection on a river is all around you.

In Cherokee County the Broad River passes under I-85's great asphalt ribbon just outside Gaffney. "Every time I drive over, I look both ways and imagine floating under," I said as we passed under.

"I'll bet you're in the minority," he said. "Most don't notice they're crossing a river these days."

There were several other bridges in the next few miles. The Southern Railroad Bridge downstream from the I-85 crossing is a beautiful WPA design, like a Roman aqueduct seen from the river. There's a stone abutment just below for an older bridge, and farther down is the crossing for US Highway 29, a modern highway bridge. Sometimes from the river the whole world looks like a ruin.

Past all the bridges is the site of Cherokee Ford, an ancient crossing of an American Indian trail and one of the most important fords during the Revolution. Warring forces on both sides crossed and recrossed the river there before and after the battles of Kings Mountain and Cowpens.

"The river at the ford is about eight hundred yards wide, and upon the firm pathway, which has been constructed at considerable expense, the average depth of water did not exceed one foot," wrote Benson J. Lossing in his 1850 *Pictorial Field Book of the Revolution Vol. II*. "Unless the river is much swollen, the ford is perfectly safe. A strong dam, owned by the proprietors of the iron-works, crosses the river an eighth of a mile above; and so shallow and rapid is the current, and so rocky the bed of the river, for many miles in this vicinity, that it is quite unnavigable, except in a few places."

A little more than a mile downstream from the ford is Cherokee Falls, one of the early mill villages of the South Carolina up-country. In the early nineteenth century there was a large ironworks there, but in 1881 the first mill was constructed with Northern capital and know-how. Before that, as Bobby Gilmer Moss reports in *The Old Iron District*, his history of Cherokee County, "the waters of the Broad River ran practically unchecked to the sea."

The mill at Cherokee Falls harnessed the power of what has been described as "the cataract" that was known as Cherokee Falls. The developers of the mill created industry in the midst of thousands of acres of what was once forest for feeding local iron furnaces. "Except for distillers, charcoal burners, and squatters," Moss writes, "the vast acres of the iron companies' forest lands were practically untenanted." The mill prospered until a fire destroyed it in 1894. The Cherokee Falls mill fire was so fierce it could be seen from Gaffney, four miles distant. After the fire, the factory was rebuilt even bigger and prospered until the collapse of Southern textiles in the late twentieth century.

Now the windows of the mill are boarded up as the building awaits the fate of almost all the old factories—demolition and salvage. Very few of the old brick structures have been reused after the fickle finger of industry abandoned much of the Piedmont. Many like me wonder once the mills go, can it be long in geologic time until the old dams as well disappear. We can only hope.

Approaching Cherokee Falls Dam, it's hard to figure out a way to portage. There are no signs pointing the way. Burlington Industries, the owner of the mill in 1989, must not have followed through with the portage path reported on a fancy Duke Energy interpretive plaque we'd seen upstream, or after selling off the mill the next owners abandoned the river trail or never finished it.

The only way around the odd, wide, multi-angle dam is to hug the right bank and work down to where the structure abuts the rocky shore. We took out, moved gear around the abutment and the exposed rock, which was dark and slippery, and slid our canoe in river.

Cherokee Falls is significant because it's the first old cotton mill we've seen along the Broad. For one hundred years industry prospered in this isolated, dramatic Cherokee County spot. Now there's a big "For Sale" sign on the mill's side. There is no industry here except for a few recreationists like us—either fishing or paddling.

Once we got a good view of the dam, we could see what terrible shape it was in. There were once "batter boards" on top, a wooden skirt designed to bring up the pond level three or four feet above the concrete structure. Many of the boards were now missing on the eight-foot dam and a gap in them about halfway across the river provided some thrills for area white water boaters. I've seen videos on the internet of local kayakers running the flume of water pressing through the broken dam. There would be none of that for us and our laden canoe, though below the Cherokee Falls Dam there are big, long shoals that also offer some good white water waves for surfing.

We ate lunch on a concrete dam abutment. Afterward we planned to pack the canoe and paddle down through the exciting shoals below. I couldn't finish my sandwich. I was nervous about the shoals. Before lunch I'd scouted the long broken ledge between us and the bottom of the shoals. It was nothing I would have thought twice about in a kayak, but paddling a loaded canoe is another thing. This sort of expedition paddling is new to me. I wasn't used to sitting upright above white water. What could happen? I kept asking myself, and I always came up with the same answer. We might fill up and have to bail the boat, or worst-case scenario, we might flip and have to work the boat over to the shore through cold early-spring river water. We had all our gear tied in. It would ride with the boat, and there was little chance the eddy below would look like a yard sale.

"Oh, just keep it straight downstream and we can ride through about anything," V said when I told him I was nervous. "You want me to take it through by myself?"

The shoals below were just as Venable said they would be. We kept it straight and hit the big rolling waves in exactly the right place, one of a dozen smooth tongues of river water breaking the ledge into multiple glassy arcs. We worked down through several hundred yards of ledges with little waves and holes behind them.

After that scrap of adventure we floated on down to the 99 Islands Dam takeout three miles below on river left. I don't know exactly how many islands there actually are in the 99 Islands area, but there are quite a few. I imagine that before it was dammed, the river there had an almost braided feel, a landscape Venable would have found familiar from the rivers up in Alaska. As we floated along, we heard gunshots and Venable identified them as having come from a pistol. "Nine millimeter probably."

The shots were coming from the right or east bank. "Target practice?" I asked. "That or somebody shooting at bottles in the river." Then the shooter fired off about twelve rounds, paused, and a deeper report followed. Venable said, "Now that's a semi-automatic assault rifle."

"So that's what a firefight would sound like?" I asked.

"Oh, I believe a firefight would sound nosier than that."

An hour later we could see the boat landing in the distance where we were meeting a friend who would take us back to Spartanburg. Just before landing we passed a great blue heron rookery on river right in a large tree along the edge of the impoundment. There maybe were ten birds with nests. Great blue herons are the large solitary waders you're most likely to see fishing on Piedmont streams, and I don't often think of them congregating in rookeries. We floated slowly past this wild bloom of blue birds above us.

In many ways a rookery is the opposite of an abandoned textile mill like Cherokee Ford, a place where our economic culture played out in the past its notions of industry and profit, often spoiling the land and water in the process. Those notions become obsolete locally, or too expensive, and the economic usefulness of a place moves on. Other forces take over—decay, rot, compost, nostalgia.

"Nature is nuance," the writer Edward Hoagland claims somewhere. I look up into the rookery tree and I see hope for the river and for us. The industry of herons is sustainable as long as the river itself is whole and healthy.

An old man solitary as a heron was fishing off the side of the boat dock when we arrived. He greeted us as we floated in, then he called off his little dog, Ginger, as we landed. His accent was old-growth Piedmont mill town. He slurred his sentences until the vowels and consonants swam together in an audible gruel. Every sentence was slow as chilled molasses.

"Fishing any good?" I asked.

"Naaaaaw," he said.

"Well, it's a nice place to spend the day," I said.

"Day's right. You don't want to be here after night," he said. "Ginger, you get back over here. Them local boys will steal your tires. The game warden parked his truck, went out to do a little fishing. When he got back they'd sawed his lock and pushed that trailer right in the lake."

Through this old man we found out about the terrible weather in the region the night before. It was frightening to hear what we had avoided.

In the barely comprehensible local dialect leaking from under his cap, he told us that bad weather had moved through the South Carolina up-country: "I'm telling you. They was hailstones big as golf balls, and they filled the back of my pickup ten inches deep."

The old man spit a clear stream in the dirt of something he'd been chewing all along. "You better be glad you weren't out in that pontoon," he said, nodding at our canoe. "It woulda tore y'all up."

Rivers, like the old fisherman or the herons who live along them, have complex histories. Cultures once clung to them. Towns and industries rose and disappeared on their banks. Now river are mostly occasional stages where weekend jubilees float through. Recreation has mostly replaced industry. Quiet has settled in the crooks and bends where mills once hummed and the workers once ached.

I'm still drawn to rivers, even though interstate highways often fulfill their original cultural niche ferrying our freight and dreams downstream. What I take away when I load my canoe and drive back to the suburbs is the lingering feeling that the world is bigger than us and in motion. One way to make sense of it is from the seat of a canoe. I float in order to feel the larger world.

URBAN REEDY RIVER

In early August I meet Dave Hargett to explore what he calls "the Parkins Mill to Conestee Reach" of the Reedy River. We unload Dave's two green solo canoes just downstream from where the river passes under I-85, and in my chest I feel the vibrations as an endless stream of eighteen-wheelers rumble down the prime artery of East Coast commerce. This is not a wilderness paddling trip, I remind myself, though I forget that for a moment when I get my first glimpse of the river. The river level looks almost ideal for paddling, unusual for an urban river in August thanks to yesterday's late-evening thunderstorm the day before.

Dave's dressed for business, a get-it-done conservation warrior clad in old green long pants and shirt and a beat-up forestry-supply cap. On top of his quick-dry pants, he's strapped on heavy hip waders. As executive director of the Lake Conestee Nature Park, the four-hundred-acre public green space downstream, Dave's on, in, or, near the Reedy River almost every day. I'd argue he probably knows it better than any other human being alive. I'm dressed more like a tourist, a recreational paddler who could have bought his outfit down the interstate at REI—T-shirt, nylon shorts, Chaco sandals, and a wide-brimmed boating hat.

Before we depart, I retrieve my paddle and my small dry bag from the truck bed. I need to take some notes as we float, and for that purpose, I've brought a notebook, several pens, and the Notes app on my iPhone. "So, do you write on that widget all day?" Dave asks when he sees me tapping away. He's packing other gear: a Swedish chainsaw tucked inside a protective orange case. "You don't paddle the Reedy without a chainsaw," Dave explains. "You might get lucky and find the stream clear of downed trees, but chances are you won't. The nature of urban streams is abundant large woody debris."

We carry our boats under the Mauldin Road bridge where the Swamp Rabbit Trail passes underneath the traffic and negotiate a steep bank of granite riprap to get to the water's edge. There we prepare to begin our river trip with a spot rich in the detritus of twentieth-century urban/industrial infrastructure—asphalt, underpass, interstate, nearby factory. I'm thinking mostly it's just plain ugly at the corner of Parkins Mill and Mauldin Road, but then Dave points out the beautiful LEED (Leaders in Environmental and Energy Design) certified-silver angular headquarters building for ReWa, Renewable Water Resources, formally known as the Western Carolina Regional Sewer Authority. ReWa's HQ facelift and rebranding offers a prime example of the complexities of the evolving relationship between communities, rivers, and our waste.

For the first century and a half of the Industrial Revolution, rivers were simply convenient drainage ditches for all our waste. Once the Clean Water Act was passed in 1972 the federal government imposed penalties for polluting. Before then, few, if any, cared what a water-utility building looked like, and nobody cared much about sewage, as long as it went away, typically downstream. "Once we paddle past the ReWa outflow downstream, twenty-five percent of the current under our canoes will be effluent from their plant," Dave says as we push off into the river. "It's bacteriologically cleaner than the river water."

For the first half mile we float through the forested floodplain portion of ReWa's three hundred acres, with its sewage settling ponds invisible in the trees on the left side of the river. I say for the first time, "You know Dave, this is really beautiful," and Dave agrees. He points out that for the next three miles we'll be paddling through a surprisingly wild spot, especially for the center of the most populated county in the state, a floodplain that is a mile wide in places and yet is still an urban stream.

Near the confluence with Brushy Creek (a tributary that drains much of Greenville's west side) we pull the canoes up on a sandbar and Dave points out we've just passed the pipe that discharges Greenville's wastewater. I comment on the color of the river water, the expected shade of red clay discolored by a slight brown sheen. I'm not complaining. Fifty years ago the river ran many colors, whatever the textile dye plants upstream were releasing that day—red, blue, brown, green. Dave explains the wastewater is mostly clear, but the river has to carry the burden of industrial dying processes still underway. "Sometimes the Reedy runs dark brown like weak coffee," Dave says as we stand and watch the river passing.

Aldo Leopold says at the beginning of *Sand County Almanac* that there are those who can live without wildness and those who can't. Like Leopold, I'm one who can't, but every time I paddle on an urban stream I have to revise my ideas about wildness. The urban Reedy is as wild as Leopold's Wisconsin River, but whether I like it or not, the Reedy's still paying its industrial dues. Dave, the scientist, assures me the dye in the river has no measurable effect on water quality downstream.

"What would you say to someone to convince them to love the Reedy?" I ask Dave as we begin to paddle downstream.

"Greenville exists because of this river," Dave says. "It's our hometown stream. Everything depended on it. It was the backbone, and despite all the abuse and insult, it has recovered remarkably. It's a great example of an urban stream."

In a place like the Reedy River, nature and culture swirl together, the river, a flowing sluiceway of beauty and ugliness, of pollution and productivity, of birdlife and abandoned plastic objects. Paddling an urban stream is as natural as negotiating the deepest reach of the wild Amazon.

We beach our canoes again. "I want to show you where our Treefrog Trail crosses a marshy bog," Dave says.

Before I step off the beach I look down at my feet and see a male yellow swallowtail butterfly perched on a fresh pile of raccoon scat, gleaning a few amino acids from the waste, a perfect metaphor for what's going on along the Reedy River. What we think of as spoiled and dirty is pulled back into the system. We feed on it through our visions of a place like the Conestee Nature Park or the Swamp Rabbit Trail. On an urban river it's all about perspective.

MAY THE WIND TAKE
OUR TROUBLES AWAY

The Okefenokee is seven hours south of our South Carolina Piedmont home and covers seven hundred square miles in South Georgia. Five hundred thousand acres of wetlands is preserved and protected as a federally designated wilderness, so we knew that some of the trappings of this particular brand of contested political space could be a privilege granted to us as citizens of this great country as an enduring perk of democracy—solitude, silence, cathedral-like beauty of a few large cypress stands, a little sense of caution from snakes and alligators, the uncertainty of weather, the discomfort of mosquitoes, and a rite of passage deepened by each self-propelled stroke across the swamp.

We needed was some wilderness relief, so our friends Brent and Angela set up a three-night backcountry paddling trip with us and Brent's sister Melanie across Okefenokee National Wildlife Refuge. The refuge, as Brent explained, "is a dark site, always listed as one of the best places in the East to see stars." Brent and Angela run an outfitter called Alarka Expeditions in Franklin, North Carolina, although Angela also has a life in music and a deep avocational love of natural history. Brent served for more than a decade as an administrator of a large national conservation nonprofit, though in the end the brushfires of wilderness politics drove him into the life of an outdoor service provider. Melanie is a retired teacher, avid birder, and a confident boater with multiple trips to the swamp.

Kingfisher Landing is the northernmost of the two eastern launching portals to the swamp's designated wilderness. From Kingfisher Landing there are two trails across the swamp, a looping northern red trail through Carter Prairie and Double Lakes to Maul Hummock, continuing south and east through

Sapling Prairie, Dinner Pond, and Big Water, and ultimately on to Stephen C. Foster State Park and the western entrance. We would paddle the green trail, heading south through Durdin Prairie to Bluff Lake and continuing east to Floyd's Island. From there, we would leave the green trail and intersect with the red trail at Floyd's Prairie and Minnie's Pond. These trails intersect with yellow and orange trails as well, forming a navigable system of entryways into and through the wilderness, but our focus would be on green and red.

Colors have become political in this country—like masks and MAGA caps—and so I could not help but project our good fortune of paddling "the green trail" for the first twenty miles through the wilderness before intersecting the more fraught "red trail," where we might encounter the complexities of partisanship.

Brad and Diane, two friends of Brent's and Angela's from the Bartram Trail Society, met us in the Kingfisher parking lot to day-paddle part of the first leg with us. When they arrived we had yet to pull the boats down off the racks and were waffling on whether we should paddle or not, whether it was foolish, with a growing threat of wind and rain from Tropical Storm Eta moving in. Betsy said her weather app was showing showers for two days with wind fifteen to twenty miles per hour with gusts up to thirty. We went as far as making an alternative reservation in a condo at the coast to ride out the bad weather. "Don't go into the swamp with a hurricane on the way!" a voice in my sixty-six-year-old brain was saying, but Brent, who had worked years protecting wilderness, really needed a shot of its renewal before winter set in. His adventure focus was honed and unceasing. "We'll go even if it's snowing," he'd written in an email a few days earlier when it looked like the weather might turn nasty.

Betsy looked at her app one more time. "The wind should be blowing fifteen but the trees aren't moving at all." With that, something magic shifted in us, and we jubilantly unloaded the gear and hauled our multicolored dry bags and kayaks to the swamp's portal, the grassy ramp into a glassy canal. The wilderness of our caution gave way to the joy of expectation. This was not Lewis and Clark's Corps of Discovery, but it was as close as we could get in the Southeast. Under hopeful blue skies, our troupe of seven entered the green trail and paddled south toward our first night's reservation for the camping platform at Bluff Lake.

It had been a wet year, and water on the green trail was high enough so that everything in the swamp was inundated, a perfect landscape to fall into the familiar long-distance, flat-water rhythms of self-propelled watercraft—the rotation of the torso, the slight sway back and forth of the boat's track through black water as the double-bladed paddle enters and exits. I've had forty years of paddling and bet I've logged a thousand miles this way, alone, focused, observant of the more-than-human world. As my friend Drew Lanham says, "All nature asks is that we pay attention."

Tandem canoes are the smallest unit of mutual cooperation. Canoes are great for hauling and teamwork, more caucus than primary. Outfitters don't call them divorce boats for nothing. A kayak puts the burden on one person. Two blades but one paddle. For my supplications before the wilderness, I have always preferred kayak to canoe. In my kayak I took control of my own pace as I hauled our gear in a fully laden, twelve-foot, orange Hurricane into the wilderness. Cutting through water lilies, I felt akin to an Eskimo hunting the ice seas, for this is the origin of my craft—an individual spirit focused on a singular task, that being, in this case, the transformation that arrived when I left the fully civilized world behind.

I paid attention as we continued forward. Walls of green and expanses of wet prairie alternated. Catbirds seemed common. Green as it may be, our trail was no Acadian watery byway, not even a pioneer passage from frontier days. When you drill down historically, the green trail is a canal dug a century ago for the early industrial extraction of peat. The peat-pit highway wiggles south, a few miles west of the modern paved road to Folkston. In spite of the singular nature of a kayak, it is still possible to build human affinity as you paddle. I pulled parallel with Brad and Diane and talked about ecological communities. They knew their botany and teased out the species rising around us on the canal sides—sweeps of mustard-yellow coreopsis, mats of blooming yellow and white water lilies, and wild Medusa heads of green pitcher plants rearing their tangle of little death kettles amid hedges of tasseling swamp cyrilla or black titi.

We crossed Durdin Prairie, and we saw our first alligator, a small one cruising through the mats of water lily leaves the size of dinner plates. The sighting amped up the group's level of swamp anxiety, but for me it was a reintroduction to one of my favorite creatures. One of my first publications had been as coauthor of a scientific paper on Morelet's crocodiles soon after I graduated from college. I had spent the summer in Belize interviewing crocodile hunters, and also participating with my friends in a crocodile survey. One component was capturing and tagging crocs. In the following decades, I had participated in two other research expeditions in Mexico and Florida and, most recently, I had written a profile of one of the most renowned alligator biologists in the South, so I had long been familiar and comfortable with the behavior of crocodilians. This first gator slipped out of sight as we passed.

About three miles in, day-trippers Brad and Diane reversed course and doubled back to Kingfisher and their car. They were our last stern line to civilization cast ashore. We stopped for lunch, a bag of fruit and power bars eaten in our boats because there was no dry land. The first meal in the wilderness is always a relief. Like sitting around a fire, eating hamburgers with friends, a wilderness meal has its own gravity. Cheese tastes sharper cut with a pocketknife. Apples carve up cleaner when the biodegradable core can be tossed in the bushes.

After lunch we were hit by the first brief but intense squall—the hurricane we had worried about and tried to reason

244

with. The first human beings we passed were soon after that, a shell-shocked couple in a canoe. The woman in the bow had her face almost completely covered by the dark hood of her rain jacket, though it was no longer raining. The man looked haunted and warned like a prophet of a looming tunnel of vegetation out of Bluff Lake, crawling with the threat of spiders.

Approaching our Bluff Lake camp, we saw our second alligator, a four-foot stationary one poised on a grass tuft. As we gathered around, Angela commented on how it had not been dead long enough for the ebony sheen to fade from its beady eye. Its black, armored skin was perfect, with no scent of necropsy. Its backbone had been exposed by something that chewed him up, possibly an illegal boat prop in the wilderness or a trail grinder. "Probably injured on the canal's bottom and climbed up on the grass to die," I said. It looked like a manhandled museum specimen, a poorly stuffed exhibit in a roadside zoo.

Near the end of our first day in the swamp, the dead gator morphed before my eyes into a strange cultural metaphor—the last four years stretching behind us, only so much political carrion, I hoped, for the vultures of history.

With each mile into the wilderness I could see the stress of the outside world draining from Brent's shoulders. "I need about a month of this," he said. Designated wilderness is a political consideration. No one knows this better than Brent. He spent decades fighting to protect what wilderness has been established since the 1964 Wilderness Act and working to create partnership that would assure more wilderness could be added, places like the swamp, whose half a million acres came into the system in 1974. Partnerships is one aspect of community. Political alliances and the acts and laws they create are often the most fragile fruit of partnerships because they are subject to constant ratification. Community is a web of assured support and relationships. Partnerships are contractual and often are built upon concessions and compromises. Friendships and communities are built on exchanges and expectations. Nothing as final as a vote can end a community. This litany of definitions was what filled my mind as we paddled the end of that first day.

In a little while we set up our tents on the sleeping platform at Bluff Lake. Melanie read from the silver aluminum logbook provided at each campsite by the reserve management to keep up with reservations. The canoeists we'd run into were out to "escape the election." Who were they rooting for?

Before dark, off to the north of the Bluff Lake camping platform, hundreds of swallows passed. We wondered if they were pushed ahead of the storm or simply out foraging at dusk. From the added elevation of the platform we could see fire snags in all directions from the great fire of 2003, something harder to comprehend while paddling the canal. Angela said, "That hummock behind us looks like a perfect place for a barred owl," and right on cue one let loose with "Who cooks for you?"

There were gusts of big wind all night and squally rain. I had a bad dream and woke up deep in the night in a panic about our boats and went out to make sure they were secured to the platform and that our wilderness transportation had not floated away. I looked up into the dark sky and thought about the four-year war on wilderness of the outgoing administration, starting with reducing the size of Bears Ears in Utah and finally opening up the Arctic Wildlife Refuge for drilling. I wondered if the next four years would see the restoration of some of the territory everyone thought had been drained away. The stars I could see were points of hope. But what of all the darkness? What of the hurricane?

The next morning there was hard paddling coming out of Bluff Lake, just like the shell-shocked canoeist prophesied. The channel in that section of cypress forest had been hit hard decades before by wildfires. Brush had narrowed the trail to a series of constructed passages, and for whatever reason, the brush cutters had not cleared the way. A snake fell on Melanie's canoe and quickly swam off. It was hard to get a paddle stroke in. Betsy and Melanie led the way. Melanie showed Betsy that snapping apart her kayak paddle and using only one blade made for more efficient turns and locomotion. It took more than an hour to paddle a mile and finally emerge into Territory Prairie. We paddled quietly once there was enough water again to get in a paddle stroke. The sky seemed huge after the constrictions of the morning's first hour. We were all more observant. Melanie was taking photos. We stopped a few minutes to watch a small flock of white ibises feeding on the floating mats. Wood storks passed overhead.

I felt deepest in the wilderness when we emerged into the long open canal across Territory Prairie. Two hours later we approached Floyd's Island through alternating burned groves and a magic stand of cypress somehow untouched by the fire. I hummed Uncle Tupelo's "Let the wind take your troubles away," and it seemed to work. The storm I'd worried about overnight still seemed miles away. Even if it did hit us, now it didn't matter. I thought back to the moment at the launch when we considered the condo at the beach. We were closing in on the halfway point of crossing the swamp and continuing on would be no harder than going back.

The paddling trail to Floyd's Island ends in a black water cul-de-sac and a portage to the other side. The one-hundred-year-old hunting cabin sits on a dry, sandy ridge in the island's middle. Pines and oaks shade the path and cabin. Somehow the fire spared this island. Once we portaged to the cabin, Angela walked Betsy and me down to see where you put back in on the other side. Brent and Angela had camped on Floyd's Island a year before after Angela's mom had died, and they'd approached from the other direction, from Stephen C. Foster State Park. Standing looking at the water, Angela had a mistaken memory.

She thought the water had risen around the island in the preceding year. Her grief the year before had clouded her idea of the trail. We took her at her word and wondered aloud if it was the wet year or climate change. I thought about the trauma of the last four years for people like us, advocates of diversity in all its forms, wildness, the fluidness of borders, the certainty of laws.

Back at the cabin, someone from a previous trip had tried to chop the cabin's corner post for kindling with the ax, and out back I found a slaughtered rat snake. The pump was broken. Palmetto bugs scuttled out of the cabin corners where we shined our headlamps. We slept in our tents inside the three empty, musty rooms. Near dawn another barred owl called.

The metaphor "drain the swamp" actually has its origins in the marshy wetlands that Washington, DC, was built upon at the beginning of the nineteenth century, but soon after, it became a demand flexible enough to drown any corrupt political position, right or left. High taxes? Drain the swamp! Graft? Drain the swamp! Everyone from Ronald Reagan to Elizabeth Warren has called for the current standing political water to be channeled away. There was one very swamp-like area of the swamp where I thought about drainage a great deal: the huge mystical cypress head we paddled through on the middle fork between Floyd's Prairie and Minnie's Lake was a primordial dream. As Betsy and I steered ahead of the other three, our boats glided back and forth between the green, algae-covered bases of six-foot-diameter fluted cypress, some perhaps predating the founding of the Republic. Somehow this Doobie Brothers' black-water swamp had survived the big fire of 2003. Each swamp cypress was festooned with Spanish moss and soaked with rain. By midday, as we glided through, pushed along by the first current we'd felt in three days, the sun was low enough that the scene looked like an ice storm as the rays electrified each branch with light.

Betsy had other pop-culture memories as she floated through the cypress. She told me it felt just like the Six Flags Over Georgia ride "Tales of the Okefenokee," which operated from 1967 to 1980 and was based on Uncle Remus stories. The water ride coasted through various scenes in the swamp, each one dramatized by singing animals and what one account calls horrifying sentient carrots. "I remember lots of rabbits," Betsy said. "You don't see many rabbits in a swamp."

We took a break midday on a platform with a porta-john and picnic table. We basked like gators in the sun. A half hour after we arrived, we heard the whine upstream of an approaching motorboat. The boat pulled even with us and slowed. The young men didn't seem to be fishing, maybe out joyriding instead. They eyed our colorful boats and pointed. They coasted past, gunned the throttle, and continued up the Middle Fork of the Suwannee River.

We all sat up, startled out of basking by the intrusion. What does it mean for our larger sense of community that these two young men in their motorized johnboat, slowing down as they passed, grumbling to themselves, and glancing our way, were the only scary moment I had in the swamp? Not the alligators, sightings of which I craved and strained through my consciousness like strong tea for their wildness every time I saw one; not snakes; not mosquitoes; not weather; but a pair of white men with a two-stroke engine like the one that had likely minced the back of the gator we'd seen the first day.

The last night, we set up our tents on dry ground again at Mixon's Hummock alongside what's known at the Suwanee River Sill, a low earthen dam built in the early 1960s to raise the water level and reduce fire frequency in the wildlife refuge. The embankment cut through our campsite, and we crossed it going back and forth to the boats for our gear.

Mosquitoes nearly carried us away at dusk. After we ate dinner and night had fallen, I walked everyone out on the dock and showed them the red-eye shine of an alligator across the river narrowed down by the sill. In the 1970s in Belize a crocodile hunter had told me that in the old days before the crocodiles were exploited, the eyes on a healthy wetland would look like "stars in the night sky."

Another barred owl visited us near dawn, and I woke up with the bird calling in the dark above Brent and Angela's tent—the four-note call responding to another across the river. In four days paddling we had passed through many watery communities, but this owl call had been the thread connecting each night, a hopeful sign. That last night we communed with each other and with the wild world that protects and preserves us—gators, owls, even mosquitoes. Like natural systems, community remains healthy when intact, but changes in the margins.

On the last morning, we paddled forty-five minutes from Mixon's Hummock, unloaded the boats at eleven, and shuttled with Okefenokee Adventures from Stephen C. Foster State Park to Kingfisher Landing, completing a half circle of the swamp. In a little more than a hundred years railroads and highways had circled the swamp. Mining, development, and private exploitation of timberlands had tightened the noose like water circling centrifugally down a drain. Swamps are drained by the same means they are most often recreated—a series of purposeful canals, scars deeper than the water table through wet country.

In the front seat, Chip, the swamp guide and shuttle driver, gave Angela a dissertation on Okefenokee history, ecology, and particularly environmental politics. All masked-up and feeling the g-force of reentry, I didn't really listen, but from the back of the van I did catch a phrase or two. I watched Chip's right hand punctuating each sentence—"titanium mine...coal-ash dump... water table sucked dry...cypress clear-cut for bags of mulch..."

Chip dropped us off at the end of muddy Kingfisher Road. We loaded our boats and gear, took a ceremonial shot of Shackleton scotch, and hit the road back through pecan- and cotton-growing South Georgia in intermittent torrents of rain finally spinning off Tropical Storm Eta for sure. The heavy weather we had feared all along had finally arrived.

CANOE AND ALLIGATOR: A MEMORY

We untied the cross ropes and the bow and stern lines on Ab's old aluminum Grumman canoe and shouldered the battered boat down to the black water's edge. A man-made water-control dam had deepened the strand and created the pond where we stood; the dam had slowed the water draining from the immense swamp beyond, and when Ab first saw the map earlier in the afternoon, he had said to Curry that Bullhead Stand looked like a perfect spot for alligators. The edge of it was as good a place as any to begin the ranch survey. "Our alligators," William Curry had called them as we stood in the Babcock Ranch office and gazed at the map.

Ab motioned me toward the canoe's bow, and soon we pushed off from the shore. I sat on the narrow aluminum seat and cast the headlamp mounted on a yellow miner's helmet out over the water with each shift of my searching eyes. Unlike human eyes, the eyes of alligators shine red when hit with a light. Alligator eyes are set high on their heads and directed forward, so the animals can float near the surface of a pond and expose only their eyes and snorkeling nose. The eyes shine red because of reflections off a third eyelid, or "nictitating membrane," which adjusts the alligator eye's focus for underwater vision. Ahead of me pairs of red beads slipped across the surface of Bullhead Strand. I spotted with the light and directed Ab as he paddled us quietly over the surface of the pond toward the floating alligators. Ab didn't have to explain what we were doing. I had hunkered other nights in the bow of a canoe and searched for alligators on a dark pond. I'd even looked for crocodiles with him in Belize and the Florida Keys. Each outing with Ab was a privilege, often funded by some small grant he had secured to do his research, or, as in this case, a commercial contract because a ranch wanted to know something about "their" wildlife and was willing to pay a wildlife biologist to find it out.

Shining alligators is old craft. It is not only how people account for them through study or census (as we were doing), it is how people hunt them. Since the invention of artificial light, millions of alligator and crocodile eyes have shined red in headlamps and flashlights. The crack of a rifle or shotgun often followed the light, and the alligators felt their skulls shatter. Until the introduction of lanterns, and more recently strong battery-powered lights, there was very little that could threaten an adult alligator floating far from shore. The atavistic refuge of water would not last.

Ab has been hired by private ranch owners to survey the ninety-thousand-acre Babcock Ranch, to see how many alligators are in its numerous ponds, sloughs, creeks, and swamps. I was working as his research assistant. If it was a good night, we would catch, measure, and weigh enough alligators so that Ab could extrapolate the information recorded on survey sheets into a portion of a population model for the ranch. A bad night would force us to return and try again.

There was no moon that first night on the ranch, and my headlamp drifted around the pond's black edges where the cypress stood. A net of mosquitoes and gnats swirled and danced in front of the lamp. In the old canoe's stern Ab pulled the battered aluminum paddle silently through the black water and duckweed. If one had been watching from shore, one would have seen us disappear into the darkness led forward by the beam from my headlamp.

Some historians have compared the slaughter of alligators with that of the buffalo. Some say as many as ten million were killed by hunting in the nine "alligator" states (North Carolina, South Carolina, Georgia, Florida, Alabama, Mississippi, Louisiana, Arkansas, Texas) between the early 1800s and the 1950s. By 1960 their numbers had declined, along with the average size of individual alligators killed, and wildlife biologists began to be concerned.

Usually alligators are hunted for skins, which for centuries have made prized leather for shoes, belts, and handbags. Usually the actual killing of the beasts is done by subsistence hunters; it is the middlemen, the hide merchants, and the large corporations processing the skins where the money concentrates. Hardly anyone ever got rich hunting alligators in the wild. This pattern still persists in the developing world, where crocodilians are sometimes hunted to the edge of extinction. Sometimes the meat is eaten (mostly the tail) and many say it "tastes like chicken." In restaurants all over Florida it is possible to get alligator meat on the menu, broiled, stewed, or fried as nuggets. I have never tasted it.

By 1973, when the Endangered Species Act was passed, alligators were included on the list of endangered Southern wildlife, and the legal hunting of them came to a halt in the nine Southeastern states where they occur. The protection had been good to the huge reptiles, and they made a comeback, so management policy in the late '80s had moved from protection to conservation. The Babcock Ranch survey was part of Florida's loosening government hold on the alligators in the late '80s.

We were on the water, looking for alligators. All history, theory, and speculation were on hold. At the moment, the reality of grabbing alligators in the dark seemed as safe and predictable as riding a bicycle blindfolded across I-75 outside Sarasota. "In the 1960s, a popular book about crocodilians had said they would disappear from the planet by the year 2000," Ab whispered, sweeping his own light across the surface of the pond, a powerful Q-beam he turned on and off to check the distances. The surface of the black water ahead of us showed red eyes like stars in a night sky. "Back then I believed that book. It's obvious the alligators didn't get the word."

The pond was thick with the sounds of tree frogs, and insects spun a universe around my headlamp. Even with all the noise, Ab tried to paddle quietly and joked intermittently about the Florida Freshwater Fish and Game Commission record for hand-grabbing alligators: over six feet if you were grabbing from a canoe. Anything over five and a half is legend. Five, respectable. Under five? "Automatic. Part of the job."

"The last of the ruling reptiles," I remembered Ab saying Wilfred Neill had called them. Though not *Tyrannosaurus rex* huge, *Alligator mississippiensis* is still a formidable creature. Reaching lengths of nineteen feet, males can weigh as much as a car—two thousand pounds. Their slightly smiling, toothy jaws have the crushing power of a hydraulic press.

I shone my light out over the water. Tannin dark. I narrowed from forty pairs of eyes to two, illuminated twenty feet away. They were too far apart. Ab had taught me well: if I could make out the distance in inches from the tip of the nose to the eyes of an alligator, it would be close to total length of the animal in feet. The one I'd spotted was seven inches from nose to eyes. Some of the animals, Ab had told me when he first hit the pond with his light, were well over seven feet, and we would try to noose them later. I finally narrowed down and chose one animal. My light was the only one on, and Ab waited for my directions.

"Headed in just right," I said, lying across the bow of the canoe.

"How big?" Ab took long strokes for silence.

"A three-footer, maybe." We cruised silently up on the red eyes.

"Is it still up?" Ab ruddered the canoe ahead.

"Still up..." We were up beside it. I grabbed and caught the gator behind the jaws. Not a three-footer at all, but more than four. It was like holding onto a running outboard motor with the throttle stuck out full blast.

"You got him!" Ab paddled hard for shore. "Hold on!"

Though a rare event, alligators do eat people wading, water skiing, or even swimming near them. The gator I was holding in my grip was four feet long, so I was in no danger of being eaten. What I was more worried about, as the alligator thrashed about in my grasp, was being maimed for life: losing a finger, a hand. We were in the country of the alligator in an unsteady canoe, and Ab's voice kept me honest and sure-handed: "The alligator," Ab had said before, "is a predator by nature, and I can think of no compelling reason people should not be considered appropriate prey by a big alligator."

Literary history has not helped with people's irrational fear of alligators, and here I don't wish to deepen the myth of alligators. It's almost as if early literary accounts help to show how the alligator seizes on our imagination, if not corporeal selves. I told Ab about how the early naturalist William Bartram encountered an alligator on the St. John's River in north Florida early in his *Travels* (1791). Bartram described traveling up the "St. Juan's" River, where he spared no imaginative detail concerning "the subtle and greedy alligator."

The animal Bartram encountered sounded more like a biblical leviathan than a biologically described species: "Behold him rushing forth from the flags and reeds. His enormous body swells. His plaited tail brandished high, floats upon the lake. The waters like a cataract descend from his opening jaws. Clouds of smoke issue from his dilated nostrils. The earth trembles with his thunder."

Bartram wrote about a particular alligator stalking him, presumably for the fish he had caught for supper. The naturalist spotted the alligator in the water near his camp, discharged the contents of his gun in the creature's head, and proceeded to "cleanse and prepare my fish for supper." While Bartram scaled the fish, he saw the alligator again, "through the clear water, the head and shoulders...moving slowly toward me." Bartram stepped back, but "with a sweep of [the alligator's] tail, he brushed off several of my fish." William was quite shaken by the alligator's boldness, and he decided there was no safety for him in his camp and spent the night on watch. He built a fire and "prepared myself in the best manner I could, I charged my gun, and proceeded to reconnoiter my camp and adjacent grounds."

Bartram went on to describe a scene he later witnessed, many alligators feeding on fish in the river: "Should I say that the river (in this place) from shore to shore, and perhaps near half a mile above and below me, appeared to be one solid bank of fish, of various kinds, pushing through this narrow pass of St. Juan's.... The alligators were in such incredible numbers, and so close together from shore to shore, that it would have been easy to have walked across on their heads had the animals been harmless."

The "army of fish" were fed upon with such veracity by the "devouring alligators" that the naturalist seemed content to settle back into his camp for the night. Though the alligators never attack again, Bartram's whole experience with the river and the Florida wilderness was colored by their presence. The terrible night was filled with their bellowing. Ab said Bartram's account reminded him of the worst kind of romanticism about wildlife. It was indeed true that Bartram's descriptions were so vivid that Coleridge made extensive use of *Travels* to sculpt his imaginary kingdom "Kubla Khan," and Wordsworth used Bartram's accounts of Florida to make his own poems more descriptive. "Let the croc beyond the croc pass without further discussion," Ab once wrote in an introduction to crocodilians that I have drawn heavily upon for my own understanding of alligators.

When the water was shallow enough, I jumped out of the canoe and sat on the thick, wet gator's neck. It soon calmed down and I did too. Ab wrapped gray duct tape around its jaws for safety and set to work. I held the creature still as possible, and Ab measured body length, head length, checked its gender (this one was a female, established by way of an obscene probing gesture concerning the animal's cloaca), and recorded the data on his survey sheet, already wet from the alligator's earlier mad thrashing. The data would help Ab determine how many animals of each size and gender were on the pond, by way of statistical modeling.

We released the alligator back into the pond and called it a night. Curry's ranch cottage was waiting for occupancy. Our first Babcock Ranch alligator splashed out of the shallows with a thrust of her powerful black tail. The tally sheet that night showed we had spotted twenty-one alligators, six under three feet, and fifteen over. The alligator I caught was not close to any record, and no account inspired by William Bartram could make me into a leviathan wrestler in anyone's eyes but my own. "A good four," Ab wrote in his log, my alligator quickly disappearing into one mark on a scientific survey sheet. "A good four is all."

EIGHT

RECENT RIVER POEMS

Thinking Like a River

is watery intimacy, is a side
bay full of invasive memes
and a burbling current slipping
under the mind's railway bridge.

Out there, it's big water.
If you didn't reach it today,
don't worry. You will return,
even if your mind sinks.

The Habits of Crayfish

Crab, prawn, what do you
Think of your inland country
Cousin? This poor man's lobster

Pensive and stable,
Washed with conflictions,
Currents, contradictions,
Streamside custodial pleasures.

Crawdad, you are surely more
Than a raccoon's appetizer,
Creek trash left for the next
Flood to sweep downstream.

In the moss you strive,
Though we would never know.
Mudbug, bony with solitude,
Are our habits less linear,
Though no more serious?

Suspension Bridge

Between who I am
and will be—
Bouncing at the ends
more than in the middle.
The river far below—
the worst part
is the squeaking
old cables
and the sign—
"Slippery when wet."

No Water in the River

River, where do you live
When the rain stops?

Your ribs are showing.
There's dry moss on your shins.

Trout in a Tank

Fingerlings, flush
past my human
shadow. Hunger,
show the essence of their
desire. For a quarter,
a handful of feed.
Toss it—satisfied?
Never enough,
for you, or for me
walking above.

Intellectual Watershed

A friend says I sell
my brain short
when I claim
not to be
as intellectual
as poet so-and-so.
My brain is a piedmont
seep, more spring
run than main stem,
more meander
than reservoir.

CODA

MEANDERS, TOEHOLDS, SCOUR HOLES, AND OXBOWS: SOME NOTES ON A RIVER LIFE

Remembering poet and novelist Jim Harrison
(1937–2016) and his *Theory and
Practice of Rivers*.

In June of 1969 the Cuyahoga River in Cleveland, Ohio, burst into flames when a passing train threw off sparks and ignited oil and debris on the stream's surface. For an environmentalist like me, the idea of a burning river is both an outrage and a prophecy.

I was fifteen years old in 1969, and if I yet had a political agenda, I was unaware of it. I have no memories of Earth Day, or burning rivers, or demonstrations, though my teenage rivers and creeks in the Piedmont of South Carolina often flowed red like murky fire. My environmental awareness began in ignorance and love; I didn't suffer from the childhood disease so common today, what Richard Louv has called "nature deficit disorder." Every afternoon was a joyous surplus for me; home from school, I roamed through broom sedge meadows on the edge of Spartanburg, South Carolina, where subdivisions now stand; I explored the semi-wild creek valleys of the Piedmont cloaked with second-, third-, and fourth-growth woods. In the small creeks at the bottoms of gullies, I captured crawfish from under rocks and fished for native knotty heads in the plunge pools using a can of sweet corn. In the shallow, muddy reservoirs backed up behind textile-mill dams built to generate power in the late nineteenth and early twentieth centuries, I fished for catfish and bream, and I swam there, too. These explorations weren't without risk. Yellow jackets hovered over my sweet corn and occasionally stung, and about once a year some young boy would drown in these millponds of the up country.

In my childhood, rivers, streams, and the wooded riparian zones surrounding them were my royal roads to personal escape, my portals to watery freedom from the chaos of homelife. I walked riverbanks and waded their shallows to forget the trouble of my family—my father had committed suicide when I was five, and my mother, unable to cope, had started drinking, and the family never pulled out of poverty. I realize now that rivers and the beauty of the outdoors were a form of mitigation for me.

By the time I went to college in 1973, a few years after the first Earth Day, escape morphed into beauty and excitement when I discovered white water paddling through a college outing program.

Back then that I was learning to love rivers, but it's difficult, but probably not impossible, for modern humans ever to know a river the way a crayfish knows one, or a trout, or a mink. We are never tied so entirely to the river as these aquatic creatures have been throughout their history. At the dawn of our species, and even up into our midmorning, we too were connected to a landscape in this intimate way, but probably not to rivers. We are creatures of the open plains, or at least that's what we became once we climbed down from the trees. Our closest living primate relatives, the chimpanzees, live in forested country along rivers. We have ascribed to native peoples the power to be "of" a place, to be in it entire; about ourselves we say we are "from" somewhere.

In *Weed Time*, my first prose book—I had published several poetry collections—there was an absence of rivers. At the beginning of that 1993 collection, I say, "Living in the Smokies there are metaphors for the soul's journey all around." But the metaphors I chose to focus on back then were not watery. Instead I found meaning in other traditional nature- writing tropes like bird migrations, the changing seasons, migrating monarchs, gardening, and the rituals of daily settled life such as coffee making. Back then I was looking for literary energy in domestic rituals and the land. I was paddling almost every day some literal river or stream, but none of them made it into that book.

Nine years later, rivers figured prominently in my second book of prose, *Waist Deep in Black Water*. Five of its eighteen essays were either set on a river or used a river for important action. In the last essay I tried to articulate my watery connection: "I love rivers because they are real and not only metaphorical.... I write about rivers because the ones I know best give me hope of recovery of the land after great abuse. Even in the face of such abuse, a clay river...endures, and our relationship with it endures."

Chattooga, Circling Home, The Best of the Kudzu Telegraph, My Paddle to the Sea, and *Begin with Rock, End with Water*—all these books since had rivers at their center. Looking back, I found that these works seemed almost a flood, six books in a little over a decade, but I think of them now as a headwaters, a high valley of infinite springs pouring forth into a series of channels I still do not control. Some of this flow will survive me; some will drift into eddies of obscurity.

"Erosion, transportation, deposition." That's the way of the river, and it's all important as metaphor. River systems flow from high to low, and the change creates energy; with energy, channels shift and meander, according to resistance.

Say it—*No ideas but in change*: source (erosion), transfer (transportation), response (deposition).

The features left behind always get poetic names: meanders, toeholds, scour holes, point bars, bed load, thalwegs, and ox-bows.

My best teaching has happened in boats, or in vans on the way to get into boats, always in places outside of the traditional class-room. When I think of my teaching, it's the January short terms and the learning-community classes with labs that I remember most, or the field trips elsewhere with students. In other words, this memorability often has to do with moments that can't be evaluated by usual means.

In 1999 I developed a science-humanities learning commu-nity with a Wofford College colleague, biologist Ellen Goldey, and taught it for almost a decade. We called this arrangement of Biology 104 and Humanities 101 "The Nature and Culture of Water," and we met as separate classes every Tuesday at 9:30 and 1:00, but every Thursday, because of the required biology lab, we had the students for the whole day. We carried out some of the traditional science experiments you would expect in a class about water—water-quality testing in particular—but we also traveled a great deal in boats, paddling the Chattooga; Lake Conestee; the marshes of the Baruch Institute in Georgetown, South Carolina; and Lake Jocassee; we read a range of books, stories, poems, and plays about water; we wrote poetry and personal essays instead of critical papers.

What did we experience about the connections between wa-ter and life? We learned that artists have often found such con-nections, that "life is like a river," goes far beyond cliché—whether reading Flannery O'Connor's story "The River," Ron Rash's poems about Lake Jocassee, or James Dickey's novel *De-liverance*. "In a life properly lived, you're a river," Jim Harrison said in an interview. "You touch things lightly or deeply; you move along because life herself moves, and you can't stop it; you can't figure out a banal game plan applicable to all situations; you just have to go with the 'beingness' of life." I have tried to live my life properly and I have wanted my students to learn this lesson as well. I've wanted them to know what it was like to be a water-bird, floating on the surface of their experience, like a blue-winged teal.

The meaning of rivers deepened for me in the 1980s, after I'd been paddling about ten years. I would drive west from the Nantahala Outdoor Center where I worked in Wesser, North Carolina, to Copperhill, Tennessee, where I would enter a surreal landscape. This was the Copper Basin, an area mined since the 1840s and where, by the time I began driving through, the acid from smelters had stripped thirty-two thousand acres of all life. It was said that the astronauts from the surface of the moon could see Copperhill like a scab on the earth.

There was something deceptively charming about the names of places—I passed Copper Basin, Ducktown, Turtletown—but I found that feeling undercut by the neon-red clay and the stunted pines visible along US 64 in the 1980s. The place felt western, like an artificial Utah in Tennessee. How did it get that way? What were the forces that formed it? I never thought, back then, to explore a landscape in terms of environmental justice or to question my responsibility toward rivers. I was in a hurry to get to recreate. The idea of the past labor of a mining culture was hidden or, better yet, lost on me, masked by my passion for kayaking.

Copperhill was simply the gas station and motel I passed before I started my descent to a beloved Ocoee put in. But these upper reaches of the river were within the scab. The wild Ocoee I paddled gathered itself partly from that ruined thirty-two-thousand-acre landscape—Walkertown Branch, North Potato Creek, Burra Burra Creek, Grassy Creek, Davis Mill Creek—and downstream from those braided industrial waters floated me in my recreating joy for many summers.

273

One sun-drenched day in the mid-1980s, at the height of my recreational river coma, I was sitting in an eddy halfway down the Ocoee at the top of a large rapid called Table Saw when three unexpected kayakers slid in beside me. One of them proved to be Yvon Chouinard, the founder of Patagonia, quickly becoming a reluctant billionaire by way of his outdoor-clothing company.

This memory is an example of my environmental blindness to the full nature and culture of rivers back then. Many of us were still experiencing rivers mostly as recreation, and seeing Yvon Chouinard brought that home because he had helped bring the recreation revolution *to* the rivers. We were floating above so much human history and environmental misery—erasing or softening or ignoring the alteration of landscapes with romantic notions of wildness and adventure.

Since the mining ceased in 1987, millions of pines have been planted, and the basin has been "seeded with acid-tolerant grass." In the center of Copper Basin the old Burra Burra Mine has preserved its unreclaimed three hundred acres. A few of the mine's structures remain—the hoist house, boiler building, powder house, and machine shops. There is even a museum in the old engineers' office building, and the parking lot overlooks a big sinkhole opened up when the Burra Burra collapsed.

The Ocoee was, by the time the Burra Burra closed, the epicenter of Southeastern industrial rafting—a recreational industry that created enormous profits through the use of laborers (raft guides and support staff) jokingly called "outdoor-recreation migrant workers." Rafting, canoeing, and kayaking looked like "clean recreation" back then, before the calculation of carbon footprints. Yvon Chouinard rode that recreation boom to wealth and a new kind of business model. Now, in 2018, he is nearly eighty years old, and Patagonia's mission is to "build the best product, cause no unnecessary harm, use business to inspire and implement solutions to the environmental crisis." Now every day is Earth Day in Ventura, California, corporate home of Patagonia.

Janisse Ray in *Drifting into Darien*, her narrative about the Altamaha River in South Georgia, puts it this way: "I know this river story has already been written, over and over it has been told...but those who were not transported by water will never know what really happened."

If you think like a river you might understand *Virginia Woolf* drowning herself in the Ouse, or Thoreau setting out for a week with his soon-to-be-dead brother down the Concord and the Merrimack. To think like a river you must have been on/in/under one. You must have been close enough to hear the flood, far enough away to worry at the absence, and troubled enough (as Bob Dylan says) to "sit down on a bank of sand/and watch the river flow"; confused enough to ask someone, as the Talking Heads instruct, to "take me to the river/drop me in the water"; you must have felt, like Langston Hughes, that you knew rivers; or like Norman Maclean, looking back on a life of joy and tragedy and seeing that "a river runs through it"; or believed, as T. S. Eliot did, that "the river is a strong brown god"; or sensed what Whitman meant by "pent-up, aching rivers" within him; or felt, as Emily Dickinson said, "My river runs to thee."

———

In another dream I've had about rivers I'm driving past a flooding one. I get out and look down into the colliding currents. It's obvious I can't paddle such difficult surging water, but just as I'm readying to drive away, a single kayaker starts down with great skill and caution. When I look close, I realize it's me.

Sometimes risk flows hard up against death, the ultimate scour hole. I have lost two friends to death by water in kayaks, have searched a week on a river for the body of a total stranger killed in a beginner's kayak clinic, and have been on a raft trip where two clients died negotiating a flooded river. I've made several stupid errors of judgment that put me and loved ones at risk, and the only way I could have avoided these dark situations was if I had never put a boat on a river the first time.

I've talked with students through the years about the difference between "risk" and "perceived risk." Of course, in outdoor recreation we want the perceived risk to loom large and the real risk to be manageable. Sometimes the wires get crossed and tragedy results.

In our environmental-studies program at Wofford College, every one of our majors takes classes in environmental science, environmental social science and policy, and environmental humanities and arts. I teach the humanities classes.

What good does it do for a scientist to hear stories about rivers? What can a poem possibly contribute to politicians' understanding of water issues in their region? I think what the arts-and-humanities side helps us to do is cultivate love and maintain a healthy respect for, and fear of, rivers. If we love rivers we're going to fight harder before we make decisions to pollute or straighten or divert them. On the other hand, if we fear or respect rivers (as I believe we should) we'll understand that river systems are much bigger than us, and they aren't entirely for our use. Rivers function quite well on their own with systems much older than us. On the east side of the continental divide, rivers have flowed to the Atlantic for hundreds of millions of years; we've only been floating and crossing these rivers for perhaps twelve thousand years.

Today the Cuyahoga is designated an American Heritage River and is much healthier than fifty years ago—but even though it doesn't burn today, its waters are still mostly unacceptable for recreation, showing high levels of fecal coliform. The waterway still receives discharges from sewer overflows and wastewater from plants and factories along its shore. Swimming or even wading in the Cuyahoga is "currently discouraged."

Earth Day began in 1970 as a response to deep human degradation and insult of the natural world. In the years since, we have made some progress in our relationship to water, passing the Clean Water Act, the Wild and Scenic Rivers Act, the Fishery Conservation and Management Act, the Safe Drinking Water Act, and others—but much more remains to be accomplished than appears to be assured.

The art of paddling wild rivers always looked like a loss of common sense to those who don't love white water, much as suicide looks to those on the outside, caught in the backwash. Why did I want to throw my body into a plastic boat and invite the river to twist me around a steady rock? Hiking is much safer, as is biking. Why not take up one of those?

Yes, there are other ways, most of them good, to get close to the earth, to be alone with it—but rivers have been mine.

ORIGINS OF WRITING AND PUBLICATION HISTORIES

One
From the Center

Until 1983 I was primarily a poet. I had only attempted a few short stories in college, but I had no sense of reporting or writing pieces that were just then beginning to be called "personal essays." Then, in 1983, I began to work at the Nantahala Outdoor Center (NOC) in western North Carolina, and the experience was formative for me in so many ways. It was the first time I really felt a part of a deep intentional community. I began to write short lyrical prose pieces for *The State* paper in Columbia, South Carolina, for their Sunday supplement magazine edited by Claudia Brinson about various topics, including paddling. I was paid for my work, which was something new for me, and I was told I could write about whatever I wanted. My first piece was about remembering when dunks were illegal in college and high school, and the only way to score close to the basket was by layup, and other pieces soon followed about natural fibers, the collapse of Sunday as a well-defined Southern day of the week, and driving the Blue Ridge Parkway. Then, in December of 1984, I wrote for the first time about my passion for kayaking. The piece was called "Why I Love Falling Water." These early prose pieces showed the bones of my poet self. The title of the collection is a riff on this early piece.

"Pilley's First Law of Rapids," "Down the Sometimes River," and "Waterfall Logic" were published in *American White-*

water, the official magazine of the American Whitewater Association, between December of 1986 and August of 1993. These pieces came out of my contact with the rivers around the Nantahala Outdoor Center and with the people I met. I think they have the same voice as my *State* magazine pieces, but I was learning to write prose and add a little more reporting.

"Silver Creek Paddles" owes a great deal to my early infatuation with John McPhee and his love of prose craftsmanship. McPhee has a brief passage about the Nantahala. It occurs in his essay "Reading the River," published in the 1975 collection *Pieces of the Frame*. McPhee describes the Nantahala, a river he had only heard stories about, as a place where "canoemen gather and stare fondly from its banks at its homicidal gradient." As McPhee describes the river, it is a place of mystery and challenge, especially when the cold water drawn off the bottom of Nantahala Lake makes contact with the warm North Carolina air, where "the cloud hurtles and roils along" downstream. "Into the instant river the canoemen fly," he says. "Shooting downriver and around bends, they desperately call one another's names, trying to keep contact in the mists."

I used a beautiful wooden paddle manufactured by Silver Creek the years I shot downriver on the mysterious Nantahala and other rivers. Silver Creek's little shop was up Silvermine Road. I interviewed Homer and Mar King during 1985 and early1986 for what I hoped would be my first long feature. I wanted to write about them and their paddles in *Southern* magazine. A fragment of the piece I wrote finally ran in October 1987. With this writing, I discovered how hard it is to "report" like John McPhee, and also, that as a freelancer, you have little control over how your piece is edited or presented. My original Silver Creek paddle is in the Sowell Collection archives at Texas Tech University in Lubbock, Texas.

The essay "Death by Water" was solicited by the writer John P. O'Grady for a special issue of the MIT journal *Terra Nova: Nature & Culture* and appeared there in December of

1998 after he heard me tell the story of assisting in the recovery of the body of a dead beginning kayaker on a river during my days at NOC. Though written later than the earlier pieces in this section, "Death by Water" goes further toward deepening my understanding of how writing about water might work in my own psychic accounting. The piece appeared in my book of essays *Waist Deep in Black Water* (University of Georgia Press, 2002).

What emerges from these prose pieces is a sketch, an outline, of the paddling culture at the end of the 1980s on the cusp of great change. The pieces often feature the good people I worked with and called friends. I had started coming to NOC in 1975, only three years after its founding, and I began working there in 1983. In those days the community was still alternative, flourishing deep in the North Carolina mountains, an escape from the corporate mainstream, a true "Magic Mountain." In the years hence, several of the marriages and businesses and people described here are no longer with us. The spirit of the times still lives, though, in us all, and I hope in these pieces.

Two
First River Poems

"At Cherokee Ford" and "The River Falling" were two of my first published poems. I wrote both of them when I was in college. "At Cherokee Ford" was written as a geology assignment, about 1975 or 1976, and appeared in *Blair & Ketchum's Country Journal* in 1981; "The River Falling" was written that same year. Neither one was written from the seat of a boat, so they have a different perspective to other pieces in this collection. Both of them appeared in my first book of poems, *Quarries* (Briarpatch Press, 1984), and then later in my selected poems, *Abandoned Quarry* (Mercer University Press, 2011).

"Along the Little Betsie" was written in 1988 while I was teaching at Interlochen Arts Academy. I wrote the poem to explain to my poetry students the difference between language and the real world. It appeared in the *Cimmaron Review* the year it was composed and was a favorite at readings I did in the late 1980s. It also appeared in *Abandoned Quarry* (Mercer University Press, 2011).

"The Fear Program" was written in the 1990s, thinking back on all the beginners I'd taught to roll a kayak. It touches on some of the same feelings I expressed through prose in "Death by Water." It also appeared in *Abandoned Quarry* (Mercer University Press, 2011).

"Above Bone Ring Lake" is a eulogy written in the summer of 1991 in Wyoming, a few months after my housemate at NOC John Dobeare died in a kayaking accident. It appeared in *Petroglyph* in 1994.

Three
Excursions

"Sardis" was written because I had developed a joy in exploring the idea of connecting the literary with the fluvial through paddling trips. I always wanted to paddle through William Faulkner's Mississippi "Big Bottom," and in April of 2004, as I embarked on a book tour for *Chattooga* (University of Georgia Press, 2004), one of my friends invited me down and set up a canoe trip. The essay was finally published in *Prairie Schooner* in February of 2011 and won their Glenna Luschei Award as the best work to appear in the magazine in 2011. The essay also appeared in my essay collection, *Begin with Rock, End with Water* (Mercer University Press, 2012).

"Gradient" was written about a paddling trip to Maine in May of 2002, one of the most challenging writing assignments I made for myself in my career—a river, a craft (the wood-and-canvas canoe), a person I admired, a physical challenge. I worked on it many years and finally got it close enough for it to appear in

Begin with Rock, End with Water (Mercer University Press, 2012).

"Lake Conestee" was solicited for the anthology *Voices of the Earth: American Writers Respond to the Earth Charter* (University of Georgia Press, 2008). It marked a departure for me as it was some of the first writing I had done about my teaching.

"Confluence: Pacolet River" happened because my friend Barry Lopez was editing an anthology called *Heart of a Nation* (National Geographic Books, 2000). In 1999 I agreed to write a piece for the anthology. The editor said I could write about any place in the whole country—and was very surprised when I decided to write about my home river where I'd never put a boat in. The piece appeared in my book of essay *Waist Deep in Black Water* (University of Georgia Press, 2002).

"Youghiogheny" was a real challenge, but in 2001, after *Heart of a Nation*, National Geographic Books asked me to write a second river piece, to paddle the length of the Youghiogheny River and report on the trip. I wrote the piece for their anthology *Adventure America* (National Geographic Books, 2002). This was the high-water mark of my white water experience. The piece also appeared in *Begin with Rock, End with Water* (Mercer University Press, 2012).

"Sols Creek Falls" probed the mystery of a local waterfall, and I published it in *The Smoky Mountain Times* in July of 2000. The piece also appeared in *High Vistas: An Anthology of Nature Writing from Western North Carolina and the Great Smoky Mountains Vol. II*, edited by George Ellison (Natural History Press, 2011).

Both "Paddle to the Sea" and "River Time" were written for *The Kudzu Telegraph*, a column that I maintained weekly for five years (250 columns) between 2006 and 2010. I don't know how many river pieces I wrote over those five years, but it must have been dozens. That would be an interesting project to pull them together. I had two more in this collection but ended up cutting them. "Paddle to the Sea" and "River Time" were both written about the "scout trip" I did for my book-length narrative, *My Paddle to the Sea* (University of Georgia Press, 2011). "River Time" is dedicated to the memory of Grady Anthony.

"$35 Million River" was written around 2008 when I started to visit the US Whitewater Center in Charlotte and had very mixed feelings about artificial river channels. It was originally for an Association for the Study of Literature and Environment (ASLE) conference panel in 2007, but a magazine editor heard the presentation and asked me to expand it, took the piece, but then cancelled after they held it for a while. I finally published it in *Begin with Rock, End with Water* (Mercer University Press, 2012).

Four:
River Poems Downstream

"No Water in the River" was written in the drought year of 2006.

"Ridge Music" was written in fall of 2008 on a trip to Interlochen Arts Academy. That week I stayed in my old friend Mike Delp's river house on the Boardman River. It also appeared in *Abandoned Quarry* (Mercer University Press, 2011).

"The Half-Finished House" was written in October of 2002. The poem is for Betsy and it appeared in *Town Creek* in fall of 2007. It also appeared in *Abandoned Quarry* (Mercer University Press, 2011).

Five
Ripples Outward and Inward

Around 2005 I got wind of an amazing man and an amazing environmental-justice story in my hometown of Spartanburg—the "ReGenesis Project." I decided I would check it out from the seat of a canoe—and paddle through a Superfund site. Brown University's student-run environmental magazine *Watershed* published "ReGenesis: Seeking Wildness in a Damaged Southern Landscape" in winter 2006. The piece later appeared in *Begin with Rock, End with Water* (Mercer University Press, 2012).

Over Christmas of 2004 I took my family paddling waterfalls in Mexico. "A Week of Mexican Waterfalls" was written about the trip but wasn't published until *Yemessee* brought it out in 2012, edited by my friend and former student Will Garland. The piece appeared in *Begin with Rock, End with Water* (Mercer University Press, 2012)

"Meet the Creek" was another essay about teaching. It appeared in the anthology *Teaching About Place*, edited by my ASLE colleagues Laird Christensen and Hal Crimmel (University of Nevada Press, 2008). The piece was written in collaboration with my colleague biologist Ellen Golden to explain our humanities-biology learning community at Wofford College organized around the theme of water. We team-taught this course for five years in the early 2000s, funded by a National Science Foundation grant. This piece must have been written around 2003.

The drafts I have of "Watershed Thinking" are undated. I believe the piece was written in the early 2000s as I was working on the environmental-studies program at Wofford College. I think I delivered it as a speech somewhere, or maybe published it in a newsletter, about that time.

I turned fifty in October of 2004, and I wanted to paddle the Chattooga on my birthday and run Class V Bull Sluice. I did it, but I ended up not writing about paddling the Bull. I wrote instead about "the urge to merge" and about getting old and out of shape. Because I had just written a book-length narrative about the Chattooga and *Deliverance* (*Chattooga: Descending into the Myth of Deliverance River*, 2004) I was invited to speak at a special James Dickey conference that fall, and Clemson published a special issue of its proceedings and included my essay

"On the Chattooga," in *The South Carolina Review* in the spring of 2005. The piece also appeared in *Begin with Rock, End with Water* (Mercer University Press, 2012).

Six
The Mad Kayaker

I wrote "The Mad Kayaker" poems over about fifteen years and finally gathered them in a chapbook published by Eyewear in London in 2018. Before the chapbook, individual poems appeared in *praxas* and *The South Carolina Review*. They were written during my fifties and early sixties as I began to notice that white water kayaking was no longer the center of my physical life, as it had been for two decades. I was growing older and I'd had several close calls with river accidents (see the book-length narratives *Circling Home* and *My Paddle to the Sea*) but I still loved the ways that falling water could reshuffle my brain. What else can I say? I am the mad kayaker.

Seven
Mostly Flat Water

"Keowee" appeared in the elaborate and beautiful anthology *Bartram's Living Legacy* (Mercer University Press, 2010) edited by Dorina Dallmeyer. Sometime around 2008 I chose Lake Keowee and the drowned Keowee River as the Bartram spot I wanted to visit and write about from a contemporary perspective. Choosing an impoundment on a drowned river gave me a chance to paddle and argue good-naturedly about literary postmodernism with a colleague.

With "The Upper Broad River: A Pastoral" I returned to the Broad watershed with my friend Venable Vermont, the super-sized hero of *My Paddle to the Sea*. We took the trip together in March 2010 and got in a little trouble, which sometimes happens on rivers. The piece appeared in the anthology *State of the Heart: South Carolina Writers on the Places They Love,* edited by my friend Aida Rogers (University of South Carolina Press, 2013).

In "Urban Reedy River" I returned to Conestee Nature Park in 2013 to canoe with my friend Dave Hargett as one of a series of narratives in the coffee table nature book *Web of Water: Reflections of Life Along the Saluda and Reedy Rivers* (Upstate Forever and Hub City Press, 2014).

"Canoe and Alligator: A Memory" is an old story lifted from a draft of an unpublished manuscript, "A Stand of Cypress," about an alligator survey in South Florida. This version dates to about 1992. I include it here because I wanted to remind myself of my former life as an alligator research assistant and that all dangers on rivers and lakes are not created by rocks.

"May the Wind Take Our Troubles Away" is the newest piece in this collection. We found ourselves among alligators. The narrative was written after a four-day wilderness paddle into the Okefenokee with my wife and three great friends a few days after the election in November of 2020.

Eight
Recent River Poems

These poems were all written in my field journal or on my iPhone in the Notes function between 2006 and 2019: "No Water in the River" (21 July 2006), "Trout in a Tank" (19 July 2006), "Suspension Bridge" (9 June 2009), "Habits of Crayfish" (8 June 2011), "Thinking Like a River" (26 September 2013), and "Intellectual Watershed" (December 2019). "Habits of Crayfish" appeared in *Clover* in 2014.

Coda
"Meanders, Toeholds, Scour Holes, and Oxbows…"

An early version of "Meanders, Toeholds, Scour Holes, and Oxbows…" was prepared and delivered as a faculty talk at Wofford College as early as 2010, and then a first version was presented at Allegheny College as the Pelletier Library Lecture "One Watery Theme: Reflections on Twenty Years of Floating, Teaching, and Writing About River" in October of 2012. Then the final version was prepared and presented at the ninth annual Earth Day program at the University of Georgia on April 19, 2017. This final version appeared in *The Georgia Review* in spring 2018. Thanks to Stephen Corey and Douglas Carlson for the edits.

BIOGRAPHY

Place and wildness, and particularly rivers, have been critical themes in John Lane's poetry, personal essays, and fiction for forty years. The North Carolina native has lived on a wilderness island off the coast of Georgia, studied crocodiles in Central America, surveyed monkeys in the remote rain forests of Suriname, and paddled rivers in all regions of the US, Mexico, and South America.

An avid paddler, Lane's outdoor-adventure prose appeared through the years in *Outside, American White Water, Canoe, South Carolina Wildlife*, and many other periodicals. His long essays, "River Wild," on paddling fifty-nine miles of the Youghiogheny River, and "Confluence: The Pacolet River," appeared in the anthologies *Heart of a Nation* and *Adventure America* from National Geographic Books.

He published a book-length personal narrative about the Chattooga River called *Chattooga: Descending into the Myth of Deliverance River* to critical acclaim. He also published *Waist Deep in Black Water, Circling Home, My Paddle to the Sea, The Best of the Kudzu Telegraph*, and *Begin with Rock, End with Water*.

Lane worked almost a decade at the Nantahala Outdoor Center store in the 1980s and early 1990s and has since led writing workshops on rivers, both nationally and internationally. He is emeritus professor at Wofford College, where he taught creative writing, environmental studies, and directed the Goodall Environmental Studies Center. There he helped imagine and direct the Thinking Like a River Initiative. In the past decade he has been named one of seven regional Culture Pioneers by Blue Ridge Outdoors, and he has been honored with the Water Conservationist Award from the South Carolina Wildlife Federation, the Clean Water Champion by South Carolina's Upstate Forever, and inducted in 2014 into the South Carolina Academy of Authors. He lives with his wife Betsy Teter near the banks of Lawson's Fork outside of Spartanburg, South Carolina, where they were among the cofounders of the Hub City Writers Project.